Masculinities
and Other Hopeless Causes
at an All-Boys Catholic School

A Book Series of
Curriculum Studies

William F. Pinar
General Editor

VOLUME 40

The Complicated Conversation series
is part of the Peter Lang Education list.
Every volume is peer reviewed and meets
the highest quality standards for content and production.

PETER LANG
New York • Washington, D.C./Baltimore • Bern
Frankfurt • Berlin • Brussels • Vienna • Oxford

Kevin J. Burke

Masculinities
and Other Hopeless Causes at an All-Boys Catholic School

PETER LANG
New York • Washington, D.C./Baltimore • Bern
Frankfurt • Berlin • Brussels • Vienna • Oxford

Library of Congress Cataloging-in-Publication Data
Burke, Kevin J.
Masculinities and other hopeless causes at an all-boys Catholic school / Kevin J. Burke.
p. cm. — (Complicated conversation; v. 40)
Includes bibliographical references and index.
1. Masculinity—United States. 2. Homophobia—United States.
3. Single-sex schools—United States. I. Title.
BF692.5.B87   155.5'32—dc23   2011030992
ISBN 978-1-4331-1538-7 (hardcover)
ISBN 978-1-4331-1537-0 (paperback)
ISBN 978-1-4539-0239-4 (e-book)
ISSN 1534-2816

Bibliographic information published by **Die Deutsche Nationalbibliothek**.
Die Deutsche Nationalbibliothek lists this publication in the "Deutsche
Nationalbibliografie"; detailed bibliographic data is available
on the Internet at http://dnb.d-nb.de/.

Cover concept by Lauren E. McLennan

The paper in this book meets the guidelines for permanence and durability
of the Committee on Production Guidelines for Book Longevity
of the Council of Library Resources.

© 2011 Peter Lang Publishing, Inc., New York
29 Broadway, 18th floor, New York, NY 10006
www.peterlang.com

All rights reserved.
Reprint or reproduction, even partially, in all forms such as microfilm,
xerography, microfiche, microcard, and offset strictly prohibited.

Printed in the United States of America

For Lauren with love, Mom in admiration and Dad wistfully

Table of Contents

Acknowledgments ix

1. **Practice and Discourse in an All-Boys Catholic School** 1
   Introduction 1
   Catholic Education and Local History 6
   St. Monica Catholic High School 9
   Catholic Wonder Tales: The Saints 11
       The Brown Scapular of Our Lady of Mt. Carmel 12
       St. Monica of Cascia 15

2. **Masculinity Foretold, Told, Retold** 21
   Gender/Sexuality 21
   Gender and the Body 23
   Masculinities 26
   Discourse 28
   Power 30
   Schooling 32
   Religion 37

3. **Crossing Over** 45
   Lenses 45
       Critical Autoethnography 47
   Wearing the Required Uniform 51
       Details 55
       Entextualizing 57
       Beyond School 60

4. **Cafeteria Catholics** 65
   Fag Discourse 65
       Lunch 66
       The Same, Only Different 67
       Girlfriends 69
       Religiosity 73
       Athletics: Pink Jerseys and Other Gay Shit 75
       Dicks, Man 81

5. **Squishes: The Abjectified** 91
   Hockey 91
   Pollut/ed/ing Women 94
      Anxiety, Sickness, and Crap (Literally) 96
   Your Boys 99
   Tradition and (Un)Available Women 102
   Squishes 104
      The Buffer of School or School as Buffer 106
      Where This (Almost) Breaks Down 108

6. **Kairos** 115
   Space and Time Apart 115
      Prayer 117
      God's Time 120
      My Kairos 123
      Plano, IL: Off the Bus 125
   Kergyma: A Conservative Project 127

7. **Make Me a Fucking Sandwich** 137
   Making Sense of the Research(er) 137
      Shalom! 139
      Seduction, or Burke! Where You Been? 143
      Bullied 148
      (En)Title(d) 152
   Implications 153
      "Flash" Interviews 154
      The Field of Catholic Education 155

   Bibliography 159
   Index 165

Acknowledgments

I owe an immense debt to early and constant readers of this work, most particularly Avner Segall, who was kind enough to mentor me from the inception of the project and stuck around to talk me through the framing of the piece, as well as the process of shaping it into some semblance of a book. Nancy DeJoy has been a thoughtful and careful critic throughout the process and taught me most importantly, to think about what was being invented and revised throughout. Thanks also to Stephanie Nawyn for her textual suggestions from the field of sociology and to Lynn Fendler for early and vital access to her text and expertise on Foucault. As one shaped by intellectual betters constantly, I would be remiss in not gratefully noting the contributions made by colleagues and faculty at Michigan State who provided not only thoughtful feedback but also brilliant conversation and attentive ears.

I continue to be blessed by the presence of members of the St. Monica family in my life. None of the access I gained would have been possible without the facilitation of Fr. Tim and the principal of the school. The Blaszaks and the Gilberts in particular made an interloper feel very much at home in the social maze of the adult world at the school. I am hopeful for the intellectual growth of future generations of Monicamen because they remain leaders there. Fr. Rich was a wonderful theological foil throughout the year. Gratitude is owed to the entire community of teachers and coaches for tolerating the curious and intrusive presence of a researcher scrutinizing from the hallways and desks of the place. Thanks, too, to Mr. Kurek, Mr. Kellam, and Mr. Summerfelt for making the rules of lacrosse almost navigable by the end of the season. I must admit, too, to missing seeing Brendan Sr. on a daily basis, as both model of work but also fatherhood.

And of course there are, most importantly, the students—now graduated and off into the re-gendered world—who welcomed me in ways I couldn't have imagined possible (nor could I have conceptualized much of it as welcoming without their helping me make sense of it all). So thanks to Brendan for trusting me, and Tim, Kimani, and Joe for letting me tag along all those months. Thanks to the lunch crew, to the JV lacrosse team for suffering my learning how to coach, and to all the Monicamen who came down to roof houses with us in the summer.

Finally, thanks to Kevin Walsh and Dena Johnson for helping me regress into the mold of a high school student and to Lauren for enduring the move to Chicago and gamely attending Homecoming and football games while pretending what I was writing made sense in its early instantiations.

Chapter 1

Practice and Discourse in an All-Boys Catholic School

Introduction

One thing I've never learned in all my years of meandering unsupervised through the world of boys was how to predict what they might do, singly or in groups, what startling kindness or humdrum cruelty they might choose to engage in.
Michael Chabon, "Manhood for Amateurs"

We believe, not because we want to know, but because we want to be.
Thomas Merton, "Confessions of a Guilty Bystander"

It is the group that is the bearer of masculinity, in a basic way.
RW Connell "Masculinities"

Father Tim[1], resplendent in white alb, draped in priestly vestments fitting for the relative doldrums of Ordinary time in the Catholic Church's liturgical year, marooned as we are between the passing of Christmas Day and the last whimper of its attendant season, brings a close to the Eucharistic portion of this first Friday Mass of January.

"Behold what you are," he intones.

A white orb of unleavened bread the texture of brittle wafer, held aloft in two hands, shadows his face as he addresses his 701 students, who are seated uncomfortably in chapel shirts and ties and, perhaps more importantly, hardwood chapel pews. Their shifting, their attention is itinerant, but they are held awake by their discomfort. Anyone slumped forward—asleep or meditating on the Paschal mystery—is shooed upright by hovering religious brothers in black cowls.

Dramatic pause.

"Become what you receive." Eyes closed for a beat, and there in his hands still, before he places the simple mixture of pressed flour and water back into its filigreed bowl, resides the Body of Christ. Transubstantiation: the Catholic dogmatic belief that the priestly caste has the power to invoke—and return the congregation for those brief instances back to the Last Supper of the historical/Divine Jesus Christ—words to make bread flesh. It would seem necromaniacal if it weren't so much a part of the rhythm of being faithful to the Church. And thus, written into the code of my life—and that of most of the boys here—through hours and decades of inhaled incense and expunged sin. But man, if you think too hard about it: to be a God-eater?

Given my druthers I might, as resident oddball—not faculty, not staff, not-quite student—suggest that religion classes at the school address the great debates of the monks Radbertus and Ratramnus. Both, rather unimaginatively wrote works called *De Corpore et Sanguine Domini* (Concerning the Body and Blood of Christ). The latter in his ninth-century folly—pilloried for its blushing scientism—suggested that there might just be a difference between the sign and that which it signified as regarded the holy practice of the Sacrament of the Eucharist; the former, a fellow monastic and Benedictine demurred: sign and signifier were too much for poor, faithful minds to process. God merely veiled the presence of His flesh in the mystery of bread and His blood as wine because humans—we weak-willed masses—couldn't handle the cannibalistic implications (Bakhuizen Van Den Brink, 1974). This, at least, might spark some interest in Mass, aside from the occasional senior fainting in his pew, or the odd bloody nose. But then interest, I've found in my four months in the school, is largely moot; theological questions remain subservient to the Purpose: to expose the boys to the practice of the mass(es). Thinking about it (religion, as with schooling) really isn't the point; doing it is.

Flanking Fr. Tim at the altar are Fr. Paul and Fr. Murphy, each dressed down, as it were, in stoles embossed in rich reds and golds with the seal of the Augustinian Order: a heart, aflame, bisected diagonally by a Celtic inspired cross and an arrow. The violence of the image, facially, is stark. And as Murphy and Paul bob and weave through the rhythms of the final blessing of the day, they beat with an external heart afire, presumably for the Lord. It all might seem very *Temple of Doom*, were it not imbued with the resident trappings of the sacred and the transposition thereof awash as we are to be in sin and unworthiness.

Mass, today, has been long. A two-hour phenomena admixed with a speech from an alumnus (St. Monica, class of 1980) who sings "This Little Light of Mine" and awards, given at the front of the altar of the marble-and-brass chapel attached to the extreme northern end of the high school, for students of the month. The boys wilt at the shoulders hoping, at least, that first period (they've told me this repeatedly) will be further foreshortened by the extended chapel time.

And then, with the procession of the cross from chancel to nave, we are sent off, to go in peace to love and serve the Lord.

Mass dismissed, the boys shuffle by me, dragging their feet on their journey back to class, in that funk of sleep and deadened eyes born of the disappointment at a near-snowday and the literal beginning of the second semester. In fits of pique they tear off their chapel ties and unbutton top buttons, free (sort of) at last. Nods in my direction and mixtures of "What's up, Burke?"; I get up to leave, to write, finding the expanded words that Father Tim engraved into the sacredness of this passed Mass in its context. St. Augustine, the adopted founder of the Augustinians—stewards of St. Monica of Cascia High School since its opening in 1905—in a fourth-century reflection on Jesus' Sermon on the Mount is to have preached, "Behold the mystery of your salvation laid out for you; behold what you are, become what you receive" (Jepson, 2008). Salvation: in the reflection upon, and shaming of, the earthly flesh, that one might become God, or at least God's hands on Earth, loving and serving. This is my data, a study of beholding (boys), of shaming (boys), and the salvific properties of schooling (boys). I can only hope, by way of fidelity to a critical lens that I've more Ratramnus in me than I yet suspect.

What follows is a fiction, full of truths. It is the gathered fruit—bruised and overpolished—of a semester spent shadowing four students in the senior class of St. Monica High, an all-boys secondary school on the southwest side of Chicago. As a man, a researcher formed by his experiences in a similar institution less than two miles distant, I came to the research—just as I come to its telling—an interested (if not interesting) party. My history, a mixture of pride and the growing disdain of a man increasingly discomfited by the Home (the school/s) of his childhood, is rolled up in all of this data. It is this history, too, in the converse, that dictates that to which I am too close—too snowblind from experience and fondness and a self-conscious (and unconscious, too) distancing from the past—to realize I will not see. This is the insider missing the forest for the trees, I suppose.

To present the data without acknowledging the impossibility of the work of removing memory (as it blinds and reveals)—that of the researcher and the neighborhood surrounding him—from the study would be dishonest, would be the worst kind of dissimulation, "pretend[ing] not to have what one has. To simulate…to feign to have what one doesn't have" (Baudrillard, 1994, p. 3), a move toward "substituting the signs of the real for the real" (p. 2). Rather, my hope is to engage in the process of "genuine reflexivity...achieved by subjecting the *position* of the observer to the same critical analysis as that of the constructed object at hand" (Bourdieu & Wacquant, 1992, p. 41), knowing well that "one cannot disassociate the construction of the object from the instruments of construction of the object and their critique" (p. 30). Here all is constructed and conflicted, but these need not be agonistic relationships.

In the interest of frankness then, this study fits awkwardly under the umbrella of a critical post-modern autoethnography, trained on the discourses that lead to the construction of masculinities and spiritualities, composed of data collected through field notes generated during a semester's stint as a participant observer at St. Monica, filtered through the eyes of an interested and nascent/troubled researcher. Rose (1989) helps here, suggesting the tenor of these clashes, noting "It is an unfortunate fact of our psychic lives that the images that surround us as we grow up—no matter how much we may scorn them later—give shape to our deepest needs and longings" (p. 44). I have, in some ways, gone home to my research amidst a swirl of self-scorn at the needs and longings bound to be uncovered by the work.

The sieve, particularly as regards critical engagement with schooling, and most particularly schooling in/de/formed and shaped by religious doxology, can never be fine enough. This I believe. Mine is, (un)fortunately rusted and holey, a product of a lapsing of faith in the rituals of a theology (of God, of race, and of place, too) that troubles me; patched with new screens, of different materials constantly, shiny theories of resistance and schooling, the work of this study has become a pastiche of confused ideas of manhood, religiosity, and the gerrymandered lines between research and living. Hint: there may not be a difference. It's all been very messy. Which is good. But it makes for fitful sifting.

From August of 2009 until January of 2010 I 'enrolled' three days a week as a senior student at St. Monica. I was able to follow the daily course schedule of four different students (one a month), collecting data in school situations, broadly defined (e. g. athletic contests, intramural activities, in hallways, the dining hall, the classroom, etc.). In the process I found strong support for Nespor's (1997) suggestion that "what kids value most in school are opportunities for interactions with peers" (p. 124). As a pseudo-peer my involvement on a personal level, as a "classmate" provided a ready lens through which to examine/experience the play of ideology, institutional, and individual power at the nexus of student-to-student interaction.

This study, then, was an attempt to examine the ideologies of a school; of a Catholic school; of an all-boys Catholic secondary school. It is a project meant to elucidate how religion (as proxy for patriarchy,[2] quite often) helps form assumptions—thus presented as (im)possibilities through the official and unofficial curriculum—through schooling about what it means to become a man in this certain context in its specific history. It is, further, a project that I hope examines how these officialized discourses are reshaped—made sense of, made nonsensical, too—by the young men of the school in their daily lives. In the process I seek to explicate how students come to make sense of and exercise—through resistance, capitulation, and otherwise—their own power amidst the discourses of the school around/through/and by religion and gender and, necessarily, sexuality.

I am concerned in this work with myriad versions of masculinity.[3] This text is about what is in play as regards the development of gender and sexuality when religion and gender are the explicit terms around which a school is organized. It is necessarily then, perhaps more honest in acknowledging that the religious shapes assumptions of gender and sexual possibility than texts that fail to account for the ways in which schooling in America has ever been informed by the religious. It is important to note that a significant gap in the literature exists—excepting in particular Pinar (2006)—as pertains to engaging curriculum in any manner of depth as regards the *intersection of religion* and schooling and how this comes to crystallize as important to the development of students as sexual and gendered beings. The distinction is vital, and one that begs further examination precisely because our schools as institutions are embedded in a society informed so blatantly by Judeo-Christian religious thought—argument as to the degree of interference in the public realm is renewed cyclically—whose notions of what is acceptable for men and women came about largely as a result of church practices and teachings. Gender differentiation, indeed, is exacerbated by religious discourse and this has to do with, for example, what is said about and against gay marriage, but also women's (and conversely nearly always, men's) roles in the/any-given church. This book seeks to bring both religion and schooling into consideration. And it's vital then to note that this is not a book about religion but about the construction of masculinity in a religious school as impacted by the ideals and ideologies made present through, at least partly, the specifics of a Catholic context.

In order to make sense of the study I utilize R. W. Connell's notion of multiple masculinities, with a Foucaultian focus on discourse and power.

"Behold what you are" (in shame); "become what you receive" (passively). This is, imprinted on the holy features of a religious ritual, the largely unspoken assumption upon which so much of schooling is based. There is pushback, though. Mount Carmel High School, an institution similar in profile, location, and history to St. Monica began me on this journey. Their twinned histories, as well as the genera of Catholic schooling, in this ethnic enclave at the very edge of a city will follow shortly. A vignette first, a flash to childhood:

> As I walk through the front doors of Mt. Carmel High School, wrapped in a surround of college-gothic fascia, beset by a solid stone cross, a simple glance up confronts thirteen-year-old me with the mantra of the place. In stolid brown letters—no script, no trilling "L's"; no flying buttresses here for this, it might seem, is business, the external all pomp—I read: "You came to Carmel a boy. If you care to struggle and work at it, you will leave here a man." Second person. Direct address. It is as if a Carmelite priest himself is telling me so. Entreating me even. Confronting. And though I did not attend Mt. Carmel,[4] I will never forget that inscription, for it has come to mean so much—most especially as I read it here, as I seek to critically examine its message—to me, to the men in my life educated within those walls and gone through doors—marked by very similar crosses—much like them.

This work was born of a desire to dig more deeply into the kinds of struggle, and work that might just occur to produce (various versions of) the man abstractly referred to on the frontispiece of Mt. Carmel High School and other schools like[5] it. Make no mistake, please, the above epigram is not meant to encapsulate the ideology of all Catholic schools, but rather serves here as synecdoche for the manner of assumptions perhaps made (and un(der)explored) by religious and non-religious schools as regards the work of becoming a man in a religious context. What I saw, gathered and created, with/through/by the school and the boys housed therein over the course of the semester was a great deal of all manner of banal cruelty tempered by equal measures of startling kindness, much as Chabon suggested in the epigram at the head of this chapter. What follows is my attempt not to predict such acts, but to describe them in a richness of theory brought to bear upon the work of becoming what was received and conceived and deceived at St. Monica High School in the Fall of 2009.

Catholic Education and Local History

Parochial schools, on the whole, provide education for roughly 11% of the K-12 school-aged population nationwide, affecting directly—pedagogically—somewhere in the ballpark of 5. 2 million young men and women ("Digest of Education Statistics," 2009). Sifting further, we find that Catholic schools account for about one third of this number, enrolling something close to 2.2 million students in the 2008–2009 school year. St. Monica is one of 461 single-gendered, Catholic K-12 schools extant in these United States. Its ilk provides a version of the above promise of a gender-separated education for roughly 215,000 American students (McDonald & Schultz, 2009). These numbers are not meant to provide fodder for an argument about representation nor representativeness; rather they are meant to help explicate a simple and oft ignored point in educational research: Parochial schools exist and are an integral part of the education system in the United States. And yet very little theoretical (let alone critical) work about what these schools do (well or poorly or uniquely) is present in the literature. What does get written often amounts to cheerleading for the cause (Kearney, 2008; McCloskey, 2009) or is limited to/by statistical analyses of test scores. That is, the vast majority—to the extent that it exists—of empirical (theoretical, or otherwise) research on parochial Catholic education is A) written by Catholics to B) justify and/or C) prove the efficacy of Catholic schooling as a (favorable) alternative to public schooling (Bryk, Lee, & Holland, 1993; Grace, 2002; Hoffer, Greeley, & Coleman, 1985). That this work exists is less troubling than that a critical literature that interrogates foundational assumptions of self-consciously religious education is largely lacking, particularly in light of the possible implications of intentionally organizing a school around religion, specifically segregated by gender.

Catholic education is part of a larger network of schooling, as Catholicism is also, we can argue (and feminists do) a part of larger and dangerous discourses about gender, sexuality, and masculinity (Chernin, 1994; Daly, 1973; hooks, 2002; Krondorfer, 2010; Salzman & Lawler, 2008; Spong, 1992) and thus this work is not just about religious schooling. It is about indoctrination/socialization which all schooling, in the end, must be. As is any project which seeks to impart knowledge of any kind upon and to children. Though we can argue that religious ideology is different in kind from the desire to "create a moral, disciplined, and unified population prepared to participate in American politics" (Carper, 1998, p. 16), the processes by which devout followers (dilettantes, agnostics, and atheists too) of Christ and willing citizens of the United States are produced in schools are similar. Indeed Horace Mann and Noah Webster saw their common schools movement as inherently tied to "the principle of virtue and of liberty" in order to help students form an inviolable attachment not to religion but to country (Nord, 1995, p. 75). It was a religion of country as divine over the Godhead. That said, it is still important to understand the unique historical circumstances out of which the American system of

Catholic schooling grew as a way to grasp the kinds of historical discourses which (may) still affect practice, pedagogy, and mythology within such schools. Because, after all, for Foucault, knowledge is always produced in history under specific conditions.

Catholic schooling as a formal network in America began in New York City under an Irish immigrant, Bishop "Dagger" John Hughes. Traditionally the founding of the current network of 7248 schools has been seen as a reaction to Anti-Catholic violence as well as an objection toward a perceived Protestant bias inbred within the curriculum of municipal public schools in the 1840s—rooted specifically in mandatory study of the King James Bible (Nord, 1995). Lazerson (1977) further suggests that Dagger John turned to the creation of separatist schools "to preserve minority rights" (p. 302) of ethnic Irish and German immigrants.[6] Coupled with state injunctions that sought to protect the rights (often repealed and reinstated almost on a rolling basis as control slipped in and out of the hands of Know-Nothing/Nativist legislatures in subsequent years)[7] of the now burgeoning Irish Catholic immigrant population, this alternate model of schooling created the flashpoint by which public schools were free to move from a Christian denominational spirit, to the new doctrine of late 19th century Americanism. So we can say, though these two systems of schooling have since diverged, they share historical and ideological roots.

The Irish in Chicago faced similar issues of resistance as their perhaps more cosmopolitan cousins in Gotham on their path to assimilation. The Protestant founders of Beverly Hills-Morgan Park on the far Southwest side of Chicago had a hunch the Catholics moving from the inner enclaves of downtown might be trouble. As the Rock Island rail line expanded transportation possibilities out to the unincorporated area of glacial ridgeline—originally called Washington Heights and later Blue Island—that had served as a German Lutheran stronghold from the early 1870's, a wave of Irish began to flee their slums and tenements in search of land and security. When, in 1924, Fr. Michael Hurley was finally able to secure a small parcel of land just west of the newly laid tracks at the lip of Lake Michigan's ancestral southwestern shores, old-guard residents were up in arms. So much so, in fact, that a cross was burned on the future site of St. Barnabas Catholic Church. The Protestants sensed a demographic shift; the Irish Papists (truly a race at the time, though since faded to an optional ethnicity for most Chicagoans to trot out in mid-March) multiplied at nearly improbable rates after all. And the neighborhood began to go Kelly green. Catholic parishes—Christ the King, St. John Fisher, St. Walter, St. Cajetan—sprung up throughout the neighborhood to serve the burgeoning Irish commuting set, and the Lutherans and Methodists fled to the newly founded suburbs immediately to the west. It was the neighborhood's first version of White Flight (Oswald, 2001).

The high schools, serving the bursting parishes and their expanding middle-class aspirations for advanced education, came next, dotting the southwest side. Within a seven-mile radius buildings, sprouted as various Catholic religious orders jostled for the souls and minds of the young immigrants. They included: De La Salle (1889), Our Lady of Mt. Carmel (1900), Mother McAuley (1900), St. Monica of Cascia (1905), Maria (1911), Leo (1926), Hales Franciscan (1946), Mendel Catholic (1951), Academy of Our Lady (1952), Brother Rice (1956), St. Francis de Salles (1958), Quigley South (1961), St. Lawrence (1961), Queen of Peace (1962), and Marist (1963).

So a young (white, ethnic) Catholic had options. None of the secondary schools, at the time of their founding, though, were co-educational. In the fifty odd years since Marist opened, however, a number of schools have closed or been forced to merge into mixed-gendered schools in an attempt to survive dropping enrollments. This as tuitions rise in the face of sagging religious vocations and the skyrocketing costs of actually having to *pay* a faculty. Some stalwarts, including St. Monica remain, however, becoming in ensuing years increasingly, doggedly even, committed to their founding ideals of single-sex education. Just what those ideals are, and why they necessarily exclude girls (or certain perhaps non-conformist boys) relies either on a commonsense allusion to the-way-things-have-always-been, or is attributed to research (often cited) from education psychology circles that points to gender difference without questioning its (and single-sex schools') role in creating those same differences.

St. Monica Catholic High School

The research site, St. Monica, is a secondary school run by the Augustinian fathers, who took over the school after the Archdiocese of Chicago closed Quigley South,[8] a seminary high school that had been operating on the location into the early 1990s. St. Monica of Cascia sits[9] on the northwest corner of 79th street and South Western Avenue at the crossroads of Chicago neighborhoods marked—pocked, perhaps better describes it—by the effects of Irish/Polish/Italian ethnic-turned-white-flight begun during the 1960s and more or less completed in the early 1990s when Irish political bulwarks kept Beverly to the south white (and as of the early 2000s, cul-de-sac'ed off). Too, Midway airport maintained a western border as big box stores developed near the airfield and began to replace hastily constructed slum housing and four-hour-nap hotels. Lake Michigan provided an incontrovertible lapping eastern border and heading north up Western Ave. will take one on a tour of what (some) whites might describe as progressively worse urban blight until the street regentrifies north of Madison avenue, the people getting paler and the homes brown(ston)er. Make no mistake: it has been the continual disinvestment in the infrastructure of these neighborhoods by the city of Chicago beginning most prominently under the first mayor Richard Daley that has pushed property values that were already artificially low in the Black Belt[10] conspiratorially low.

This is important, not because I will be able to address fully the very real and troubling racial context that underlies any discussion of education in this region of Chicago in particular—I won't—but because it is one layer of the history of the place, of the school. And it is part of the silences that construct the discourses into/through which the young men who attend the school grow. That is, if they are anything like me: a white son of the South Side (or the Sox-side for your typical baseball fan), a Catholic, and immersed in the mythology of Christianity, of Irish Chicago, of racial Beverly then they will know only that their school is largely white though the neighborhoods that surround it no longer are. So on with the business of life, back south down Western toward home, or west and north to Midway to Scottsdale or Hegewisch to the isolated neighborhoods kept white by powerful ethnic politburos. A quick look at the demographics of the school tells me that, at least on surface I may be correct as St. Monica—all-boys, 9–12, and enrolling 701 young men—serves a population that is roughly 70% white. One of the fairy tales of the place is that this is normal. It was certainly normalizing for me at Marist. Feminists have long suggested that gender (and any attempt at analyzing the production of it) requires the adoption of an intersectional lens (Baca Zinn & Thornton Dill, 1996; McCall, 2005; West & Fenstermaker, 1995) and so any examination at the school and gender it would appear, requires an attending to race as well.

Fr. Tim McDonnagh O. S. A.[11] is the former principal and current president of St. Monica. He is also an alumnus of the school and a native of Beverly. When I proposed the study of masculinity and spirituality—ostensibly in all boys Catholic schools writ large, but located in its particularities—at St. Monica, he was incredibly welcoming and eager to engage in the project seeing it as a way to improve the school which, based on his personal history with the place, is very dear to his heart. After a tour of the building—which I remembered vaguely from events there when I was a child and my brother was enrolled—he handed me three documents meant to help me familiarize myself with the pedagogical approach of the Augustinians, the history of the school itself, as well as the personal life of St. Augustine. This was actually my second encounter with the beginning of my education about what it means to be a "Monica man." On the exterior of the building is a frescoed rendering of the motto of the school—and ostensibly of the Augustinians—"Veritas, Unitas, Caritas." Truth then unity then love. A convenient trinity of Latinate terminology. The order of the terms is not accidental, and we need only turn to the Gospel of John for verification. Christ as the Way, the Truth, and the Life (John 8:12) provides a process, through a mindset, toward an end goal—and in true Christian triplicate, all three are one. So it is with Truth, presumably attained through the brotherhood of the school, achieved in the work of love. Therefore, for the young men of St. Monica affixed on the walls is a constant reminder of just what is to occur upon entering the school: the search for one Truth (Christ), achieved in lockstep (Unitas) with God (who *is* love, again from John, 4:8). This is one of the very first (and most prominent for administration and alumni, at least) stories with which the students of the school will come to interact, even in passing, throughout their days at Monica; too the notion of Truth, Unity, and Love becomes one (three?) of the ways that the experience of the school, of the ideology and the discourse and thus the way power and gender get played with at St. Monica will come to de/limit the world for students, in turn seeking to form them as beings in that schooled world as well. In a way, my education at the school had, in these initial meetings, already begun.

Catholic Wonder Tales: The Saints

> It is only with the gradual rise of the Christian Church, which began to exploit magic and miraculous stories and to codify what would be acceptable for its own interests that wonder tales and fairy tales were declared sacrilegious, heretical, dangerous, and untruthful. However the Church could not prevent these stories from being circulated; it could only stigmatize, censure, or criticize them. At the same time, the Church created its own "fairy-tale" tradition of miraculous stories in which people were to believe and still do believe.
>
> Jack Zipes, "Why Fairy Tales Stick"

Uh-oh.

Picture me, please, slowly twisting one of the two scrolls which encircle my neck. Nervous. Another finger has been pushed out of my own weakening dyke of faith by the pressure of this overwhelming rationality, historicity, inscrutable reason. I am digging, as I read the above, into my own past, wondering at the constructed "marvelous but fallacious instrument of collective memory" (Versaci, 2007, p. 90) that has cast various shadows upon my faith in God. Perhaps and probably the tension in my hand, as I finger the scapular at my throat is rooted in my belief that stories are what I have faith in and my (theological) stories come from an inherently political institution, very much rooted in the contentiousness of the human affair of creating the soul to repress and then save it (Daly, 1973). The Catholic Church, is thus actively engaged in reifying its own power through the work of "teach[ing] that which is other, opposite, and inferior" that we the humble laity might "cease to be other" (Nodelman, 2008, p. 68) through assimilation into a conservative ideological project. One way to bring the flock into the fold is through church doctrine, another is through schooling; the third is in the stories we tell about fantastical plebes (like us) made holy, beatified. All this in Jesus' name, of course.

I have, as Trites (2000) recalls "grow[n] to maturity trained in the ways of such institutions" (p. 22) raised in a very specific language of belief, outlined by ideology but highlighted through the dazzling firework-ed stories of saints and sinners (martyrs, heroes) who have become easier to love than a Church that deeply troubles me, that continues to alienate. Make these stories mere fairy tales and all I have left is a great anger at the re/op/pression of a tradition-bound and woefully immodest clerical-patriarchal hierarchy and its very human drive for power.

Shit.

The Brown Scapular of Our Lady of Mt. Carmel

> The fairy tale was intended to play a major role in the socialization process.
>
> Jack Zipes, "Why Fairy Tales Stick"

> Ideology is not a political policy...it is a climate of belief...[and] we believe some ideologies so deeply that we consider them Truth.
>
> Roberta Seelinger Trites, "Disturbing the Universe"

> Truth...is not necessarily the same thing as fact.
>
> Rocco Versaci, "This Book Contains Graphic Language"

I was nine when my older brother, thin, invincible and prone to passing out with the light on while I pretended to sleep on the bunk below, rolled me my first brown scapular. This was the Communion of our neighborhood. As much as alcohol and racism and the vestiges of an Irish ancestry branded us South

Siders, this simple piece of cloth made us men of Christ. In her gift to St. Simon Stock—this is how it's told to us[12]—in the unfathomable Middle Ages (knights and damsels and chamber pots in my mind), the Virgin Mary bestowed favor on all those who wore her scapular in *good faith*. Chief among the fringe benefits of belonging to Mary's club is the stipulation for free passage to heaven. This ensured all those venal sinners out there fortunate enough to get a twenty-seven-cent string with two elaborately screen-printed guesses at images of a saint and the mother of God that they could avoid centuries of severe hair-pulling discomfort in Purgatory. It also pardoned the mortals their rages, defilements and sexual dalliances.

They, scapulars, tear off easily. This is relative of course. Say rather: they tore off easily when my prime occupation was front-yard football. Here would-be tacklers went for hoods, ankles and scapulars; anything to slow you down in the frost of a November Chicago night.

Always after it happened, after the game ended of course, the dilemma was burial or holocaust. Sacred objects such as these, blessed by priests even, cannot be thrown in the trash to languish with coffee grinds. Like flags or pets, they require proper disposal. Mine usually ended up in the Coleman grill on our back porch stuffed in with years of accumulated palm fronds. We never cooked outside, it was either too cold or the yellow jackets had taken over. So my faith lay—more or less intact—nestled in years of accumulated ash, entombed in rusting chrome.

But it's odd that they broke so readily, come to think of it, because once in fifth grade on the West Side, I had to really work to cut one off to sate a heathen referee.

"No jewelry."

First of all, only gays wore jewelry. I learned that on the playground early on. An earring in the wrong ear marked you open for ridicule for life. Oddly, rat-tails were socially acceptable. Secondly, it was more than ornamental. It was faith, it was home and if I collapsed on the court and died that day I'd be going to hell for hitting Kim Vick in the forehead with a marker on the playground that morning. Her welt—it really was impressive; even said "c-r-a-y-o" before disappearing into her hairline—and my severed scapular spelled an eternity of fire. I cried in the stands, sawing at the thread with a key. I'll haunt him, I thought, already gnashing my teeth.

As I got older, though, this kind of blind faith in a hellfire as well as a heavenly backstage pass started to make very little sense. Some digging brought me to a conflict of stories as allegory and the Bible as Truth. Then there's this: St. Christopher, I have only recently discovered, may never have actually existed.[13]

After St. Christopher was officially discredited (or defrocked, maybe de-realed, I don't know the terminology) screwing over nervous travelers for centuries to come, I decided to look up St. Simon, just to check on his relative reality. I'd been wearing the scapular gifted to him by the Virgin Mary for years.

I found things.

Some I knew: *He founded the Carmelite order of priests and brothers.* Good men. Spiritual, practical. Fans of football, basketball and minor emotional abuse—nothing traceable or too deep, mostly guilt. Mt. Carmel high school near us claims a cadre of professional athletes and the neighborhood abounds with the brown and white of the Caravan faithful.

I didn't go there for high school. I chose Marist (a mashup of Mary-in-Christ) for academics. This reasoning was only barely acceptable. It created problems. A friend's father reminds me of my poor choice whenever I see him.

He was English. Pale, bad teeth.

He was a hermit. Who wasn't? Skellig Michael in Ireland was beautiful. I can romanticize honeycombed cells: men cloistering on a wind-torn cliff overlooking a wild Irish sea.

He lived for a decade in a tree trunk—yes, IN a tree trunk—*subsisting on leaves and roots. It was at this point that the Virgin Mary appeared to him and gave him the Brown Scapular to spread to all who needed saving in her grace. He returned to his home speaking in tongues of his vision, carrying a brown cloth, preaching the word of salvation through enrollment in Mary's corps…*

My eyes stopped there. I heard a cartoon screeching—the kind usually preceding a collision—in my head. Flashes of fumbling madness came. A vision in a tree, in a tree(!). Transubstantiation has become reasonable and I'm reincarnated a failed Catholic wearing a useless bauble, the vestiges of a mad saint. Always the hypocrite, I left it there, limp, meaningless for the first time; my faith still embodied in fraying cloth.

As I said…

Uh-oh.

This could be paralyzing, I suppose, but part of the work of an academic involves holding commonsense notions up to the—hopefully—prismatic light of scrutiny that we might better, as a community, recognize the truths and falsehoods—conflicted and conflicting—that alight within unquestioned belief. It is our task, Eagleton suggests, to become trained readers in order to "read for…silences" (as cited in Trites, 2000, p. 52). For me the search thus framed is for the discourses of faith that might have been spawned by/in/through the scapular (and objects and tales of faith that function as socializing influences just like it) rather than the fact of the holiness of the object itself. Or at least I hope so.

Because I am necessarily bounded as a scholar by my history that then affects "my choices" which are "thus a blatant example of how my conclusions are limited by the boundaries of my knowledge" (Nodelman, 2008, p. 102), some personal history will matter here. To this end, Trites (2000) helps us understand that any examination of religious ideology, of how it might get promulgated through a "discourse" of religious fairy tales requires that we look at how such a discourse, filtered through ideology, "transmits and produces power…reinforces it, but also undermines and exposes it, renders it fragile and makes it possible to thwart it" (2000, p. 114). My truths about religion are runthrough by the transmittal of power and its renegotiation manifest in the brown scapular and particularly the silences of the history of the thing. What I came to wonder, at St. Monica High School, an institution very similar in profile and Catholic representation, to Mt. Carmel, are just where the fairy tales that push ideology lie—in both senses of the word, I suppose—for students. That is, what silences ought I be reading in the literature of my research site that create specific religious and gendered discourses, ideologically narrowed, by their authors. And more importantly, why are they constructed as such. To what end? For high schoolers are, in the eyes of both church and society, still children—legally defined, even—and to read the literature of the school is to read "what producers" of knowledge, ideology, religion…men "hope children will read" (Nodelman, 2008, p. 4) but also what they hope will not be read. It helps to begin with history and, I suspect, the wonder tales of the place.

St. Monica of Cascia

Born to Antonio and Amata Lotti in 1381 in the Italian hillside town of Roccaporena, Monica Lotti began her healing miracles as an infant. In her parents' fields a "laborer working the ground with the Lottis cut his hand and, running back to the nearby house for some bandages…was startled to see a swarm of bees circling little Monica's face" as she lay sleeping." Though Monica's face was not disturbed…the man instinctively began to wave away the bees with his hand—his injured hand," which was, upon the abrupt exit of the docile bees, of a sudden, healed (Di Gregorio, 2003, p. 5). Years later, after much study, the teenaged Monica announced to her parents that she wished to join the Augustinian convent in the neighboring city of Cascia. "As attentive parents," swarming bees aside, "who knew well their daughter's natural goodness and fervent religious spirit," Monica's mother and father "may well have anticipated this piece of news" (p. 8). Which is why, the author notes, it is odd that they instead forced her to marry a local man named Paolo Mancini, thus altering the course of our story significantly.

John Shelby Spong (1992), in his search for religious truth among the repressive tradition of a Church regarding women, asks, "What does it take to understand the mythic dimensions that fill our religious story?" (p. 12). A healthy suspension of disbelief, one supposes, or the unwillingness to break down the fourth wall that keeps priests on the stage of the altar and we fallen/failing laypersons in the pews facing their ministrations. Less glib, Spong suggests that "origin tales," such as those of Monica here, and St. Simon earlier, "are commentaries on adult meaning" (p. 59); they "are not history but are a form of myth-making" (Connell, 2002, p. 69). Set within an argument for a contextual reading of the scriptures placed firmly within their Hebrew Midrashic[14] tradition, he pleads for a similar reading of the sacred texts (and stories) that come to constitute the constellation of the Christian mythology. Which—considering the relative lack of options for women in Italy in the 14th century and their general dearth of power within the family structure—still makes it an odd choice for Monica's parents to have pushed her towards marriage considering the violence rife in the Cascia region at the time; violence that would claim her "quick-tempered" husband's life. Her story from here is filled up with trying to keep her young sons from retaliating for the murder of Paolo, which worked, on a technicality: they both died of "a deadly illness" (the Plague, perhaps) less than a year after their father's murder (Di Gregorio, 2003, p. 19).

On the one-hundredth anniversary of the founding of St. Monica High School, an historical shrine—a walk-through yearbook if you will—was constructed in the open foyer at the entrance of the school's current location. There, at the center as one enters the hall of pictures of distinguished—and not-so distinguished—Monicamen, is a plaque that tells the crib notes story of the historical St. Monica of Cascia. In this version, Monica is born amidst an early mob war and after her husband's death, her sons are "lost in the mists of time." At which time, then, Monica was free after her period of mourning to enter the convent of St. Augustine—though the nuns were reluctant to take her for fear that the violence that clung to her family life might follow her into cloister. From there the religious tale begins with devotion to the sacred heart of Christ—invoked repeatedly as the "restless heart"[15] by St. Augustine, her patron and ends with the stigmata. After forty years behind the walls of the convent:

> she spoke of her willingness to relieve Christ's suffering by sharing even the smallest part of his pain. Her offer was accepted...and Monica was united with Jesus in a profound experience of spiritual intimacy. In this moment of ecstatic union, a thorn from Jesus' crown penetrated Monica's forehead and the wound...remained open and visible for the next fifteen years until the day of her death. (Di Gregorio, 2003, p. 39)

Thus, then, we come further through mists of time to a school named for a stigmatic, a child beset by bees, a mother of the mob. And on Novena Thursdays, before school, attendees are blessed by an ornate cross, the centerpiece of which contains the fragment of her ancient finger bone in some relic-ed homage to a phantasm of long-ago faith, whose remains come to color the discourses of the boys in that early morning chapel, yes, but also those who don't feel the call to pre-dawn devotion but still attend the school. For St. Monica's name is invoked consistently in interesting ways that indeed shape the discourse of religion made possible, but also of gender. At least for the administration. The boys, largely, I come to find, except in one specific alternative space, see her only in name, in statue, and in the Prayer of the Peacemaker they must recite (or pretend to) during opening announcements each day.[16]

When I talk about the study of masculinity and spirituality—or rather, masculinities and spiritualities—as formed, reformed, and deformed in the context of an all-boys Catholic school what I am studying, ultimately, is the play of discourses of the place. As "gender is not fixed in advance of social interaction, but is constructed in interaction" (Connell, 1995, p. 35) we must consider, as above, the "multiplicity of discursive elements that can come into play" (Foucault, 1998, p. 170) at the nexus of the individual negotiating a given day, a semester, a life of schooling; Catholic and gendered schooling. Because I am in agreement with Biesta's (1998) analysis of Foucault's take on discourse(s) as coming to be through the intersubjective where "the subject is always already on the inside of history, on the inside of language, on the inside of the discursive and nondiscursive practices in which she constitutes her own subjectivity and works at the limits of herself," (p. 11), I choose to attend to the history of the school, of the neighborhood, and my-coming-to-self as a presage to the discussion of how the Monicamen came to make (non)sense of their gendered/schooled experiences. That is, there is a reason that only men are able to turn wafer into flesh, wine into blood, and this is historically rooted, yes, but the ways that the boys shifting in their pews come to accept or challenge, sleep through or ignore the doctrine of transubstantiation is part and parcel of their homelife, their relationship with friends and enemies within the school, and their negotiation of the fairy tales about religion or white flight or who St. Monica might or might not have been. That is, their masculinity is informed by all of these things, sure, but they are not passive in this information chain and are ready practitioners of a nuanced negotiation of becoming men. None of this, either, is fixed as Bourdieu and Wacquant (1992) remind, noting "social laws are temporally and spatially bound regularities that hold as long as the institutional conditions that underpin them are allowed to endure" (p. 52). The discourses of Church, school, and society (of which the first two are both part and co-constructors) hold those priests on the altar, and the boys in the pews. However, in word, in deed, in cruelty and kindness, the young men of the school are constantly working (even in acquiescence and resistance to prayer) at the limits of (becoming) themselves.

Notes

1. All names have been changed, including those of the school and its patroness.
2. I've chosen, here, not to use the concept of "big 'P'" patriarchy which is probably most tersely defined as "a single overarching structure of domination between men and women" (Mac an Ghaill, 1994, p. 10) because of course this is not always about what I would render as an overly simplistic relationality between and among men and women. And of course the hope is to complicate notions of both power and gender through the research here. It is vital, though, to note that the Catholic Church is (and has been) institutionally calcified as a patriarchal institution, from the structure of the clergy to the language of the Mass over the centuries. It is, in short, an organization run by, and in many ways created to perpetuate the status of, men while defining what's possible in the process of becoming a man as well. The school (and its boys and this researcher) are subject to these realities. Some of what is talked about, then, is how patriarchy comes to simplify and complicate our lived existences.
3. The problem of defining masculinities in relation and opposition to femininities in the school would bring welcome complexity to the analysis here. In following the thread of the research and in conversations with students and faculty, it became apparent that to be true to the data, though, it was apropos for this study to name everything performed in and in the name of the school as a form of masculinity. This reflects, of course, a (probably) troubling and (certainly) limiting view of what is possible in the actions of those defined as boys and men, particularly by their actions in school. But it also remains consistent with the ways the boys and their faculty understood and came to relate to the world of St. Monica.
4. Each Catholic school in the area holds an entrance exam. Every school's test, aside from those on the North side of the city, occurs on the same day—generally on the second Saturday of January. Where you test, in essence, is where you will attend. So the lives of 7th and

8th grade boys and girls, like myself, become a-brim in the fall semester with open houses as they are wooed by pep bands, insufferable hallway tours, and the not-so-subtle architectural lessons like that I learned in my brush with the Carmelites here.

5   The word 'like' is tricky here. While each school would argue that it has a unique charism informed by historical and theological as well as ongoing pedagogical ideals, I mean to draw attention to the similarity in approach to gender-segregated schooling as well as a rough correlation which runs along the lines of a self-conscious Catholicism. Too these schools are drawing from roughly—and competitively—the same demographic of student: white-ethnic, working class, parochial school educated. The difference falls out in the details, or so I hope this study will illuminate.

6   The Italians, too abject, were left out of the equation at the time. Useful to note, too, that Mother Elizabeth Seton's school—considered the originator of Catholic education—predates Hughes' attempt at creating a system of schooling by thirty years. We might rightly ask why this narrative is less well known, perhaps a manifestation of very real gender troubles in/with the Church and the stories it (and historians) chooses to tell.

7   Indeed it was around this time, Carper (1998) reminds us, that Illinois and Wisconsin made it mandatory for children between 7 and 14 to attend sixteen weeks of public schooling a year. The Bennett and Edwards laws, respectively, were meant to undermine sectarian religious education as Catholic and Lutheran schools were seen as corrupting the ideal of evangelical Christianity espoused through public schooling.

8   My brother attended Quigley South; my father Quigley North. Neither were options when I got to high school age and so I went to Marist, an all-boys' Catholic school south and west of St. Monica which has since gone co-ed, like a great many Catholic secondary schools, in an effort to remain financially viable. My sisters all attended all-girls' Catholic schools in the area and my mother went to St. Scholastica (what a name!) on the north side of the city, itself single-gendered, too.

9   I mean this, actually, in two ways. The building of the school is named after the historical figure Monica Lotti, true, but it also contains a shard of her finger bone, a relic housed in a shrine within the school's chapel.

10 Philpott (1978) provides a ready history of the creation of this geographically restricted region set up by city policy to contain blacks who migrated north during the Great Migration of the twenties and thirties. Daley, in fact, is said to have built the Dan Ryan expressway, specifically for the purpose of maintaining a western border to the thing, an eight-lane moat reinforcing a very real color line (Royko, 1971). It didn't work. In part because of "blockbusting" real estate agents who capitalized on the FHA's "red-lining" policy restricting lending (and pushing down property values) in areas containing "inharmonious racial groups." But it also failed because Daley's own official and unofficially bigoted policies led to further racial discord which allowed for the exploitation of a great fear of miscegenation. The Black Belt, thus, expanded west beyond the Dan Ryan, and south beyond Hyde Park because of panic-peddling agents, cultivating the seeds of prejudice among ethnic whites who justified their flight along economic lines.

11 O. S. A. is the abbreviation for the Augustinian order and it stands, as one might imagine, for "Order of St. Augustine." The charge of the Augustinians involves "the gospel imperative of love of God and neighbor—which Augustine sees as one, since we love our neighbor in God and our God in our neighbor—" which "becomes for the followers of Augustine their particular charism in friendship and hospitality" ("The Augustinians," n. d.).

12 Doctrinal and historical information available at: http://carmelnet. org/scapular/scapular. htm. A caution: This is not stuff for the faint of faith, or the skeptical, or the lapsing. Particularly in light of assumptions collected by Clark (2003) that suggest "anything associated with childhood…exists only to be outgrown" (p. 65), which might best have cited 1 Corinthians 13 for its inspiration: "When I was a child, I spoke like a child, thought like a child, and reasoned like a child. When I became a man, I gave up my childish ways."

13 http://www.catholic. org/saints/saint. php?saint_id=36. In some sense, I suppose it doesn't matter, but it is hard to explain Catholicism as monotheistic when we already have the Trinity and then these sub-deities and their cults running around making up miracles, wonder tales. Their spread, then, as with my own experience of the scapular story runs along very similar lines with Zipes' (2006) theory of mimetic cultural transmission. The thought is that notions such as "belief in life after death" caught on by "parasitiz[ing]" (p. 4) the imaginations of early Christians. And so it might be with various Lives of (now fictional) Saints. These stories of miraculous saints whereby in the Catholic church of my youth, after death, a person could only be beatified if three miracles were attributed to them; the number, I believe, has since been lowered. We expect less of our saints, I suppose. Or our capacity for storytelling is running out; perhaps our dubiousness has been piqued by cases like St. Christopher.) are what get illustrated in text and stained glass. They are exciting, mysterious. Troubling.

14 "Midrash represented efforts on the part of the rabbis to probe, tease, and dissect the sacred story looking for hidden meanings, filling in blanks, and seeking clues to yet-to-be-revealed truths" (Spong, 1992, p. 18).

15 At the beginning and end of each school day, we were entreated to recite the following prayer in call-and-response form:
"You have made us for yourselves O' Lord…"
"And our hearts are restless until they rest in you."

16 St. Monica, messenger of peace and herald of reconciliation. Despite hardship and suffering you lived the Gospel message of compassion and forgiveness, and showed the power of love to conquer hatred, and to establish harmony. Help us to follow your example, and to be instruments of Christ's peace. Pray that our hearts may be always open, and our arms extended to pardon those who do wrong, and even to embrace with mercy those who inflict injury. Pray that God may use our humble gestures to touch hearts and to sow peace. Amen.

Chapter 2

Masculinity Foretold, Told, Retold

> Masculinity is foretold, told, and retold, instated, regulated, and enforced.
> Ken Corbett, "Boyhoods"

> Words caused things here.
> Michael Ruhlman, "Boys Themselves"

Johnny: "Where you been, Mr. Burke?"
Me: "I was at the hockey game."
Johnny: "My Mom wouldn't let me go."
Me: "Why not?"
Johnny: "'Cause she's gay about me going out on school nights."

Gender and Sexuality

Some memory-work to begin:

In August of 1998 I'd splintered off a piece of my radial head (elbow) bone. This left me, in-sling, and more-or-less helpless to dress myself for the first two weeks of my freshman year of college. And there I was, living on a floor—at my new Jesuit university-home—with twenty plus eighteen year old "men," trying to figure out how not to get labeled "gay" were I to ask one of them—strangers all—to help me put pants on. This concern, that a simple action—asking for help, albeit in somewhat extraordinary circumstances as far as potential intimate contact went—might make me "the fag" of the floor came from somewhere.

My sense is that it—this fear?—was rooted in my four years in the crucible of performative masculinity that was Marist High School: 1,200 boys and the only women in sight were Religious and/or faculty. Limp a little bit on a given day…gay; use a three syllable word to answer a question…gay; wear maroon shorts to soccer practice…gay; ask a guy to help you get dressed…super gay. It was, as if, as Pascoe (2007) suggests, we all had a unique form of Tourette's. But the labeling served a function: it kept us in line. We were practicing some version of what Butler (1990) calls "the repeated stylization of the body…which define[d] 'masculinity' and 'femininity'" (p. 33).

We were homogeneous; we were straight; and shit were we worried that you—or anyone—might not know. Mac An Ghaill (1994) stresses that "heterosexuality is a highly fragile, socially constructed phenomenon" that is, though, presented as "fixed...apparently stable...and unitary" (p. 45). Absent, both on my all-male floor and in my same-sexed high school were women as potential heterosexual partners (Cameron, 2006; Pascoe, 2007) that we—insecure and embedded in a culture fraught with, and run through by, homophobia—might assert our heterosexual identities through the protection of a ubiquitously present girlfriend. And so we flailed, lashed out, belittled. That to be gay was to be less-than was selfsame, foregone. Indeed Butler (2008) as philosopher and credited as founder of the very notion that we might queer gender/sexuality, notes in reflecting on the response to her seminal (these problematic words of ours) work, *Gender Trouble*, that she initially "sought to understand some of the terror and anxiety that some people suffer in 'becoming' [or being made] gay,' the fear of losing one's place in gender" (p. xi).

This was all a part, we could argue, of our "gender-role socialization" which for boys "is often characterized by negative prescriptions: Don't be a sissy; don't engage in feminine behavior" (Harris, 1995, p. 43). Whether or not a broken elbow and the resulting temporary lack of facility with a zipper was feminine mattered little: it was made strange and thus negative, which led to a very quick slide to "gay" on the hall. Epstein and Johnson (1998) propose that "in schools...sexuality is both everywhere and nowhere" (p. 108). And it is through expression/repression of sexuality that gender comes to be represented and regulated often in the hallways (and dorm rooms) of schools, an idea which Butler (2008) attributes to the conditions of "normative heterosexuality," where the "policing of gender is sometimes used as a way of securing heterosexuality" (p. xii). Thus I was made the "fag" where by dint of being different from me, any individual on the floor could assert his straight status in contrast to my sudden suspectness. All that for getting dressed, to say nothing about what I actually wore.

The point, though, is this: gender, sexuality,[1] masculinity, they are always in process, they are constantly being reworked. To be "fag," for Pascoe (2007), is not to *be* at all, but rather to inhabit—to be forced to colonize, like a penal immigrant sent by the British Crown to Australia—that agonistic space, usually temporarily. "Fag," she notes," is not necessarily a static identity attached to a particular (homosexual) boy. Fag talk and fag imitations serve as a discourse with which boys discipline themselves and each other through joking relationships" (p. 54). Further:

> [The] fluidity of fag identity is what makes the specter of the fag such a powerful disciplinary mechanism. It is fluid enough that boys police their behaviors out of fear of having the fag identity permanently adhere and definitive enough so that boys recognize a fag behavior and strive to avoid it. (p. 54)

I have come to find in my work, too, that they—these boys—do not only discipline each other but also most anyone who inhabits their world. So it is that Johnny's mother—from the epigraph above—becomes/is made gay through her parenting. This is something of what Connell who has written extensively about, and is the genesis of multiple masculinities (2002) calls the "social embodiment" of gender, which "may involve an individual's conduct" and its regulation by other individuals, certainly, "but also may involve a group, an institution, or a whole complex of institutions" (p. 48). Families. Kinship groups. Schools. Religions.

Gender, thus, is not "something one passively 'is' or 'has'" but is rather something one does (Thorne, 1993, p. 5). And it is ever (re)created in the tensions of activities, in the webs of language, as above. This is Butler's (1990) "gender performativity" where gender "is produced as a ritualized repetition of conventions…socially compelled in part by the force of compulsory heterosexuality" (p. 31). In this view where "nothing human is 'outside' discourse," and "society is unavoidably a world of meanings" made through language, gender "meanings bear the traces of the social processes by which they are made" (Connell, 2002, p. 65).

What to do, then, with this growing sense that all language, particularly that which seeks to regulate action, is both "productive as well as reflective of social relations"? (Pennycook, 2001, p. 50). Perhaps begin with the body.

Gender and the Body

Though it is important to acknowledge that, as Pascoe (2007) asserts, "bodies are the vehicles through which we express gendered selves" researchers concerned with masculinities and gender had best recall that bodies are also "the matter through which social norms are made concrete" (p. 12). That is, they become a part of the language through which gender is written and read. One major critique of early literature on masculinities is that it located a masculinity firmly in the male body without looking "at the masculinizing process outside the male body" (p. 12). The interplay, by implication—the interstices—between the physical and the social(izing) begs attending. A body, in this understanding, is both, in my case male by my various presentations of self,[2] but also made male by a whirlwind of socially generated discourses that are ever swirling around and upon me constantly affecting my performance of gender. This is the body as an "'array of intersections'; articulated [in] moments in networks of relations and understandings'" (Nespor, 1997, xiv).

It is also a body which is very much affected by the educational world it inhabits. Schools in particular are good at "policing [children's] bodies and presentation[s] of self" (Ferguson, 2001, p. 65).[3] Ferguson rightly trains her sights on the (im)possibility of being young and black and male in schools and sees a consistent linking "of meaning in the connection between black male bodies and fear" (p. 67). This surveilling, and coming to fear, is applied in similar ways for Mac An Ghaill (1994) to working-class white males who in his study of a school in England, though "born into male bodies" consistently battle with administrations' notion of what a boy in school ought be. This he came to view as a frustration on the part of adults at the boys unsuccessful "accomplishment of culturally appropriate versions of masculinity…within shifting sets of social constraints" (p. 89). Many of those constraints deal directly with presentation of the body or rather with how meaning comes to be grafted onto this presentation. Ian Harris (1995) whose research is on male interpretations of cultural messages, frames the discussion as one of control, or its lacking. As "gender identities are molded by cultures which hold beliefs about appropriate male" presentations of self "younger men not in control of their own destinies take direction for their behavior from adults" (p. 51). And adults in a schooled setting present a decidedly jaundiced view of the male body: it is to be controlled and in control, straight or it will be straightened. Or so the rhetoric suggests.

Much of that discourse comes to be outlined by a doctrine of Spartan "hardening" through self-denial; particularly in light of sport(s) an area explored by Messner (2002) who notes junctions where the body becomes "a machine, or a tool, to be built, disciplined, used (and if necessary, used up) to get a job done" (p. 58). More militaristically (though not less incisive) Miedzian (2002) in her work seeking to understand male tendencies towards violent behavior suggests that, "from the youngest age…boys are raised as soldiers"[4] (p. 56) disconnected from the emotionality tied to femininity and encoded with the "John Wayne syndrome" which demands of them a hardness, toughness, unemotionality, ruthlessness with a constant stress on aggressive competition (p. 35). All of this is a part of the "masculine mystique" (p. 16) engendered through familial relations, media influence, and societal interventionism. Ferguson (2001) notes that this increased root in physicality requires then "the active development of a defense system against encroachments from others" where a masculinity embodied "is constructed as the practice of power plays and brinksmanship" (p. 43). In sum, boys are to be—in school in particular—aggressively in control of their bodies; that is manifesting aggression, often, through control of their space and that of those around them.

Sex (and sexualities) of course is the not-so-hidden discourse here. Corbett (2009), in a unique marriage of queer and psychoanalytic theory, asks that we consider the ways "in which boys' bodies are either erased or glossed" through an elaborate "phallophobia" (p. 218) which dictates how/that sex is not talked about openly or, rather, frankly in schools. Sex is certainly talked about in schools, but often only obliquely through official channels.[5] That the male body is sexed, even as it is instrumentalized for the punishment of the athletic field, for example, can be readily seen in something as simple (and culturally loaded) as a choice of mascots; there is a reason St. Monica is the Mustangs and not the Geldings and it is all rolled-up in the implied prowess bought through the performance of the honed male body. I choose, at this point, however to delay the discussion of sex and the body in the interest of picking it back up as it relates to religion and the imposition of doctrinal/assumed virginity as austerity/conquest.

One way to make sense of this embodied/imposed gendering of the male body is suggested by Connell (1987) who posits a "gender order" by which dynamism of gender-definition is possible on a societal scale under "the current state of play in…macro-politics" where "the formation and dissolution of general categories and ordering of relationships between institutions" come to represent the macro-politics of gender (p. 139). That is: gender is an always changing thing, dependent on individual actors affecting large-scale definitions which in-turn then (de)limit the possibilities of both individuals and groups to express and live gendered lives. It's a feedback loop, always closed, ever recursive and massive in scope.

Such a structural understanding eliminates (fails to illuminate fully) for this researcher the possibility for individual agential activity. For in the end those who create and do and recreate gender do not live macro lives and the slippage at the boundary of when structure ends and the individual begins is problematic and often undertheorized. What we're talking about are the vulnerable joists here, the vagueness of just what it means to be "between." Cherryholmes suggests (1988), "meaning is," indeed, "always in constant play" (p. 47), which supposes in some ways that which is gendered cannot rightly be ordered, for it is always ever disordered by the very nature of a constantly mutable meaning. They are, meaning and gender, ever between. What this study came to be about, however, is how meaning is made and maintained; this is about the play.

The tension in structural definitions such as Connell's suggests that gender is both constructed, yes, but then—with struggle, perhaps—categorizable. And the production of a gender order is what happens when the doing and the done combine to build a socially normative set of behaviors. In other words the "structure" of gender "becomes an object of practice, because the choices and actions of today's [actors] re-create [extant] divisions of labor and power" (Messner, 2002, p. 11). Thus understood, it becomes possible for Connell (2002) to suggest that "bodies have agency *and* are socially constructed" (p. 47) and further that:

> gender is the structure of social relations that centres on the reproductive arena, and the set of practices (governed by this structure) that brings reproductive distinctions between bodies into social processes. (p. 10)

One helpful (or not, I suppose) religious metaphor might be the Christian definition—for this study is, after all, rooted in a particular religious context—of free will: we are all actors of our own accord under an omnipotent God who understands and experiences time and space differently than us and already knows how we will act and though He (because, well, so often He[6] is represented as male) has lived our choices for us already—and they are then somehow fixed in a time we have yet to come to know—we are free under that structure to make decisions that we have, in a sense, already made in a time we cannot hope to comprehend. Still, it is with Connell's theorization of multiple masculinities that this study was begun and it is to hir[7] foundational critique of a limited view of masculinity as singular and unified that we rightly and respectfully now turn.

Masculinities

Connell (1995) troubles the idea that masculinity is a unitary, singular, concept. Ze proposes an expansion of the range of gendered possibility present in the enacted world thus through a discussion of the problematic nature of sex-role theory. The "basic tendency in sex role theory to understand men's and women's positions as complementary" (p. 25) belies studies that note that "sex differences, on almost every psychological trait measured, are either non-existent or fairly small" (p. 21). These small differences, however, in the male and female sexed-bodies, ze argues, are "culturally cued" to be exaggerated (p. 21) and so the difference that makes a difference is projected/encoded as across genders, rather than within them. The male role, as socially embodied, could remain singular and separate from the female role unless we begin to envision a theory of multiple masculinities rooted in the notion that "gender is not fixed in advance of social interaction, but is constructed in interaction" (p. 34). And so it is with masculinities which are indeed myriad and unsettled and always in negotiation. "To recognize diversity in masculinities is not enough," though; "we must also recognize the relations between the different kinds of masculinity: relations of alliance, dominance and subordination" (p. 37). Further, "in recognizing different types of masculinity, then, we must not take them as fixed categories" (p. 38).

Connell (2002) also posits the existence of "core" and "peripheral" institutions within society that affect (and guide, and fasten, we ought assume) the societal gender order, of which these masculinities are, for hir purposes, a part and to which they co-contribute. Core institutions like "the military, the state [and] corporations…retain…a patriarchal legacy of male power, control, and exploitation" while "other institutions (educational and familiar), though still retaining a patriarchal legacy, are more contested" (Messner, 2002, p. xx). Though in this model the latter remain more malleable than the former, they all still produce multiple masculinities that are arranged—and this is where I will eventually depart from hir—hierarchically (Connell, 1995). At the apex, in societal terms, is hegemonic masculinity characterized by dominant or compulsory heterosexuality (Rich, 1980) which "in a given space and time, supports gender inequality" (Pascoe, 2007, p. 7). The purpose of multiple masculinities as a theory was to provide a "fluid and conflictual" model but it is, Pascoe feels and I agree, most often "used to construct static and reified typologies" (p. 8) which essentially slot men and women by activity and practice into fixed but ill-defined categories. This is the danger for this author of structural theory, as I see it: deciding just where the giant invisible hand ends and where individual agential possibility begins, if at all. For in the end we might rightly decide that it's all too deterministic and one could reasonably ask, to borrow from/corrupt that great feminist student of erotic power (or the power of erotics, say), Audre Lorde (1984), if this isn't just all a reordering of furniture in the master's house and really, what difference does it make, all those deck chairs, rearranged, if the Titanic, so much hegemonic masculinity, is going to take us down with it anyway?

A more elastic concept of gender-cum-masculinity offered by Connell (2002) is that of "gender relations" (rather than "orders," the military connotation of that term perhaps coming aligned with hir core/peripheral theory) which "are always being constituted in everyday life," presumably by individual and collective actors/humans where "if we don't bring [gender] into being, [it will] not exist" (p. 54). There's between-ness (meaning in negotiation) possible here, and we're closer to what Butler (1990) saw when considering gender "a relative point of convergence among culturally and historically specific sets of relations" (p. 15). Still, Connell (2002) relies on an overarching "structure of relations" which ze insists "does not mechanically determine how people or groups act" (p. 55). Out of this ze theorizes "crisis tendencies" on both large and small scale, out of which changes in gender can come when "personal practice is structured around commitments which are both urgent and contradictory" (p. 74). We are still—though more relationally, one supposes, than in a rigid gender order—doing gender stuck on/in a web (rather than a straight—pun intended—line along a continuum) with possibilities spun out before us by the multifarious spider that is an overarching gender structure. Call it free(ish) will. What we lose, here, is just where structure and agency begin and end. Some of what Connell tries to do with hir core and peripheral theory is map this out, but what of an individual? Can he be core? Peripheral? Will I ever know if I'm hegemonic in my masculinity? Will I always be/do as such? Who determines? And when?

Discourse

Perhaps a better (or more generative, for me at any rate, and at least different) way to engage with the idea of multiple masculinities, then, is to examine it in terms of discourses. Fendler (2010) suggests that discourse, for Foucault, "is everything we can access with our minds"; discourses, further, are "continually being re-created by people as they think and talk" (p. 36). Most importantly, however, for our work here: discourse neither controls (determinism) nor is controlled by people. Here we find the fluidity between Connell's agency and structure.

Cameron (2006) in her tome, *On Language and Sexual Politics* notes that, "we [can] take it that no expression has a meaning independent of its linguistic and non-linguistic context" (p. 17) and thus language both creates and is created by a social and historical reality. Further she suggests that "every act reproduces or subverts a social institution" (p. 18). Trites (2000), similarly, suggests that "humans grow to maturity trained in the ways of…institutions" and this "training invariably depends on language of some sort" (p. 22). In this sense language is a part of discourse which for Foucault (1990a) "transmits and produces power; it reinforces it, but also undermines and exposes it, renders it fragile and makes it possible to thwart it" (p. 101). This understanding of discourse allows an analysis of the masculinities produced and resisted in a school (in the face of religious ideology) to become more "indefinite" more potentially contested; in essence it allows students the possibility to "shake them up, make them fragile" allowing for "crossovers and osmosis" (1998, p. 137). Further, Foucault (1990a) cautions that we may not find, nor necessarily look for a rational ordering nor progression of discourse:

> We must conceive discourse as a series of discontinuous segments whose tactical function is neither uniform nor stable. To be more precise, we must not imagine a world of discourse divided between accepted discourse and excluded discourse, or between the dominant discourse and the dominated one; but as a multiplicity of discursive elements that can come into play in various strategies. (p. 100)

And so I'm asking, in this study, just how the notion of working to become a man (in/for Christ) as put forth explicitly (indeed lettered on stone often) by an all boys Catholic school gets played with fitfully, through language, curriculum, and bodies that are ever filtered by/through ideology.

Fendler (2010) explains Foucault's notion of ideology this way: "Ideologies…sort and filter discourses" making "certain kinds of knowledge accessible…and other knowledge inaccessible" (p. 37). And so all schooling, religious or otherwise, in a very real sense is the process of presenting information in an ideologically specific way, to and for students. In the process, silence is created. Silence, too is of significance in the formation of discourse for, rather than delineating the end of its reaches, quietude becomes a mode of response, of resistance:

> Silence itself—the things one declines to say, or is forbidden to name, the discretion that is required between two different speakers—is less the absolute limit of discourse, the other side from which it is separated by a strict boundary, than an element that functions alongside the things said, with them and in relation to them within over-all strategies. (Foucault, 1990a, p. 27)

These discourses all, these silences, are neither static nor are they typologies useful for slotting precisely because they are fragile, temporal (or historically specific) and always in play. Neither are they the only discourses that might get mobilized within a given school at various times. Represented as/in the official texts of the place, certain curricular discourses might, though, be considered as perhaps seeking to produce a kind of hegemonic (or preferred) masculinity as suggested by Connell. In this sense, then, an all-boys Catholic school will present certain ideologies as always-already: that religion is valuable to the educative experience and that single-gendered contexts produce certain kinds of men. What is done, then, with that ideology happens in the negotiation of discourses by teachers, administration, and students. This is the interplay—the work of becoming a man, if we recall the walls of Mt. Carmel—that I came to study.

If gender is indeed something one performs and does, it is vital to examine on what stages such performance occurs and for what audiences and how these contexts stymie or encourage certain versions of self. For schools, it seems, provide unique "terministic screens" through which students come to view, interact with, perform, and resist versions of gender and religious ideology (Burke, 1966). They might be considered the structures, or perhaps *institutions* is a better term, through which (gender) relations come to be (played with).

Power

For Connell (2002) it is possible to distinguish between hegemonic and subordinated masculinities. These distinctions are explicitly power-laden. In this understanding of how power exists in the world, one preferred model of masculinity perpetuated by core and peripheral institutions (like schools) maintains itself as dominant and is held as the ideal against which all other versions of masculinity are measured. Any action, then, in the doing of gender and masculinity always occurs in reference to that which is hegemonic and defined external to (even if by and through personal action) the individual. Drastic change in gender relations occurs only when crisis tendencies come to "undermine current patterns" to "force change in the structure itself" (p. 71). The change, though we can assume, merely serves to reestablish another hierarchical power structure of gender, where one masculinity (even if newly redefined) is always held in preference above others. Wheat from chaff. The idea is that though resistance might occur, it is always occurring in relation to an oppressor by the oppressed; and though revolution through crisis might come to be, so too will a reordered structure reconvene itself when the dust settles. Nothing, to simplify, goes sideways or diagonal; all in this scenario is bottom-up or top-down. Again, while multiple masculinities and the power in the re/creation of them opens possibilities for study, the limitations of Connell's structural model lie in the assumption that power really remains in the realm of structure, for individual actors (or groups for that matter, that coalesce) who resist will always ever be exerting futilely and generally unknowingly in the rebuilding of a nearly universally oppressive (unseen and vaguely defined) structure. And the doing of gender is just the Sisyphean task of pushing boulders up neverending hills of hegemony. It is action, sure, but futile in the end.

Foucault, in contrast, saw "power [a]s exercised from innumerable points in the interplay of nonegalitarian and mobile relations" (1998, p. 166). If we're to return to Sisyphus, then, we're all still pushing boulders, but perhaps sideways, or down (running after them) or maybe up, but someone might be pushing along with or against us. In this sense, then, masculinity is always being redone, though not necessarily in reference to an always-present hegemonic ideal. Indeed Britzman (2000) asserts that it is:

> discourses [that] authorize what can and cannot be said; they produce relations of power and communities of consent and dissent, and thus discursive boundaries are always being redrawn around what constitutes the desirable and undesirable and around what it is that makes possible...intelligibility and unintelligibility. (p. 36)

Discourses, thus, and the power and resistance constantly produced within them are always unstable. "Power," rather:

> Must be understood in the first instance as the multiplicity of force relations immanent in the sphere in which they operate and which constitute their own organization; as the process which, through ceaseless struggles and confrontations, transforms, strengthens, or reverses them; as the support which these force relations find in one another, thus forming a chain or a system, or on the contrary, the disjunctions and contradictions which isolate them from one another; and lastly as the strategies in which they take effect, whose general design or institutional crystallization is embodied in the state apparatus, in the formulation of the law, in the various social hegemonies. (Foucault, 1990a, p. 92)

For Foucault (1998), and this contravenes my reading of Connell, "we must not imagine a world of discourse divided between accepted discourse and excluded discourse, or between the dominant discourse and the dominated one, but as a multiplicity of discursive elements that can come into play in various strategies" (p. 170). Indeed though Connell (2002) ultimately lands on the side of hierarchical modeling, for hir, "power is widely dispersed, and operates intimately and diffusely. Especially it operates discursively, through the ways we talk, write and conceptualize" (p. 59). And so we must not think of a hegemonic masculinity come to lord over other subordinated ones. Hegemony exists, certainly, but it is not fixed in a specific masculinity, but rather is instantiated (temporarily and conflictually) by the institutional forces of human creations and human destructions. Rather we might better think of masculinity and all of the doing of gender as occurring in terms of regulatory practices (Butler, 1990) put forth within discourses against and through which young men and boys—for my purposes here—come to exercise power and resistance. Indeed "power is everywhere; not because it embraces everything, but because it comes from everywhere" (Foucault, 1990a, p. 93) and so "where there is power, there is resistance, and yet, or rather consequently, this resistance is never in a position of exteriority in relation to power" (p. 95). Students, then, are constantly re/creating, re/interpreting and resisting notions of masculinities and spiritualties—cloaked in curriculum, architecture, dialog—that flow within the hallways of a school, or this Catholic school, St. Monica.

As "it is in discourse that power and knowledge are joined together" (Foucault, 1998, p. 170) what better place than a school to examine the nexuses of the production (and resistance) of power and knowledge? If indeed, "power is tolerable only on condition that it mask a substantial part of itself" where "its success is proportional to its ability to hide its own mechanism" (Foucault, 1990a, p. 86) then the work of this study becomes the partial unveiling of discourses wrought with/by power. The examination of masculinities in an all-boys Catholic school will come, then, to attend to the regulatory practices sanctioned by religious ideology, local history, and school curriculum, but also those practices adopted, perpetuated, and resisted by and among the students themselves, all of which work to produce educated men in reference (and perhaps resistance) to each other. The work of gender in school, for the boys of St. Monica comes in the individual reordering of the content of these discourses. This is power-full stuff.

Schooling

"The civilized body," Nespor (1997) asserts, "is a schooled body" (p. 137). Or so it comes to be viewed through a social lens that utilizes schooling as a way to define "permissible forms of behavior," where the suppression of "bodily movement and expression [comes] to code bodies as having gender" (p. 122). And it is in schooled environments that children are perhaps most strikingly socialized into the doing of the work of gender, which involves then the reification of social expectations and norms around dimorphous and complementary presentations of boy-schooled bodies and girl-schooled bodies. West and Zimmerman (1987) see the "'doing' of gender [as] undertaken by women and men whose competence as members of society is hostage to its production" (p. 126). It would be easy to argue, then, that this hostage-taking begins (or is insidiously continued) with the regulation and production of a schooled/gendered body.

Nespor (1997) reminds that schools are not a priori nor are they external to society, held responsible for its ills and salvation as they are. Rather they are "extensive in space and time, fluid in form and content; [they are] intersections of multiple networks shaping cities, communities" (p. xiii). They are formed of the discourses of a society, in other words. James Gee sees big D[8] Discourses as "ways of being people like us" (as cited in Young, 2000, p. 316) which in this case is really about, for schoolchildren, being *taught* to become like the us which determines curriculum, requires schooling, and through its processes tries to define the possibilities of being or becoming. Because "institutions define and sustain practices of masculinity in which individuals can be held accountable" (p. 316) then the institution of schooling bears examining for its de/limiting of the discourses for our purposes here around what is im/possible for a gendered and masculinized student body, in both senses of that last term.

Schools, in essence, come to define and (attempt to) restrict sexualities through the normalization and discipline of the body. Fiske (1989) writes of the use of the body to incarnate and intextuate the law where the law, and this is particularly true though oft unspoken, in religious contexts is rife with images and homages to heterosexual possibilities (only).[9] Pascoe (2007) alludes to a particular school's "parents' and policy maker's" wariness "of teens' burgeoning sexuality" (p. 50) to the point where "thinking or talking about" these developing sexual "bodies in the classrooms becomes difficult at best" (Hawhee, 2006, p. 156). And though school as a project "ultimately tries to suppress bodily movement and expression and to define appropriate bodily orientations" (Nespor, 1997, p. 122), still, in spite of this ramped up interest in and trepidation about teenage sexual possibility, schools are inherently conservative in their educative approaches to the topic. So it is that at schools like St. Monica a homecoming king and queen are still crowned—the symbolic married heterosexual couple, come to rule over a court of peers and presented—at the Homecoming football game in front of thousands of fans. A parade of sport and celibate coupling culminating in a dance where dates are of the opposite sex only and dancing is still regulated such that room for the Holy Spirit must be maintained between opposite sexed bodies on the gym floor.[10]

Here was see much of what Foucault (1990b) was explicating in his *History of Sexuality* when noting that, though "sexual union" as theorized by the Romans was "a fact of nature" and thus couldn't be a bad thing, it was really only "the possibility and the principle of the act that [were] validated" (p. 112). This was a regulatory regime where "indulgence in sexual pleasures at the wrong time [could] induce illnesses" (p. 100) both physical and moral. Thus, the presentation of heterosexual coupling serves to confirm the probability of heterosexuality in the school, but the miming (perhaps) of the physical act, as much dancing is feared to mimic, must be belayed for a time when it is acceptable, under the auspices of the sacrament of marriage. And of course, marriage, in the Church and thus the school is always-only a heterosexual possibility.

Mac An Ghaill (1994) has it that in "school microcultures of management, teachers and students are key infrastructural mechanisms through which masculinities...are mediated and lived out (p. 4) where it becomes possible that the creation of "man" in and through education "is not a fact but rather a specific solution to a specific problem" (Biesta, 1998 p. 9). What we need to decide, and this is Biesta's take on Foucault's "diagnosis of modernity...is what kind of answer man is" (p. 9) to the problem as created. Schooling is, in short, about creating problems and molding solutions to those very issues. In this light, then, it is salient here to turn to a number of studies done in K12 educational settings that address the formation of genders and masculinities by way of situating my own research at St. Monica.

Barrie Thorne (1993) conducted a two-part, two-year ethnographic study at elementary schools in California and Michigan seeking to examine "how...children actively come together to help create and sometimes challenge, gender structures and meanings" (p. 4). In the process, she sought to put an "emphasis on action and activity" as a way of rooting out how kids "do gender" (p. 5). What she encountered, recalling her assumptions about structured genders, was a stark splitting of boundaries where boys and girls came to transgress but also reinforce the physical borders of gender. "Boundaries," she notes, were "created through contact as well as avoidance" (p. 64). Though "gender boundaries" were "episodic and ambiguous" (p. 84) for Thorne, they were always split down the middle of groups of boys and groups of girls. And though the researcher reminds that "we should treat the opposition between male and female as problematic rather than known" (p. 109) the sum of the research fails to question effectively the unitary categories of "boy" and "girl" as formed in/by the spaces of school.

Ann Arnett Ferguson (2001) draws on Thorne as a way to introduce the contested punishing spaces used in an elementary school—or schools as these spaces themselves—to affix fear to the state of being young, poor, and black. Using interviews with students—in fifth and sixth grade—and administrators at an urban middle school, as well as participant-observation in classrooms and detention rooms, she chronicles the construction of a troubling pathetic, in the sense of pathos, development. Fear and containment, that is, becomes synonymous with black male masculinity through the ministrations of the school. "School rules operate[d]," for Ferguson "as instruments of normalization" (p. 52) most often through "a proliferation of surveillance and assessment techniques" (p. 53). The locus of analysis in the study lies in how "gender acts are always and already modulated through race at the constitutive embodied level as well as that of the imaginary and representational" (p. 164). And further, the researcher decides that "we come to know ourselves and to recognize others as of a different sex through an overdetermined complex process inherent in every sphere of social life at the ideological and discursive level" (p. 170). Certainly and it is vital to recall that that overdetermination is fed—would it be too cute to say determined over time—by and in schools.

This onus on race (and class) is carried through in a different way in Mac An Ghaill's (1994) examination of the making of men—at a working-class British secondary school—guided by the assumption that "schooling" is ultimately "a masculinizing agency" (p. 1). "Schools" in this view are "sites for the production of sex/gender subjectivities, 'where people conform, deviate, challenge, participate and engage with state apparatuses'" (p. 2). Set in a co-educational comprehensive school, the author comes to argue that ultimately, though mediated by the discourses that surround them (overdetermined again by the school context), "young people are active makers of sex/gender identities" (p. 179). Caught in the midst of a restructuring of curriculum in the face of new national standards, the faculty is presented as divided between the new and old guard, further fractured along gender divides. The boys at the school, then, become expert at navigating (through acquiescence and resistance as well) the vacillating gendered expectations that dot the school. They are not hostage as suggested above, but are rather able to work at the bindings of their restrictive situations.

They, these students, are makers of their own identities, of course, but also of those that are im/possible for their peers. Pascoe's (2007) work in the field at co-educational River High:

> illustrate[s] that masculinity is not a homogenous category that any boy possesses by virtue of being male. Rather, masculinity—as constituted and understood in the social world—is a configuration of practices and discourses that different youths (boys and girls) may embody in different ways and to different degrees. (p. 5)

As a graduate student, Pascoe came to understand her work as rooted in various official and student discourses. In the study, "fag discourse" came to the fore as a "trope" associated more with male effeminacy—in negative ways—than with actual homosexual activity. Indeed "the constant threat of [being made] the fag regulated boys' attitudes toward their bodies in terms of clothing, dancing, and touching" (Pascoe, 2007, p. 65). And so it is through language, that activity and possibility become limited. One way to opt out of this threat, for heterosexual/heteronormed boys was through the invocation and physical presence of "girlfriends" who "both protected boys from the specter of the fag and bolstered their masculinity" (p. 90). The only other outlet was afforded "Christian boys at River High" who had "institutional claims on masculinity such that they didn't need to engage in the sort of intense" (p. 113) discursive work of distancing from the fag as their less (openly) devout classmates.

What to do, then, with a single-gendered context? Though more the exception than the rule as noted in the statistics provided in the first chapter of this text, these schools still produce men and women—like and unlike, clearly, myself. Michael Ruhlman (1996) returned to his own all-boys—non-sectarian—preparatory institution in a work that reads as part memoir and part nostalgic argument for the value of schools that are organized around the specific principle of separating boys from girls, presumably for their—the students' or the schools'; we're never really sure—own good. "Does it not make sense," he asks, mirroring Cornelius Riordan, a professor of educational sociology "to learn more about the potential efficacy of single-sex educational environments before they become historical artifacts?" (p. 9).[11]

While I can't speak for the methodology nor the requisite "scientific" value of the text—this was more-or-less a mass-market offering—and while I'm uncomfortable with his lack of examination into the research concerning the construction of genders and masculinities, I will say that Ruhlman's forays into a school of his memory, as an ethnographer, was helpful in certain ways. What he points to in the text is a conflicted engagement with language that uncomplicatedly supports Pascoe's assertions. He records it as such when asking a student about the prejudice in the school—a bastion for the affluent sons of Cleveland—who replies "If you used the word 'nigger' or 'kike' in this school…people would be *all over* you. But people use the word 'faggot' all the time" (p. 80). Language. What's different for Ruhlman, and this is in direct response to the kind of invocation that the young men at River High were afforded in avoiding the "fag," is that "without girls, boys can't prove their sexuality during school" (p. 76).

This seems almost dismissive. Though I suppose it turns on the idea of proof, particularly in light of Pascoe's assertions that the "fag" is malleable and transferable so that nothing is ever really proven. Too, though, *homo*sexuality may well be proven in an all-boys school, but the heteronormativity of Ruhlman's study forgets this in a prurient search for heterosexual outlets. That sexuality, heterosexuality in particular, can only be asserted or proven in the presence—or through the invocation—of women fails to take into account the creative work boys do in and through language, body positioning, and emotional thrusting and parrying. It also ignores the reality of nuanced and vital homosocial activity that occurs in groups of boys, especially at an all-boys school. The questions that might better be asked in reference to the above are, to what degree and in what ways can boys prove their sexuality in the absence of girls at a school? In what ways might this heterosexual impulse—in a homosocial environment—become malleable? And what do we do with the absence-as-presence of homosexual (im)possibility in such an environment?

Still, what this becomes increasingly about is the formation of masculinities (in institutions with patriarchal legacies), yes, but also a distancing for boys from femininity, which is tied neatly to homosexuality and abject status within society, sure, but particularly in schools. Too, we note that ultimately the present work is about creating a complication of what gender really means in schools and how it comes to be formed. For my aims at St. Monica the above is about casting evermore light onto how:

> the juridical structures of language and politics constitute the contemporary field of power; hence, there is no position outside this field, but only a critical genealogy of its own legitimating practices....And the task is to formulate within this constituted frame a critique of the categories of identity that contemporary juridical structures engender, naturalize, and immobilize. (Butler, 1990, p. 7)

Religion

It is perhaps fitting that the only class I was kicked out of in my semester of observation was a theology course. More on this later but suffice to say the Augustinian friar who taught the class—on great (sanctioned) Catholic thinkers, incidentally—had issues with the presence of a researcher. Other teachers clearly, in their awkwardness in accommodating me, took umbrage to my honorary senior-student status, but endured my presence still. They, we might argue, could be fired for denying me access—Fr. Tim, the president of the school took quite a liking to me through my interactions with students and I enjoyed a kind of most-favored-nation status around the place—Brother Larry, keeper of the monastery attached to the grounds of St. Monica, could not.

At any rate, much of the juridical language of which Butler writes comes from religion and its orientation to genders and sexualities, which run interference in terms of the development of masculinities. Perhaps I should say "religions" here, but I'm thinking most specifically of the Judeo-Christian tradition as it relates specifically to my context at an Augustinian Catholic school. Certainly we can say—and there is research to suggest—that there is a pretty consistent agonistic relationship between many and varied religions as regards the development of genders and the possibilities for and demonization of sexualities, but for my purposes here I'm going to narrow to Catholicism more often than not in an attempt to remain localized.

Foucault (1990b), in his *History of Sexuality,* reminds that an early and ongoing Christian focus on sexual austerity—carried down in history through the social doctrine of assumed clerical celibacy as well as the linking of sex-and-marriage-solely-for-procreation—"should not be" viewed as "somehow 'preformed'" (p. 21). Instead, it is vital to note that the increased attention paid to sexuality and its ethics as/and development into a thing that mattered is historically rooted in pre-Christian traditions and concerns. What began as "a male ethics…in which women figured only as objects" became "an elaboration of masculine conduct carried out from the viewpoint of men in order to give form to *their* [emphasis in the original] behavior" (pp. 22–23).

Masculinity became about being, for men, in control of one's appetites, for "a man who was not sufficiently in control of his pleasures—whatever his choice of object—was regarded as 'feminine'" (Foucault, 1990b, p. 85). It was through this Greek doctrine which valued as moral the ability to control one's desires, which further came to conflate sexual activity with animalism, that Christianity was able to hijack the conflicted reality that though "sexual activity [might be] a source of therapeutic effects" it too was run-through with "pathological consequences" (Foucault, 1990c, p. 118). The most controlled and controlling being, the martyr, the saint, the priest was thus portrayed as a man having mastered his sexual desires to the point where Transubstantiation, the ability to bring God into the world for the consumption of the faithful, superseded his need to stoop to the desire for physical release. Sex was too base, essentially, for Christ.

And the austerity of masculinity, its religious pinnacle, ended up filtered down into men cloaked in the purity of white albs at the head of 701 uncomfortable schoolboys in a Midwestern American city preaching a Gospel born of

2000 years of (mis/interpreted/guided) tradition. There are no women priests in the Catholic church in large part because the sexual doctrine of women as objects and too feminine to be able to control sexual desire and its offspring, emotional weakness, remains at the whispering fore of our doctrinal engagement with the world. Spong (1992) addresses this in no uncertain terms: "Patriarchy and God have been so deeply and uncritically linked to gender by the all-male church hierarchy that men have little understood how this alliance has been used to the detriment of women" (p. 1).

Additional feminist theological scholars see this as, to understate things, troubling. Well they should. "The point," Daly (1973) suggests:

> is not to deny that a revelatory event took place in the encounter with the person Jesus. Rather, it is to affirm that the creative presence of the Verb [God, degendered and active] can be revealed at every historical moment, in every person and culture. (p. 71)

That male clergy control the dispensation of the seven holy sacraments of the Catholic Church (Baptism, Reconciliation, Eucharist, Confirmation, Holy Orders, Matrimony, Extreme Unction) a reality that functions to maintain a vision of an ahistorical take on gender and sexuality, mirrored in a man on the cross and a man, his Father, up in heaven. In this vision of religion, women are always ever handmaidens, passing revelation off to the Men who will carry the message to the masses. So it is that I wear a scapular representing how Our Lady of Mount Carmel (the mother of Christ, of God!) brought revelation to a lonely hermit in a forest. She needed him to speak for her to gain legitimacy, to have a voice. We see this consistently in the way prayer is formulated: because she was not God herself, we can only pray that St. Monica intercede on our behalf to the male God in heaven. Stigmata and all, and she is reduced to letter carrier to Christ, and because we cannot partake of the sacramental—according to Church doctrine—through a woman, then even a female saint lacks the God-giving power of a lowly male deacon, who is able to preach from the altar.

A vision of a new religion, *Beyond God the Father*, for Daly (1973) requires "freeing...women and men from the sexist ethos of dichotomizing and hierarchizing" (p. 97) in the name of tradition and Church. There is, she suggests, an artificial divide perpetuated by the Church (and perhaps, single-gendered schools), troubling because "religion" ultimately "legitimates so effectively because it relates the precarious reality constructions of empirical societies with ultimate reality" (p. 132). To call into question assumptions about gender and masculinities in a society requires, then, an attending to how religion (and religious education) serves to reinforce, indeed to sacralize,[12] harmful and deadly historical assumptions about sex, sexuality, and the dimorphous nature of women and men.

The question of women in religion, thus, becomes the question of men and women in religion. Chernin (1987) puts it this way: "When a woman seriously asks herself what it means to be a woman she is pulling at a thread that can unravel an entire culture" (p. 25). Indeed. This is, perhaps and probably, though, a good thing. Consider Daly's (1973) notion that women in Christian culture are limited to two roles, and really just one: as virgin or downfall of man (either Mary or Eve) where "the inimitability of 'Mary conceived without sin' ensures that all women as women are in the caste of Eve" (p. 82). Women are, in essence, limited to the role of mother or wife.[13] Daly (1973) suggests a revisioning of the birth narrative of Jesus—the angel Gabriel's appearing to Mary and her becoming pregnant by the male God, recall—that takes into account "the case of unwanted pregnancy...and the whole well-being of a person [as] controlled by another being" (p. 111). John Shelby Spong, a bishop in the Episcopal Church, belies the case of the virgin birth of Mary asserting, rather, a collective Midrashic revision of the person of Jesus. It was, he thinks, an attempt to cover over the possibility that Jesus "might have been an 'illegitimate' child" (1992, p. 13) whose past threatened his posthumous rise to prominence as a Jewish resistance to the prominence of the Temple Cult to the point that his followers created successively more fantastic, and thus less human, stories of his conception, birth, and life. "What does it take," he asks, "to understand those mythic dimensions that fill our religious story?" (p. 12). A robust view of historical realities, perhaps.

Why, at this point in a text about boys in a school where I seek to examine masculinities and their development, take the time to address the social context as regards women in the theological space of Catholicism and early Christianity? Not, certainly, to create a habit of parenthetical and footnoted allusions to the development of (the impossibilities of) femininity in the Church. Women, in this sense, have been footnoted enough, pushed to the margins in ways that emerge often only through good and thorough critique. No. However, in a school named for a woman, which is indeed apt to evoke her story and her intercession in its multiplicity on a daily basis[14]it seems important to address the conflicted role of women within the pantheon of Catholicism as a historical body, as well as their ongoing oppression (very visible to the boys who, though taught by women in class and compelled to pray to the statue of a woman in chapel, will perhaps *never* see one at the altar in their four years at the school, and certainly never ministering *at* it). In other words, in order to become men in the Church, it is more or less required that one accept the ways in which women are belittled liturgically as a rite of passage into Confirmed (sacramental) masculinity, which is taught (explicitly and implicitly) as necessarily oppositional of/to those mothers, girlfriends, and female avatars in stained glass at the sides of the church building, and the Church consciousness.

"The word 'religion'," James Carroll (2001) reminds, "shares a root with 'ligament,' meaning 'tie'" (p. 73). And so it is that boys-becoming-men are tied (bodily of course, but socially, and historically on top of that; say, discursively) to the religious and educational conversations that bind them to their school, to the undertheorized tenets of their faith tradition. We see some of this in the ways that the young men of St. Monica chafe at the directives of female teachers, which Connell (2002) might attribute to "a refusal of men to be under the authority of a woman…in many religions among them the Catholic Church" (p. 6). In absentia and abstractly it is perfectly fine to pray for help to a woman saint, but she of course can't give you a JUG[15] for insubordination.

These boys in a very real way are tied to the violent historical doctrine which colors red the troubled history of men and masculinity in the church. They are Mustangs for their assumed physical prowess, for it is their sex that makes them strong; it is no accident either that a rival school is the Crusaders and another the Caravan, two blatant and untroubled allusions to good Christian soldiers gone on Jihad to the Holy Land. And though "the history of [religion and] masculinity, it should be abundantly clear, is not linear" (Connell, 1995, p. 198) it is safe to draw a meandering line from the violent, assertive and brutal masculinity blessed by the popes who abided over the Crusades, to the evangelizing conquest of the New World—those conquistadores and bringers of rational civilization, a Christian God, and an unhealthy thirst for gold— on down to Vlad a senior at St. Monica, in computer science class, when asked about his longtime relationship with a girl from another school, saying "I don't give a fuck; I get what I want out of it."

And so, perhaps, he does. One argument Carroll (2001) makes is that the "Church's 'mentality of power'" will remain problematic until "a fundamental shift in its attitude toward the other, which in turn involves the issue of women's equality" (p. 572), occurs. It is this mentality of power as it formulates and foments young men in school, that has brought me to this study. I hope, now, to shed light on its workings as a way of freeing up spaces for discussion about the various workings of religions and masculinities in schools as they are brought to bear upon, and are reflected back by, masses of young men, or perhaps more fittingly, as they are extolled to (and ignored by) young men in Mass. All the while holding to the notion that Lefebvre (1991) is onto something hopeful here when he writes that:

> ideologies dictate the locations of particular activities, determining that such and such a place should be sacred, for example, while some other should not, or that a temple, a palace or a church [and school] must be here, and not there. But ideologies do not produce space: rather they are in a space, and of it. (p. 210)

It is, after all, the people who make the space. What follows is a description of that space and its people.

Notes

1. I realize, at this point, that I'm playing somewhat fast and loose with the dual concepts of 'gender' and 'sexuality'. That is, I'm allowing them to duel rather than separating them off and fixing them definitionally in the body text. This is on purpose. Connell (2002) proposes that "gender" and its attendant relations "[is] always being constituted in everyday life[;] if we don't bring it into being, gender does not exist" (p. 54). Similarly Foucault (1990a) has decided that "sexuality…is the name given to a[n] historical construct (p. 105) very much brought to life—and very different from, though inevitably coming to affect the meanings attributed to the *sexual act* itself—in social process. That is both gender and sexuality are constructed and because of the shared historical context of their development as expressive and repressive concepts, each inevitably bears heavy traces of the other. Are sexuality and gender different from each other? Certainly; they cannot be collapsed into one category (yet), though I would suggest they are mutually constitutive as a beginning point.
2. A manifestation of Cicero's claim: "Est enim actio quasi sermo corporis, by action the body talks" (Hawhee, 2002, p. 156).
3. Catholic schools perhaps more specifically and willfully than the vast majority of their public counterparts manifest simply through gendered and mandatory uniforms which bring in real ways a great deal of, well, uniformity to the unexamined presentation of the bodily self in school.
4. For further discussion of the masculine-media connection through the soldierly, see Jon Adams' *Male Armor: The Soldier-Hero in Contemporary American Culture* (2008).
5. We might also point to the histrionic rhetoric surrounding sex education in public schools where abstinence-only initiatives, though backed by little and shaky research, continue to be funded through state and federal initiatives.
6. In the neighborhood where the study takes place, the all-girls Catholic school, on alternate weeks, replaces the traditional "father, son, and holy spirit" of the sign of the cross with "creator, redeemer, and giver of life." A friend of my sister was pulled from the school by her parents in the face of such degendering blasphemy(!)

7   R. W. Connell, cited throughout, is a well-known Australian sociologist and also transgendered/genderqueer/transsexual. These various identities open up possibilities to create a rupture at the site of traditional notions of gendered pronouns. In the interest of honoring the struggle of and pursuit for a surgical solution to sex-trait identification issues, I have chosen to use the gender-neutral pronouns 'hir' and 'ze' to refer to Dr. Connell. It allows me to acknowledge that the texts referred to were written by Connell-marked-male while alluding to the now female-identified gender scholar, R. W. Connell. Butler (2008) presaged this trouble of language and pronouns noting that "I am not outside the language that structures me, but neither am I determined by the language that makes this 'I' possible. This is the bind of self-expression, as I understand it" (p. xxvi).

8   I am uncomfortable with the idea of a split between big and little 'd' discourses for the same reason that I'm uncomfortable with the notion of hierarchical, core, and peripheral masculinity. It requires what feels like an arbitrary distinction between what is major and minor with a certain willful ignorance of the shifts that occur at points of interaction. Still, the notion that schooling is about creating individuals who will become more like those bodies that have already been schooled strikes me as wisely encapsulated by Gee (1996) in this case.

9   Daly (1973) sees this as the implication of a longstanding ontology whereby "the entire conceptual systems of theology and ethics, developed under the conditions of patriarchy, have been the products of males and tend to serve the interests of [hetero]sexist society" (p. 4).

10 See also, Lesko (1988) for an example of such adult heteronormative 'playacting' in a Catholic school in the Midwest.

11 In 2005, the No Child Left Behind act was modified to allow for single-sex public education at both the classroom and school level. The legal and theoretical justification for such an amendment both were taken from research collected by and trumpeted through lobbying organizations like the National Association for Single Sex Public Education (NASSPE) which cite vast testing gains for students, particularly in inner-city contexts, when boys and girls are purposely separated by gender in educational settings. The suggestion is that gender segregated educational contexts might just be the saving grace for struggling public schools in this era of high stakes testing. Many of these claims, indeed, made as regards the benefits of/for single-gendered education run along the lines of improved test scores, most particularly for girls in math and science over their counterparts in co-educational settings ("NASSPE," n. d.). Both inherently and explicitly such work relies on biological assumptions of gender as a fixed and heritable trait. Claims focused on testing gains, however, are confounded by work like that done in England by Robinson & Smithers (1999) who note that:

> the outstanding performance of the single-sex schools in the examination league tables has much more to do with academic selection, socioeconomic background and the standing of the school itself than with the segregation of the sexes. When, as far as possible, like is compared with like, the apparent academic differences between single-sex and co-educational schools largely disappear. (p. 23)

Still, there remains, as federal guidelines now provide the justification for single-gendered public education, a certain impetus for the establishment of separate-sexed schools. And though:

> advocates of single-sex education do NOT believe that 'all girls learn one way and all boys learn another way.' On the contrary, we cherish and celebrate the diversity among (sic) girls and among (sic) boys. We understand that some boys would rather read a book than play football. We understand that some girls would rather play football rather than play with Barbies. Educators who understand these differences can inspire every child to learn to the best of her or his ability," ("NASSPE," n. d.)

such rhetoric remains reliant on a model of essential and biological differences between, rather than among the sexes. And so no complex argument about the nature of gender relations is being made. Boys and girls by this logic still remain very different at and because of the unique circumstances of their births, though variance is certainly seen as occurring within genders. Still, the assumption runs that a fundamentally different context of education will differentially and perhaps universally benefit (all) boys and (all) girls. No sense is given about how limited possibilities within and across genders become when boys and girls are assumed to be more different that similar and can benefit from being separated in school. There is very little nuance here regarding just what kind of girls and boys will be produced as women and men in and by schools that require their gender be essential(ized) upon entrance. One way to complicate this argument, to push back on it, is to examine just how gender becomes (re)formed in a school in the face of ideology that, perhaps, assumes that gender "is," rather than "does," as it were.

12 Legal debates, rooted in religious assumptions, about marriage and civil unions come to mind.
13 The opening announcements end each day with a prayer to St. Monica, as well as "Our Mother of Good Counsel," another moniker for the biblical Mary.
14 A number of classes end throughout a given student's schedule with "St. Monica, pray for us." Too, this is a near universal invocation with athletic teams at the school.
15 A Catholic school's answer to detention, the acronym means "Justice Under God."

Chapter 3

Crossing Over

We must constantly be aware of the workings of sex and gender because in the historical and cultural moment, paradoxically they sometimes make a big difference even if they sometimes make no difference at all.
                        Jane Roland Martin, "Reclaiming a Conversation"

Make it public; critically review it; pass it on.
                        Lee Shulman, "The Carnegie Conversation on Catholic Education"

Joe: "You a student teacher?"
Me: "No. I'm doing research."
Joe: "Wait, are you writing a book?
Me: "Yep."

Lenses

What follows is a discussion of the methods through which I encountered the young men, faculty, staff, and physical setting of St. Monica High School. In order to bring some manner of coherence to the decisions I made, it is necessary to take a macro view of what methodological lenses guided me through the process. On a large scale, then, I viewed this project as feminist and poststructural and, of necessity then, critical in scope.

Feminist inquiry has long been guided by the notion that the personal is political. Indeed, much of what has been written, in the first two chapters, in fact has involved stories of my life or memories, which were stirred by my introduction (back) into the community of St. Monica. This conceit felt necessary as a way of unpacking my own history, sure, but also the discursive elements that may continue to shape young men educated (and raised) in schools close to my own, both in geography and religious ideology. To write, then, a book rooted in the neighborhood, religion, and educational context of my youth requires some acknowledgment and indeed excavation of the personal-become-political choices that I have made in the research, certainly, but also in its writing up. Research, in this view, is never objective and is always messy because of the intrusion of intentions, known or unknown, of the researcher (Harding, 1987).

Strongly tied to standpoint theory, feminist methodology makes explicit the partiality and bias of the researcher as a prerequisite to any conclusions made. Too, of necessity, feminism has long been rooted in gender research. First as an assertion of a positive (and positivist) notion of women in relation to work long pursued about men, and in later waves, aimed at the deconstruction of gender normativity calcified in what was viewed as patriarchal claims to truth coursing through a priori assumptions of sex as biology and gender as socially constructed. In the end I intend to lay claim to the later historical moves in feminist gender research, which aim at explicating just how gender gets defined, most particularly in the realm of masculinities.

Later turns in feminist work addressed poststructuralism. The two epistemologies dovetailed in their twinned ideas that truth is ultimately partial (and party to power) and that context matters. poststructuralism recoils from the notion that there is an underlying—oft mystical—structure that determines human reality and is outside of the purview of and possibility for human agency. Structuralism was seen as frustratingly deterministic and poststructural investigation came to focus on the ways in which amoebic and competing realities and truths played upon and were played with by humans. In answer to Marxist dichotomous ideals of power and resistance, oppressor and oppressed, postructuralism put an onus on the constant and creative work done by individuals in answer to, and often making nonsense of, manifestations of power in life. It is useful, then, for my purposes, as I viewed the data as a collection of discursive elements, which are constantly partial, yes, but being renegotiated through the work of the individuals of the place of research. In this way data is never truly collected, but created by the researcher and his subjects even as the researcher becomes the subject/object of research as well.

And ultimately this is a work of critical, what we could call exegesis, I suppose. What I mean here is that I am working to critique the creation of masculinities and spiritualities in a school. Because this is a feminist project, I will do so by examining and explicating theories of gender construction, because it is Poststructural, I will do so in relation to the complexities of the constant re/creation of possibility through language, curricula, religion, and so forth. And because this is feminist poststructural and critical, I will refrain from providing solutions that could be universalized outside of this specific, troubling, and troubled context.

Critical Autoethnography

"Critical autoethnography is an autobiographical genre of writing. It is research that displays multiple aspects of individual awareness about the author's critical embeddedness" where the "main advantage of [the] method is to let the researcher act sometimes as a researcher and other times as a participant" (Cupane & Taylor, 2007, p. 11). I see this work as a critical autoethnography because my ability (and will, really) to disentangle my memories as a student in an all-boys single-gendered classroom in the past from those experiences of the 2009–2010 school year strikes me as always-already suspect, particularly considering the vestiges of history and the ebb and flow of familial, neighborhood, and parish ties which continually threatened to wash over me throughout the research process. To, then, claim the ability to report on the experience of the school without making an attempt to acknowledge, deal with and perhaps encode and thus fictionalize my own role as researcher, participant, and alum strikes me as disingenuous at best and dangerous at worst. There are necessarily autobiographical elements here because I will continually fail—and have continually failed—at any attempt to separate the me as researcher, the me as classmate, and the me as former student from the me who struggled to exist again in a religious/gendered secondary schooled context. To say nothing of the me who ended up collecting/creating, collating and analyzing the data.

Austin and Hickey (2008) view "autoethnographic interrogation" as ideal for the "critical appraisal of the marginalizing and privileging influences of culture in...classrooms" (p. 138). And while I take issue with a simplistic dichotomous sense of privilege pushing to the margin, I find the methodology on a whole useful for its honesty regarding the role of researcher as creator, evaluator, and participant. In this sense, then, I was free to make decisions that felt important about data creation. I am not so much concerned, for example, with what may have happened to my memory between the occurrence (in class, or at a football game) and the writing up of the action as I understand this manner of research (and really any research at all) to be a practice in elaborated/elaborate fiction. [1] Part of that interrogation requires an acknowledgment of "the reflexive processes impacting my identity negotiation while in" the school (Olivas, 2009, p. 385) as well. This is not a study not about me in other words, but rather a study about boys—and I chief among them—in a school whose story I am telling through the lens pushing at the limits of my own experience as a qualitative researcher.

Van Maanen helps here, writing that "qualitative researchers" do not "capture lived experience. Such experience…is created in the social text written by the researcher" (as cited in Denzin & Lincoln, 2000, p. 19). Or, say: any time that passes between experience and the written codifying of the memory of that experience is basically moot—in ethnography and here in autoethnography—as the "ethnographic text" becomes "a means, the meditative vehicle for a transcendence of time and place" (Tyler, 1986, p. 129) anyway. And certainly in those intervening moments anything I choose to represent in writing will "always be filtered through the lens of language, gender, social class, race and ethnicity" (Usher, 2000, p. 28). But as ethnographers always "use, manipulate, alter, edit, discard, reduce, and recycle voices" (Segall, 2001, p. 584) as a necessary and self-conscious part of the analysis of data, such filtering is problematic, yes, but less so than not acknowledging its occurrence. So it is that I have come to matter to my data just as it becomes matter-as-data.

That the research voice in this view of qualitative research "is constituted rather than discovered" (Usher, 2000, p. 34) means that this work, as a "critical conversation' will necessarily refrain from 'solving'…dilemmas" (p. 37). That is, this piece is not meant to suggest best practices in all-boys Catholic schools for educating better men, or better Christians, or different masculinities—though certainly I have only limited control over how his work will be interpreted and leveraged if at all—but rather seeks to raise questions about how these concepts and identities get defined/defied/deified in ideologies, by and with and through discourses. Which creates a problem of writing up this "experiment" best solved by offering "experiments in writing, that is a self-consciousness about writing" (Van Maanen as cited in Denzin & Lincoln, 2007, p. 19), which acknowledges that "every telling is constrained, partial, and determined by the discourses and histories that prefigure, even as they might promise, representation" (Britzman, 2000, p. 32). In essence, "the ethnographic text intends to translate even as it is meant to stand in for, social life" (Britzman, 2000, p. 28). This product is a seat-filler at a gala event, replacing absented persons, to give the illusion of fullness. It is an existence, but not the original, which it evokes (or sits in for while the original[2] freshens up in the lobby or has a smoke outside).

"My dilemma," as was Britzman's "in studying the lived experience of actual individuals" (p. 31) is now "how to order but not normalize the stories" (p. 34) encountered and created in my research. This may be, at the point the text is read, impossible. Weedon (1998), writes of a feminist poststructuralism that demands a "subjectivity which is precarious, contradictory and in process, constantly being reconstituted in discourse each time we think or speak" (p. 177). As I imagine this to be, in the end, a feminist project it is important to note, further, that such theories—and I'd include critical autoethnography here—"suggest that experience has no inherent meaning" (p. 178) and so the telling of experience is always-already laden with and fluttered by the winds of ideologies and discourses that (dis)order its likely coming to meaning in its retelling(s) (and rereading(s)). When I envisioned the project, it involved "going back" to high school to make sense of the experience of the students I'd study, certainly, but also to help myself deal with my own emergent identities as scholar and former pupil shaped by the discourses within an all-boys educational institution. This is selfish in a sense, which is ok, but it's also much of how I began to make meaning for the study, rooted in my own experiences. The study, in a way, was a search for the stories to tell, but moreso it was about learning how to tell my story as well.

This telling is important, but not without inherent limitations. Tyler (1986) is particularly helpful in his examination of the ethnographic text created in/by discourses. Beginning with Derrida, he notes that, here, discourse is that "which is 'the other as us,' for the point of discourse is not how to make a better representation, but how to avoid representation" (p. 128). "The ethnographic text," thus, "is not only not *an* object, it is not *the* object [emphasis in the original]; it is instead a means, the meditative vehicle for a transcendence of time and place that is not just transcendental but a transcendental return to time and place" (p. 129), whose purpose is evocation rather than representation. The power, then, of ethnography lies in the ways "it conjoins reality and fantasy, for it speaks of the occult in the language of naïve realism and of the everyday in occult language, and makes the reason of the one the reasonableness of the other" (p. 134). In its openness about the limitations of stories-as-told-as-remembered, ethnography cannot "dictate its [own] interpretation, for it cannot control the powers of its readers" (p. 135). Which means, in a sense, that as a writer who cares very deeply about his subjects—because I could not help but see messy and fractured pieces of myself in them, their histories, their struggles, their discourses—though I wish I could I can only somewhat control how their (our) humanity will be mis/read. This worries me.

In essence the ethnographic text is powerful in how it acknowledges the limitations of its powers to transform/transfix readers in its homage to the reality of the necessary transformation of the written subjects for the purposes of evoking a scene, a memory, a school, a snippet of dialog. And here it is vital to ask if we understand that ethnography, this occult document, "produce[s]" only "partial truths, serious fictions, powerful 'lies,'...which partial truths about our own ethnographic practices does our 'lying' reveal? Which do they conceal?" (Segall, 2001, p. 580). Essentially this is a challenge to/for reader and author for though, I know of my purposeful partial truths and powerful lies, I may not know what they come to conceal, even as I seek to flog them to reveal.

All of this is to say that, in the end, with a poststructural project like critical autoethnography, as Britzman (2000) suggests, "representation is always in crisis, knowledge is constitutive of power, and agency is the constitutive effect, and not the originator of situated practices and histories" (p. 30). Foucault, for his part, demurred about his relation to poststructuralism, particularly later in his life as his work was increasingly pushed into the category by critics. It is fair, though, to say that his approach to discourses and the push-pull mutual constitution of power and resistance is better evocative of my own sensibilities than the underlying structuralism of Connell's deferral to masculinity's cosmic tumblers, which in the face of crisis tendencies force reorganization of power relations but always settle the same, falling back into a hierarchical, patriarchal[3] form. Still, this work here, drawing heavily from both authors' theories, of necessity straddles a bit, aiming to acknowledge through such a malleable methodology as critical autoethnography, that "the art of life isn't controlling what happens, which is impossible; it's using what happens" (Steinem, 1994, p. 258). This is a way of saying, really that "the researcher has multiple intentions and desires, some of which are consciously known and some of which are not" (Scheurich, 1995, p. 240). I may not, as introspective as I envision myself being, know all that I intend. That is a "reality" with which I am willing to part here.

"The crux of the issue" for the research Scheurich (1995) cautions, "is the interpretive moment as it occurs throughout the research process" because the "researcher brings considerable conscious and unconscious baggage into [the] moment" (p. 249). Part of the "rigors" and requirements of documents with specific formats such as books, say, is a demand that a certain order be then made of all of those moments when memory and recording and interpretation collide in an antagonistic instance-that-becomes data. Or so I've convinced myself. It is important to note, then, that this is not—the book— "reality," except perhaps in the way that reality television projects and creates a certain hyper-real of acting-real for cameras, edited to fit the form of a primetime half-hour slot a "generation by models of a real without origin" (Baudrillard, 1994, p. 1). That is, perhaps, too ungenerous. This hopefully does not fall off the cliff into simulacra or Tyler's "fantasy," but still, "there is for this researcher no 'real' to be accurately captured, no 'true' representation of voice—our own or those we gather *in* or *from* the field [emphasis in the original]" (Segall, 2001, p. 589).[4] The point is, ultimately, that a certain "order has been created" (Scheurich, 1995, p. 249) here in this document. And it represents a series of interpretive research moments that have been organized through the experiences of the author into incomplete and at times arbitrary categories largely determined by the reading he has done and the life he has lived, or the reading he has not done and the life he has not lived. The telling of the story of a semester at St. Monica is partial here and it is cleaner and regimented in selfish and expedient ways. That is a condition of the form. And it "is fragmentary because it cannot be otherwise. Life in the field is itself fragmentary" (Tyler, 1986, p. 131), and we are, finally, always in a field.

Wearing the Required Uniform

8/26/09

I step into the main hallway, jostling among students who are, by and large, shorter than me, though the athletes tend to be wider in the shoulder, and I feel a slight twinge of intimidation. This hasn't happened for years. Outside it's warm and August wafts through opened external doors, all parched grasses and exhaust fumes, to do battle with the smells of the start of school: AXE body spray, and the waxed-floor-scotch-guarded-carpets miasma of chemical old-made-new again.

I am, for the first two weeks of school—before faculty are required to switch to "professional dress"—clothed in the garb of a student: khaki pants, weathered brown shoes, and polo shirt, ID prominently displayed at my collar. I have, for the two weeks prior to this moment, participated in New Faculty Orientation as well as the August faculty professional development days. I've been introduced to employees of the school—though not to the students of course—as a "Beverly guy" (which buys me some legitimacy for being local and, because it means I have ties to the place through siblings' friends and spouses) and a "researcher investigating the school." This has not, as you might imagine, eased some of the faculty's concerns that I may be a NARC.[5] Because, well, in the end I am a NARC, I suppose. Most of the coaching staff for fall sports (football, generally speaking) has given me a wide berth. The reception has been chilly though not unpleasantly so.

As I slide into my first-period class—Senior English—I briefly check in with Mrs. Marks, who startles at the sight of me but recovers and points me to a student desk in the back of the room. She gives me a suspicious look—fair enough—and I settle in. To my right I hear:

"That kid's like eight feet tall."

But before there's time to engage further, before anyone can ask me who the fuck I am (because that, I realize now, is how it would have sounded), Fr. Tim comes over the PA to welcome us back to school and in a synchronous moment that would only seem aligned to someone attending to it, I suppose, the chapel bells begin to toll the Angelus. And so it begins.

In the fall semester I attended classes (following the full daily schedule) as if enrolled as a senior at St. Monica of Cascia high school three days a week. Work obligations kept me from school at the bracket ends of the week, and so I took a bloc of Tuesday, Wednesday, and Thursday classes, which provided a kind of mid-week continuity for me and the students who came to wonder at my regular bookending absences. In the spring semester I spent my time writing up the study in an office provided me (complete with "Mr. Burke" nameplate) in the Counseling department. I was, for better or worse, separated off from the main hallway of the school (and windowless) and thus worked largely uninterrupted but for the occasional student who, avoiding class and in the know as to where I was located, would pop in to stare and laugh at the quotes I'd taped up on my walls by way of more easily visualizing just what I was dealing with in terms of data. I spent the majority of the morning writing and chose to take lunch with the students as a way to stay connected with their lives; too this gave me the opportunity to ask clarifying questions about what I was seeing as I was sifting back through the data and figuring out just what stories to tell and how to tell them.

In the fall I followed four different students, one each month, through their daily class schedules sitting, in a student desk in each of their classes. Throughout the semester I carried the same (orange) notebook and took field notes on/about/regarding/in-response-to the students, the teachers, and the classroom environments. The students, because they became increasingly curious about what I was writing—and because they asked—were given access to the notebook and would often take it from me at the beginning or end of class to see what I'd written over the course of the previous hour. It came to be that they performed, at times, in ways that would "get them in the notes." They would, later in the semester as they saw I posed no disciplinary threat, take the notebook and festoon it with drawings typical of their daily routine—mostly penises, though, interestingly, crosses as well. Also, if a student asked a question that went unanswered in the flow of a given class, I would occasionally jot notes to them in an attempt to better (by my own estimation) address their concerns than was possible in the moment, perhaps, for their teacher. This meant that I spent quite a bit of time "passing" notes to students in transgression or I suppose defiance of the lead teacher of a given class. It made me seem more student. Maybe.

I also, in the course of their asking—as with the student in the epigram at the start of the chapter—about what I was doing in the school, made a point to let them know that they would be given pseudonyms when the text was finally written up. This was my way of easing their concerns that I might be following them to report to the faculty and staff just what terrible (or mundane) things they were doing. This morphed, then, into their being able to "pick" their own pseudonyms which took on a life of its own as students would approach me daily with new names, asking how their "character" had done the day before. In this way, they presaged the idea of fiction/fantasy delineated in the methodology discussed earlier.

The decision to follow four different senior students gave me access to the widest possible range of senior classes, yes, but also served to stave off my boredom at the rhythms and repetition (and bored teaching, frankly) of the schoolday. And though the students whose schedules I shadowed often claimed me in interesting ways:

Kimani: "This is Mr. Burke. He's my white slave for the month."
I found that for the most part I took notes on other students in classes as much as I did on those students I was "following."

For the first month I was paired with Donny, a white, lower-middle-class student whose father worked as a janitor at the school. Donny was a reserve football player who was struggling with his that fact that his GPA was keeping him out of colleges. It was through his ministrations that I gained access to the lunch group that came to be important early on as a legitimating body for my introduction to the senior class as writer rather than potential liaison to the administration.

Donny put it this way, "When I first found out you were following me I was really worried you were going to step on my cheating routine." It was probably when I, sitting in between him and a friend, Colin, helped them pass tests to each other under my notebook, that I sealed my trustworthiness. This was not an attempt to fight the power, as it were, but rather seemed a reasonable action in a student day where cheating on tests was more par for the course than exceptional. I suppose there are ethical concerns that I might address here, but really, as tests rarely matched content, I came to empathize with students who cheated to get by, and so my helping in this situation (and others) really constituted a willful passivity (I just sat there as they exchanged papers) and became important for my gaining access to student trust.

In October, I followed Joey, an honors student who operated at the outskirts of Donny's social group. Joey is white and middle class and was largely, though surreptitiously, conflicted about the religious and athletic trappings of the school, perhaps part of his choosing to work at a dentist's office in lieu of participating in extracurriculars. When I proposed to the principal, Mrs. Daley, that I might follow the schedules of different students through the semester, she—this was a self-interested choice, as I, in exchange for being given access to the students and school, was expected to and did write up my findings as regarded pedagogical implications/issues/problems I perceived for the administration based on my unique viewpoint as student-researcher-observer—placed me with Donny and Joey so that I might observe different tracked levels to see if St. Monica was "educating students in the same ways in both regular and honors classes." Short answer, and not unexpected: they weren't.

By mid-semester I had become familiar enough with the students that they began asking why I was following certain students and not them. As I had only been assigned two students by the administration, and having exhausted my self-imposed one-month rule, I took two students up on their offers/demands that I follow and—in their minds—write about them. My choices were made based on a desire to see more and different classes, in Tim's case, and to shadow a transfer student of color, in Kimani's case. This is not, of course, a matter of better data, but different data.

November found me with Tim, a white football player who outsized me by about sixty pounds. He was more respectful of the workings and work of classes than Donny, though largely because he needed his grades up for a potential collegiate football career. In January he signed a letter of intent to play on scholarship at a small local Catholic university. He, like a great many of his classmates, chose to attend St. Monica because of a family legacy that spans nearly half of the school's 105 year history.

My last guide, Kimani, transferred in to St. Monica from rival Brother Field to escape poor grades and the whisperings of a racist environment after his sophomore year. Black and the child of a single mother, he often endured mockery for being too black for the white kids and too white—because of his affected tone of voice—for the black kids. His grades suffered mightily all year—he missed two football games because of academics—and I found myself bringing two pens to class with me each day to ensure that he would have one to still-not-take notes with.

Though it gives me pause that out of four students I shadowed three football players this was a consequence of my initial exposure to the senior class through Donnie, whose group of friends was on the team. Still, in an institution of 701 where nearly half of the school plays the sport, it would have been almost odd had this not occurred. Too, as I take it that these young men are more than the sum of their marked identities, the fact that they were football players, while important, means only that they will deal with the requisite discourses and ideologies of the school and religion and masculinity in unique and affected ways. The breakdown doesn't discourage me, however, as the methodology requires that I acknowledge the partiality of my own writing and the incompleteness of the picture to be described. Too, in such a small school, where I sat in on every senior class—except for one section each of French and Theology—I became party to, and on a first-name basis with, nearly every senior. Kairos[6] retreats helped with this immensely as did my work with/through Campus Ministry, where I became an adopted member because of my prior work in Catholic schools and with retreats and volunteering. Indeed, I led a group of St. Monica seniors on a service trip the summer after the conclusion of the study. I have become, am yet becoming always, very much entangled in the school, in the lives of these kids in joyous and troubling ways as we'll see.

Details

I took field notes when possible while in the school. Generally this occurred in classroom settings and not, in less formal spheres (at lunch, for example). My aim, when not taking field notes actively, was to transcribe experiences in the middle of the school day or outside of the school setting in an attempt to "capture" moments not previously crystallized on paper. Additionally, as the school day was split into six class periods, the fourth carved interestingly to include a lunch and pseudo-study hall passing time, called TDT (Teacher Discretionary Time), I was able to transcribe my handwritten notes to the computer, along with annotations and observations during the day by absenting myself from fourth period classes while still being able to spend two lunches with two different students.[7] Further, at the end of the school day, I would transcribe any experiences in the final periods of the day before leaving the school.

Saying that I absented myself from fourth period is a bit misleading. On my third day in classes, I was asked by the instructor of the senior theology class I was observing to "give him some time and space to get the guys in line." I perceived this gentle push out the door, all eyebrow raises and import, as an open-ended invitation to leave the course for good, and I took it as my cue to not come back. As Brother Larry headed all of the senior-level theology classes, I was effectively shut out from formal religious instruction, at least in its encoded, catalogued curricular form.[8] This was expedient in that I got to spend fourth period transcribing notes in the Campus Ministry office—located along the main hallway and open to the students to pop in during TDT and spend time hanging out, largely unregulated for the only time during the course of the day—and it allowed me to build a rapport with the Campus Ministry staff, which in turn gave me access to the Kairos retreat experience.

As it is certainly the case that masculinities are engaged with in different ways in various spaces, I embedded myself in as heterogeneous a set of activities as possible throughout the year. In the process of the school day I observed student interaction with faculty and official curriculum in classes, and masses, as well as those casual conversations that occurred in un(der)officiated spaces like hallways, the dining hall, and outside on school grounds.

Before I discovered and moved to my office in the Counseling department, I was able to make Campus Ministry (CM) an impromptu workspace, because of a welcoming director who graduated from the same University as I and who came to be a good friend and confidante over the course of the year. As the CM office is located in the middle of the main student hallway of the building and its doors are always open as a way of inviting students to interact with the lay ministers (and a lone Augustinian brother) I caught a great deal of student conversations there. The space served as a crossroads of sorts, with students popping in to borrow pencils, sign up for service hours, and as an excuse to ditch class. Later, as they became more comfortable with me, senior students would take their TDT (if they had forgetful or lenient or exhausted teachers) during fourth period to sit and chat around the table in the center of the room, excited to be the subject of a "book."

Further, I was able to join and observe two senior Kairos retreats[9] offered by the school and took over duties as an assistant junior varsity lacrosse coach which gave me access to unique spiritual and athletic vistas at St. Monica. In addition, I attended extracurricular sporting and social events affiliated with, though not necessarily located at, the school itself. Playoff football games took me to the outskirts of Chicago on frozen nights; basketball left me in a hot box of a rival gym, clapping through the sweat; I witnessed perhaps the most baffling phenomenon of the semester at a hockey rink in the far southwestern suburbs. I took my partner to the Homecoming dance as well as the school's Winter Fundraiser, and she was kind enough to endure Saturday lacrosse and Friday night football contests. I mention her because she became important in much of the dialogue I had with students not only as they tried to make sense of their dating lives, but also as they came to struggle with just who I might be particularly around the question of my straightness as I queered—in the sense of making strange their prior notions—their idea of what was possible for/expected of an adult in the context of a schoolday.

Entextualizing

The question now turns, I suppose, to just what I chose to write down, and when in the orange notebook. To say that I jotted what I found relevant to the question of masculinities and spiritualities in a Catholic school really isn't narrowing too much, as potentially—especially when I'm looking at discourses and have chosen to use Foucault's broadest definition of these—anything might apply in any case. So I'll say this: I took notes when it felt like students were being exposed (and/or reacting) to specific versions of what it meant to be male or masculine. I'm thinking specifically of, for example, commercials that during Channel 1, semi-required viewing at the start of first period, presented limited and traditional notions of males as sexually predatory and physically dominant or served as ciphers for military recruitment. Too, I jotted down instances of language that felt like it was being used to give shape to what is possible and allowed for a person coming-to-be a man in a school. Often enough, students in the course of the day, were they to complain about schoolwork for example, were told by faculty and coaches, both male and female, to "man-up," and get down to business. The implications of such an invocation of manhood I'll dig into more deeply in the chapters that follow, but suffice to say that such utterances weighed heavily on my consciousness as I floundered through my revisited schoolboy days.

Also, I attended to the ways in which boys in the school came to physically interact with each other, with teachers, and with the environment of the brick and mortar school. There were interesting regulations, informal and negotiated continually, around who could touch whom and how, and much of this has to do, I think, with the way that athletics and tradition play a role in de/limiting masculinities at St. Monica. This fed directly into discussions with students that I initiated about the usage of terms like "gay" and "fag" which constantly informed regular daily discourse and served as markers for possible action and sanctions surrounding particular forms of kinship. Additionally, pictures bore portent throughout the semester and the year, both those peppering the hallways of the school and those created in semi-secrecy by the boys in a unique manifestation of and alteration to Pascoe's fag discourse. More on this later.

I was also particularly drawn to discussions among the students regarding women, in the abstract but also in their lives, most particularly as they envisioned—and boasted about—them as sexual objects. This set up a ready and intriguing contrast when considering the role of the fairy/wonder tales of St. Monica and the multiple ways and times that the boys were impelled to pray to their Mother Mary or the Mother of Good Counsel throughout the day.

I chose not to conduct formal interviews with the students over the course of the first semester. Neither did I engage faculty in such staid attempts at data creation.[10] Instead, as it felt more congruous with the rhythms of the schoolday and allowed for a certain flexibility while still allowing me not to be "expert" in the sense of appearing adult (and agenda-laden), at times, when I had a moment, I would try to engage with the Monicamen in what I'll call informal "flash" interviews aimed at capturing their thinking in an instant and trying to interrogate their intentions or consideration around a specific conversation. Sheurich (1995) in a critique on the possibilities afforded through/awarded to the process of interviewing and the celebrated representation of truth and voice in its transmission to paper-as-research suggests that a postmodern interview requires "'playing around' or experimentation...[in] ways that highlight the indeterminacy of interview interactions, ways that allow for the uncontrollable play of power within the interaction...what we need are some new imaginaries of interviewing" (p. 250). In the interest of agreeing, I suppose flash interviews to have been created in brief moments where the curiosity of researcher/subject/researched bore further examination.

As such, I never entered a given day or class period—though we were particularly free during gym, as I didn't participate actively but chose to sit on the side and observe basketball or water polo, etc. and was generally surrounded by students who were 'injured' which really meant that they didn't feel like changing out of one uniform and into another—aiming at interviewing a given student. But if there was space and a student asked me what I was writing about, or I felt the need to try to clarify my thinking or purposes I might try to engage in a moment of dialog about why things were happening the way they were happening. What follows is an example, from a day in gym sitting with Tim (this was November) and Sean, the starting goalie on the school's very successful varsity hockey team and an honors student:

> Me: "So you're at a Catholic school but people don't seem too religious. Why do you think that is? I mean you can't avoid it to a cer-

tain extent because you pray in class and you go to Mass and you guys wear the crosses, but..."

Tim: "I dunno. People just do it 'cause they have to. Like I try to be a good Catholic. My mom makes me go to church but I try not to make her make me."

Me: "Why do you go?"

Tim: "Because that's part of being a Catholic."

Me: "Does the school do anything to enhance that?"

Tim: "Not really."

Me: "What does the school do well?"

Tim: "Um, like I've been around St. Monica my whole life. I mean it's fun. I've been coming to football games as long as I can remember. It just feels like home. It just feels like family."

Me: "What does the school do to make that happen?"

Tim: "Well, we're here all the time."

Me: "So it's ok for a guy to be really into hockey or football, but would you have anyone say they were really into religion?"

Sean: "You might have a few. But not many."

Me: "Why?"

Sean: "Because we're young. Like you can talk about it on Kairos, but that's because they make that all you talk about there."

The point was to engage them about an issue I was trying to sort through around the role of devotional religiosity in the school. Also, too, it was a way to help the boys become familiar with the kinds of research questions I might be asking for my "book" so that they, should they feel so compelled, could come back to me later with insights. This was a technique I employed specifically in reference to the physicality/sexuality/fag discourse questions I had. I realize that the format of these interviews isn't particularly unique, but my point in calling them "flash" is that they began and ended as quickly as students moved near or away from me in informal periods during the day (at lunch, in hallways, in Campus Ministry, in gym, within school generally, and in the stands at sporting events outside the schoolday) and their purpose wasn't necessarily determined before they happened.[11] This was the extent to which I engaged in interviewing through the process and it was the form I chose to use, typing up my memory of the interchange at the next convenient moment.

Beyond School

As the year progressed and I became more involved in and knowledgeable about the senior students' lives, I was privy to two additional points of contact with students. Once one of them found me on Facebook, and I accepted them as a "friend," the floodgates opened. It was here that they were able to find out more about my life—they often, after looking at photo albums, asked if I had a twin brother; I don't, but we do look a great deal alike—and I was able to keep tabs on their interactions on each other's "walls." I have chosen not to include too much data from this sphere—for a number of reasons, really, chief among them being my own admittedly troubling lack of theory in the field of digital rhetorics—but will occasionally utilize the site to confirm notions of relationships/friendships between and among students. Facebook was a window through which the boys were able to integrate me into their lives outside of school, most specifically surrounding the realms of dating (through pictures from various dances and parties) and drinking. These are not generally mutually exclusive, it should be noted.

The terminology used at the school among the boys to describe this kind of low-level surveillance, through which the young men kept in touch outside of (and even within by way of surreptitious smartphone access) the school's walls, was *creeping*, as in, "I was creeping your pictures last night, Mr. Burke." The term itself bespeaks a kind of discomfort with the level of exposure to the outside world put forth through digital social networking, but its connotation was in most cases utilized as a goad to both spur and limit peer interaction over the Internet. In a larger sense, I suppose I could be said to have "creeped" (never the grammatically correct 'crept" in this etymological system) the boys lives as thoroughly as possible all year in as many ways as they were willing to grant me access and in other manners over which they had no control at all.

The second point of contact, and one from which I drew quite a bit of data in the second semester came through the serpentine distribution of my phone number among the seniors. I gave my cell to one student so that he could text me scores from a big rivalry football game that I couldn't attend in the early fall; in November I gave it to another student so that we could coordinate a midweek volunteer trip to a homeless shelter. From there, after it became clear that I didn't much mind the contact and sensing that I might just be flattered by it, I guess, I began to receive texts and phone calls from various students, generally on weekends, inviting me to social gatherings so that I could "write the real book"[12] of what goes on. Tempting as that might have been, I chose to let most phone calls—and certainly any after midnight on Fridays and Saturdays—go to voicemail for the sake of transcribing the message with the idea of using it in this text. Generally the boys called and texted to talk shit[13]—more on this later—in affectionate ways and I found their contact a point of trust. This was their way of acknowledging that I wasn't a formal faculty member or representative of the school—because I had no desire to deal with them punitively, should I find out where and how much they were drinking—and letting me know they were making sense of my role in their lives. This is something I'll discuss at length to follow, my role as researcher in their lives and how they came to make sense of me, as it certainly affected the manner/kind of data to which I was exposed and thus that material with which I could co-create, categorize, and conclude.

By way of beginning, let us go now to lunch.

Notes

[1] Tyler (1986) quibbles with this term, through a bit of equivocation, in this way:

> An ethnography is a fantasy, but it is not, like these, a fiction for the idea of fiction entails a locus of judgment outside the fiction, whereas an ethnography weaves a locus of judgment within itself, and that locus, that evocation of reality, is also a fantasy. It is not a reality fantasy like 'Dallas,' nor a fantasy reality like the DSM III; it is a reality fantasy of a fantasy reality. That is to say, it is realism, the evocation of a possible world of reality already known to us in fantasy. (p. 139)

Personally I'm more comfortable with the term "fiction" than "fantasy" and so will continue to refer to the work as such, when it feels relevant. I will also later in this chapter, address the idea of television-ed fantasy/reality. In this light, I will use Geertz (1973) as a guide for he saw ethnography and anthropological research as fiction because they are necessarily shaped by their authors and largely determined by the linguistic context and tradition through which they are created.

[2] Britzman (2000) continues, questioning the very idea of an 'original.' "Ethnography may construct the very materiality it attempts to represent" because:

> those who populate and imagine it (every participant, including the author and the reader) are, in essence, textualized identities. Their voices create a cacophony and dialogic display of contradictory desires, fears, and literary tropes that, if carefully 'read,' suggest just how slippery speaking, writing, reading and desiring subjectivity really are. (p. 28)

Which is to say, one supposes, that what is written loses the original at the slippages of the joists of memory and textualization, and textualization and a reading. Ethnography is, ultimately, an encomium for the representation of an idea.

3   Hartsock (1987) is useful here: "The construction of self in opposition to another who threatens one's very being reverberates throughout the construction of both class society and the masculinist world view and results in a deepgoing and hierarchical dualism" (p. 169). Of course Connell is not talking about a dualism here, but the ever re-settling hierarchy suggests that what really matters in the end, regardless of how many "masculinities" are discussed, is which one is hegemonic and which others are collectively, then, subjugated.

4   It is apropos at this moment to acknowledge the irony of citing portions of a piece by a colleague and reader of early drafts of this work to discuss the ways in which we fail to attend to the violence we do in the necessary skewering (and decontextualizing) of that which we cite from the research community, often in the same pages upon which we take great care to honor the supposed "completeness" of voices we present/constitute in/from field research. I hope he might tell me at this moment, "well, we all lead conflicted lives."

5   "NARC" is the truncated form of 'narcotics agent.' It's used to denote an informant or a potential snitch of any kind or form.

6   More on this to follow, in-depth. However, a brief sketch by way of providing context in the interest of expanding later in the piece. Kairos is a religious retreat popular at Catholic high schools and colleges. It is derived from the Greek, term—one of two—for time. Chronos is seen in this distinction as quantitative and or linear in measure while Kairos is more felt or experienced time. In its religious context, then, it is referred to as God's time, a retreating from the rigors of chronos.

7   Regular Student Schedule
1st: 7:55 – 9:00
2nd: 9:04 – 9:54
3rd: 9:58 – 10:48
4A: Lunch 10:52 – 11:16 TDT 11:20 – 11:44 Class 11:44 – 12:32
4B: TDT 10:52 – 11:12 Lunch 11:16 – 11:40 Class 11:44 – 12:32
4C: Class 10:52 – 11:40 Lunch 11:44 – 12:08 TDT 12:12 – 12:32
4D: Class 10:52 – 11:40 TDT 11:40 – 12:04 Lunch 12:08 – 12:32
5th: 12:36 – 1:26
6th: 1:30 – 2:20
* For the first semester I attended first through third, as well as fifth and sixth period with the students. During fourth, because of the unique configuration/usage of time, I went to lunch at 11:16 as well as 11:44 (in order to sit with two different groups of students) and used the rest of the time to type up my notes from the first part of the day/visit with students informally in Campus Ministry. In the second semester I wrote in the morning, cut down to one lunch period, and spent the rest of fourth period visiting in Campus Ministry. Afternoons were free to revise writing and to pull students from class to aid me in my analysis of the data.

8   The senior theology requirement had recently been changed to a survey of great Catholic thinkers, a theme which coincided neatly with the textbook for the course of the same title. Ah curriculum. By way of introducing the class, Brother Larry celebrated the shift. "The old class was about love and intimacy. It was called 'Christian Vocations.' I said 'if we don't change it, I quit.' It was ruining my reputation as a teacher. It was light.' All we talked about all semester was love and intimacy." There's a great deal worth pinging here, of course, but as I lasted only three days in his class it's perhaps most relevant to note that love and intimacy are considered trivial. This is most striking in light of the fact of the class's former title which could have encompassed more than love and intimacy had the instructor so chosen; it would seem the Church ought best concern itself with vocations, considering their dearth—at least as far as entering the religious/contemplative life is concerned—in the last forty years or so. Still there is a certain salaciousness with which love and sex are discussed in a schooled, particularly a religious-schooled environment, which centers on a coming to control (and being controlled) (Nespor, 1997) rooted in, particularly in this case, a masculine idea of "domination of oneself by oneself" where to be at the demands of sexual pleasures was to be "immoderate...shameless and incorrigible" (Foucault, 1990b, p. 65). And so the choice to teach vocation as love and intimacy, then to frame it as a burden, is a bit of a red herring, understandable considering the Church's ambivalent (problematic and horrific) response to allegations of clergy sex abuse over the prior decades. A friar (a generic term for any male in a religious order) like Brother Larry is not supposed to be interested in the sex, in the pleasure, in the intimacy of his students and so chose to frame his previous course as an inconvenience, and consequently 'light,' perhaps using it to impose "social and sexual normality" centering on control of desires through "discipline and punishment" (Fiske, 1989, p. 90). This might, too, all be sour grapes because he kicked me out. But, from what the students reported, they really only watched movies in the class anyways. So there you have it.

9   My affiliation with Campus Ministry opened doors for me in the school. Fr. Tim, a former Campus Minister himself, asked me to run reflections tied in with the Kairos retreats after my participation on them in the first semester and later he and the director of Campus Ministry had me speak to all of the sophomore students on their required in-school retreats about bullying, or rather, not bullying I suppose. It was through this office that I came to spend Wednesday evenings with some of the boys serving at a local homeless shelter; too it was here that I ended up advocating for taking a group of students down to Southern Missouri on a summer service trip with members of my family. This became, before coaching began, my niche in the officialized discourses of the school. I was easier to place, in other words, as a researcher/campus minister than as a pseudo-student/hallway wanderer. This put teachers and administrators at ease with me because I came to be seen as 'contributing' to the community, an image furthered after I submitted a report in January to the administration based on my observations of classes in the first semester and cemented with my role as coach. The students tended to be more dubious for longer; they were constantly renegotiating my place amongst them.

10   This would be an important aspect of further research, but I didn't much have the time during the school day to engage with faculty in anything more than informal chit-chat, due in large part to my remaining loyal to the student schedule which only afforded me four minutes between classes. It would be interesting to get faculty's sense of their own conveyance of masculinities and spiritualities and then compare that with the ways students read such messages to check for dissonance, resistance, reprisal, etc.

11   This is, maybe, not entirely true. I had multiple purposes, as I've written, for the interviews so I suppose I should say that the intent of any given flash was as malleable as the time and space in which it was instantiated, reliant on who was present, and perhaps the weather as well as the food in front of us, or the score in the game we were half-watching while we talked.

12   There were times when I thought about the possibility of attending a party for the sake of data collection but ended up deciding to err on the side of legalistic concerns (minors and alcohol and all those wonderful trappings) though it would have been enlightening to see the boys in an 'altered' state, under the influence of alcohol (and harder drugs) and girls. Two texts which skirted this line, Rebekah Nathan's (2005), *My Freshman Year*, in which the author returned as a "freshman" to the dorms of the University of her employ and Jeremy Iversen's (2007) *High School Confidential*, where the author posed—successfully by his account—as a California public high school student over the course of a school year, set a precedent for at least considering the idea. However, as a guest with no purchase on the space and access to students granted me, beyond of the good will of St. Monica high school, and considering just how open to 'creeping' the young men's Facebook sites were as well as their penchant for posting essentially everything that occurred on a given weekend, it seemed wiser to limit myself to school sponsored events.

13   This is, in essence, a form of what Willis (1981) found among his lads in the influential work, *Learning to Labor*, where "taking the piss" or "having a laff", (p. 12) meant good-natured (for the most part) ribbing and mockery served to mark lines of connection and brotherhood among male friends in the school. As I held no known, and certainly no exercised, official disciplinary role within the realm of the school, the boys felt increasingly free to integrate me into their routines involving the thrust and parry of affectionate linguistic challenge. This extended further into the sphere of physicality—touching, hugging, mock tackling—as the year wore on as well.

Chapter 4

Cafeteria Catholics

Fag Discourse

One can never really 'go native'...at the same time, it is the experience of living village life that offers the insight and vantage point needed to ask relevant questions and understand the context of the answers given.

Rebecca Nathan, "My Freshman Year"

Ought not education to bring out and fortify the differences rather than the similarities?

Virginia Woolf, "A Room of One's Own"

Abjection is the affect or feeling of anxiety, loathing, and disgust that the subject has in encountering certain matter, images, and fantasies—the horrible—to which it can respond only with aversion, with nausea and distraction. Kristeva (1982) argues that the abject provokes fear and disgust because it exposes the border between self and other. This border is fragile. The abject threatens to dissolve the subject by dissolving the border.

Robyn Longhurst, "Trim, Taut, Terrific, and Pregnant"

The purpose, until now, has been to describe the general conditions of the research. From here we will telescope in on the mise-en-scene of life at St. Monica High School from the view of an outsider with insider tendencies. The overall hedge is always that same-sex educational settings seek to set limits on gendered possibility at the assumed rigid lines of sexed difference. This is the frame, the limits of which are described by teacher discourse, religious ideology (manifest not only in the masses and classes of the school, but also by the cluttered accoutrements of hallways and rooms peppered with iconic imagery), and historico-traditional ideals of what a Monicaman must become over his four years. Masculinities are fostered here. Specific targeted masculinities are preferred. Where it gets messy is when the boys get ahold of their own discursive possibility.

Lunch

Huey is pounding the table again. Both arms, fists clenched, whatever detritus left from the twenty or so minutes of consumption, rattling with his mock-rage. He's a big kid, a former fullback and a weightlifter; there is a force to this.

"Goddamnit, Burke. I said it 'cause I wanted to say it. I will fucking tackle you, gayboy."

This is lunch. The closest we'll come to the unfettered physicality of Bakhtin's (1998) "carnivalistic act" (p. 253) beyond the athletic fields that ring the physical space of St. Monica the school. Here we are all freer from the sweeping scan of classroom surveillance and besides mostly we outnumber the dining hall monitors who are by and large too put out by the added duty to care immensely about what's going on. Some of the football coaches quietly dip into their spit cups by the windows behind us. They ignore most any uproar short of punches thrown.

This space, this time in lunch, is where the constant "mock crowning and subsequent decrowning of the carnival king" (p. 252) can be said to occur most demonstrably within the building of the place. It is the apex of the verbal jousting that ebbs and flows throughout the day. And yes, it is gay. Or rather, it is always about being and not being made gay, wielding that word and its close cousins and all their attendant meanings, like goads. There are gauntlets all over the floor.

It is here that fag discourse reigns, and it is here further that hierarchies are too unstable to endure. Boys will adopt the gay pose, boys will emplace it on others, boys will hook it on chairs; it's everywhere and it's in reference to straightness, yes, but not as its abject opposite necessarily. This, I think as we throw out the remains of another meal together, all those cheese cups and polymer chip bags,[1] laughing too loudly at something or other on our way to fifth period, is Foucault (1998) and power, "the name one attributes to a complex strategical situation in a particular society" (p. 166). For it is only in knowing (how to alter and manipulate) the rules and strategies of the discourse that one will thrive; there is no opting out. And it is at lunch that these complex power strategies come to be constantly renegotiated, flouted, and reconstituted in ways that call into question Connell's (1995) hegemonic masculinity where, by all rights ze argues, "through the everyday working of institutions...the dominance of a particular kind of masculinity [should be] achieved" (p. 213). It's just not that simple, I think as we flow out the double doors and into the athletic wing, headed back to class with the verve of the well-fed (or at least the overly fed on processed food, say). The crown just never settles.

And despite the violence of it all, I'm really not too concerned about Huey. In the end he's more prone to pull me into a one-armed embrace as we walk back to class, whisper "I'm just kidding," and then push me into the oncoming pedestrian traffic of a hallway-period change than he is to actually tackle me. The physical I'll deal with later, though. For now I'm more interested in the play of language, this "struggle for control over the meanings and pleasures" (Fiske, 1989, p. 70) of it.

The Same, Only Different

Like Pascoe (2007), I see this work as looking at "masculinity as a variety of practices and discourses that can be mobilized by and applied to both boys and girls" (p. 9). Unlike Pascoe, I am not housed in a co-educational environment (excepting faculty and staff) and so of need must focus in on how the boys[2] navigate un/accept/ed/able practices and discourses. As her work was the text that made my own feel possible, I will take a moment to pay homage to a good and thorough and like-minded study, while reserving the necessity of diverging from her path at two critical points that rely on the unique situation of St. Monica High School for their articulation.

So it is that I agree that "it is important to look at...masculinizing processes outside the male body" (p. 12), most particularly in terms of discourses. Pascoe found in her study that for high school students, males in particular the terms, "*gay* and *fag*" were used "interchangeably when they referred to other boys" (p. 37) and fag discourse, which she came to call this mode of relating to and regulating each others' actions/possible selves involves "the fag" being "not only an identity linked to homosexual boys, but an identity that can temporarily adhere to heterosexual boys as well" (p. 53).

This lexicography often seemed to devolve into a kind of Tourette's for the boys, a phenomenon to which Pascoe refers. Though I found that the students at St. Monica used the term in more creative and wide-ranging manners than explicated in her study, it was, yes, mobilized to regulate an assumption of a "lack of masculinity" where perceived "*male effeminacy*" (p. 59) occurred as with Luke (in reference to a classmate worrying about college applications), who noted with bombast, "They know you get your hair done, so you're a faggot and won't get in," or Kobe, who, in answer to my question about a classmate's name which kept eluding me, said simply, "That's Zach. He dyes his hair and tans. That's gay." What finality.

But, this wasn't just always about keeping *classmates* in line, and this is something Pascoe chooses not to address. The discourse itself at St. Monica came to be associated with, or rather came to flesh out any manner of frustration or perceived helplessness for the boys. Early in the first semester, when I was just getting my student legs under me, Qualter, a senior who spent most of first period reading the *Chicago Tribune* (and the majority of the rest of the day wandering the hallways), turned to those of us sitting behind him and, in reference to a popular Chicago hockey player, with a certain exasperation said, "Dude, that's fucking gay. Burish got hurt." Similarly, when grades came out he told me that his low average had to do with the student teacher (a woman) "being gay as fuck" about him turning in work. I should note that as a student, he was always marked by his lassitude and so these statements weren't growled; it would have been hard to categorize them as anything other than offhand. Note here that a woman was made gay, as with Johnny's mother in chapter 3, but so too was the situation of an injury. This latter example points to a notion of the term that is rooted in something other than the lack of masculinity for it is not Burish who is gay for being hurt, but rather the fact of being hurt in the abstract and his assumed resulting absence from the team that is gay.

Later, trying to get a handle on just how the discourse functioned, I pressed a student, Dunbar, on the issue after he called something "gay."

Me: "Why's that gay?"

Dunbar: "Well, it's not really gay, just stupid."

This is not necessarily out of the purview of any given teacher's (or parent's or coach's) experience in the hallways of a school or at home or on the field of sport where the conflation of gay with undesirability or stupidity[3] occurs frequently. What the boys indicated, and what Pascoe further suggests, though, is that this usage is not necessarily intentionally (read: maliciously and/or purposefully) homophobic[4]—though it certainly could be read that way. Rather, it came to function as a way of reordering the unexpected in a given day or it could become utilized as a stock rejoinder as when a teacher, responding to a student question about parking told him, "Well, we have assigned spots." The student, non-plussed and really only half-paying attention to the answer as he walked out of the room, said, "Oh. That's gay." Similarly, when Chunk, a senior who came to be a confidante through our work on a Kairos retreat, asked why it was important to study World War II and was told by the history teacher that "A lotta people died in [WWII], why?" he just said, rolling his eyes, "Gay," and got back to the serious business of not paying attention to class. Also, in the parking lot after an intramural game Nico pointed out his car to me as we walked back to class, "You see my hoopty over there, Mr. Burke? With the lights flashing?" Unsure, I asked, "Is that a Mitsubishi?" to which Kimani, who had wandered up behind us said, simply, "Yeah, it's for faggots." So fag discourse is not something that lends itself only to the regulation of possible masculine lives, but it does serve as an important part of providing limits to/for that particular situation.

The school, mind, does nothing to make fag discourse an explicit part of the curriculum. It is, as it were, the hidden curriculum of the place. That, of itself, does not make St. Monica unique. However, what I intend to argue here is that the single-gendered context requires the development of strategies for utilizing "fagging" differentially than in a co-educational context. This, in turn, affects the ways that masculinity gets folded into the origami of a Monica student becoming a Monicaman.

Girlfriends

Returning to Pascoe (2007), we find that there were two unique points of departure through which boys could opt out of active participation in fag discourse at River High, the school where the author conducted her study.

"The ways boys talked about heterosexual practices and orientations in their interviews reveal[ed] that their public sexuality was as much about securing a masculine social position as it was about expressions of desire or emotion" (p. 89).

In this sense, the Monicamen were a bit different for they, in the absence of openly gay students (there was an active gay presence at the school Pascoe studied), talked only fleetingly—and in rehearsed and specific spaces—about sexual conquests, which were always assumed to reside in the heterosexual realm anyways. And so relationships and sex—this I will discuss at more length in a later section of the text—weren't often evoked in the process of fag discourse. We might think of it in legal terms. In Pascoe a boy was straight-until-proven-homosexual; at St. Monica every student was straight. This latter assertion we can assume to be untrue considering representative statistics on gay populations in the larger society. However, it does bespeak a kind of intolerance written into the code of the school—through religion and neighborhood politics most assuredly—that coming out most likely also meant getting out (of Monica and Beverly).

"Girlfriends," then, didn't protect "boys from the specter of the fag" (p. 90) in the same ways at St. Monica as they did for Pascoe (2007). This is partially due to the fact that girls were physically absent from the hallways of the school and thus couldn't be regularly brought out on display by the boys during the day. And so they weren't "treated" in the same ways "as resources to be mobilized for…masculinity projects" (p. 107) because in most cases an invocation of a girlfriend in the midst of the schoolday would actually lead to an accusation of softness and a lack of proper confrontational masculinity. It would have indicated an inability to properly respond to an accusation, in other words.

Kimani, for instance, stopped me in the halls one day to tell me he'd seen Ben, a friend from the football team, "shopping at Hollister with his girlfriend." Shaking his head in mock sorrow and looking at me with knowing eyes, he smiled into, "I was like, that's so gay." Note that it's not the act of shopping necessarily that is gay here—as Kimani was of necessity at the mall, too, if he indeed saw Ben, and would have been presumably shopping himself—but rather the state of shopping with a girlfriend that is considered abject. This is indicative of homosocial elements present, which fed into a certain jealousy of women/girls taking time away from "proper" male friendships. This discourse ran throughout the hallways and extended, of necessity, into social lives outside of the school day. More on this later.

For now, however, it's important to attend to the discomfort the young men had in discussing sex and relationships involving women on the whole, a product, I would argue, of the abject status of "being in a relationship" conveyed through fag discourse at the school. Odd, this. But to be in a heterosexual relationship was "gay," most particularly if one actually talked about it (even if boasting of sexual prowess unless pressed for details by someone else) and especially if the relationship took away from time with one's "boys."[5]

A quick note here on this concept: There was a level of homoerotica present in visceral ways that the young Monicamen related to each other. We will delve more deeply into the relational split between one's time with the boys (who are similar and understand me) and girls (who are different and problematic) in a later section. But it is intriguing here to play with the notion that the way that the boys policed each other's relationships external to the school played into—and perhaps could be argued to have come out of—early Greek notions of ethical systems of manhood rooted in notions of self/other mastery, the codification of which led to "an elaboration of masculine conduct carried out from the viewpoint of men in order to give form to *their* behavior" (Foucault, 1990b, p. 23). In some ways, then, these titillating lines of questioning about my heterosexual relationship beyond the homosocial bonds we'd formed in my short time in the school was part of their coming to re/order me in the scales of mastery/domination related to the formation of acceptable behavior sexually and socially. I was not, in essence, outside of their rules of conduct and my between-ness (student/faculty) was what they were testing.

Cameron (2006) writes about the need in "homosocial encounters between men" to "carefully manage" interactions as a way to "ward off the spectre of homosexuality." One way to do this is to assert one's own "heterosexual masculinity by contrasting" the self "with men who are taken" or constructed through talk as "insufficiently heterosexual or masculine" (p. 174). This then leads to "what Eckert means by the 'heterosexual market,'" which is "a set of social arrangements whereby girls and boys, though still socializing mainly with peers of the same gender, reorient their relationships around the norms of heterosexuality" (p. 175). How to do it: put the fag on someone else, often through verbal sparring or even through dominative (and homoerotic) physicality.

Two different exchanges were illustrative of an initial foray into carnal curiosity, followed by increased discomfort when the rules of the discourse weren't properly engaged. Both came following the Homecoming dance, which I attended with my girlfriend as a way to connect with the students, yes, but also for the purposes of study.

Generally the workings of fag discourse operate in a certain circularity. If one is called gay, it is on him to "tag" the next person, thus removing the label from himself. We'll see a literal/physical form of this later when the boys created pictures-as-tags representing a kind of fag discourse, but in the case of verbal interdiction the "tag" worked like a kind of gay hot potato. The idea was never to allow the latest round of fagging to land on one's person for long. This verbal play was maintained by the assumption that to be "gay" in any sense was a negative thing (we might point to Church and social teachings regarding the abject status of a gay individual as a few of many sources for these perceptions) that might lead to a boy's being suspected of actually *being* gay were he not sufficiently bothered by his character-impugned. So it was that in any conversation, often everything anyone did could be called into the field of play as "gay." It just meant that the person throwing the barb could easily distance himself, and quickly, from the latest salvo coming his way.

I chose not to engage in the game in this way, invoking special status as a researcher to, instead, grill the boys on why they said things rather than playing along with actively fagging another student. At lunch the day following Homecoming, the same student who was excoriated for shopping at Hollister turned and with what might best be described as a shit-eating grin nudged me:

> Ben: "You pound it out after the dance, Mr. Burke?"
> Me: "What's that mean, Ben?"
> Ben: [Laughing nervously and looking around for support] "You know...You gonna make me say it?"

Indeed I was going to make him say it. The boys were fascinated by my relationship very briefly, mostly in its physical particulars, but really only, I learned, in an attempt to draw me into some form of the back-and-forth of making-the-fag, the terms of which they were familiar with and could better dictate. Now it could be that, because I was seen as an adult, they were only comfortable pushing so far but that doesn't strike me as an issue considering how settled they were in asking initial questions. It was when I didn't take the bait and chose to steer away from the call-and-response of the fag discourse that they lost their bearings, as evidenced by this exchange from the same day in History class:

> Packer: "You got some hot squish,[6] Mr. Burke. You should be honored. Did you post up that squish after the dance?"
> Chunk: "Yeah, did you post it up?"
> Me: "What's that mean?"
> Chunk: "Getting some."
> Me: "What's that mean?"
> Chunk: "Hooking up."
> Me: "What's that mean?"
> Scott: [Annoyed] "Sex, Burke. You faggot."

Here I benefited from the ability as researcher to play dumb for the purpose of trying to draw students from euphemism to technical terminology. Also it was a way to avoid engaging in speaking about whatever carnality they were searching for, but it was also a way to avoid getting drawn into, for a time at least, until Scott put a coda on the conversation, the inevitable fag dialectic. It mattered not in the end that I had a girlfriend or that I might have slept with her after homecoming, I was still a faggot for not taking up the linguistic challenge. And though I opted out (or at least tried to), always, of engaging actively in the discourse, I was still made gay in spite of the situation of my girlfriend. Women or the possibility of heterosexual sex, in the end, were never feasible excuses for rising above (or sidestepping I suppose) fag discourse. The value, above all, was getting the "fag" off of oneself and onto another. There were no time-outs to the game (save Kairos), either, and so the boys were constantly on-guard out of a perceived necessity to keep the specter at bay. In a sense, then, at the school we were all faggots, just as we were all Catholics. The latter, though, wasn't seen as nearly so dangerous as the former, and so denouncing one actively while perhaps resisting the other passively sufficed in the establishment of an order among the boys that said it would have been gay to be outwardly liturgically faithful, but an uneasy truce could be agreed upon around scapulars and tattoos of crosses.

The idea, of course, is that linguistic facility was important for navigating the school day. Further ways of interacting regarding heterosexual assertion were affected by the single-gendered nature of the school; were St. Monica co-educational, the above might have played out very differently. The Catholic heritage of the school further formed discourse for the boys.

Religiosity

Pascoe found that "religion played a key role in how or if boys deployed practices of compulsive heterosexuality to shore up masculine appearance and sense of self" (p. 112) but noted that "the table at which the Latter Day Saints convened during lunch was "one of the least homophobic and sexist locations on campus!" (p. 112). This she viewed as initially surprising but found through her work that "Christian boys at River High had institutional claims on masculinity such that they didn't need to engage in the sort of intense interactional work…characteristic of contemporary 'compulsive masculinity'" (p. 113). Her postulation is that "because the Christian institutions of which these boys were a part have remained relatively stable regarding issues of gender difference and [sic] equality, these boys had less need for interactional practices and gender power" (p. 113).

Perhaps so. But I think we can argue that the Catholic church is no less Christian than the Mormons and yet, fag discourse and all its attendant trappings were alive and well at St. Monica and indeed came to affect the actionability of most any boy within the school. One argument we could make is that the boys attended St. Monica not so much for its religious character (though their parents might certainly have been enamored of the Catholicity of the place) as for its tradition, athletics, or because of a lack of (perceived and this was often racially charged as noted above) good public school options. These are sentiments encapsulated by Joey, a student who lived within a half mile of me at the time of the study, who when asked told me he "came to Monica cause there were Monica dads on the block." Alums, fathers, athletes all and a tradition continues.

Conversely, as the boys at River High were choosing to sit together in a community of Christians at lunch they were putting their faith at the forefront of their activities; certainly it's possible that they felt no need to dig deeply into the inborn homophobia of "fagging" another student. Or perhaps they did so indemonstrably, deferring to Holy Scripture for their prefabricated moral guidance. We don't know based on Pascoe's work, as she wasn't privy to much of their world.

Boys at St. Monica weren't sitting together at lunch or in the fleeting moments between classes to share their faith, necessarily, or because their being Catholic was their unitary and consolidating shared trait. This happened largely in a separate space on Kairos reatreats which we'll talk about later. So to try to deflect based on religion wasn't an option left open to them. We are all (assumed to be) Catholic, the line might go, so quit being such a faggot. I'll get more in-depth into the state and function of religion as interpreted by the boys when volleyed by the school—in myriad ways, of course—as we progress, but suffice it to say that Jaime, a student from the nearby Westlawn neighborhood (where a great many students grew up), was fairly representative in noting that "yeah [he] went [to Monica] cause it's Catholic, but for [his] mom mostly." Raff, a sort of henchman for Huey at our lunch table, told me once, "Not a lot of guys are very religious. Like the school is, but we aren't." Or at least they skirted a line of appearing not to be religious within the school, though outsiders might view it otherwise for various reasons.

The above is interesting particularly in light of a trend among the seniors who, upon turning eighteen, flocked to local tattoo parlors to "get inked." This was for many of the guys, a rite of passage, and a number of them chose ethnic or familial markings (one boy had the initials of his father and stepfather, both of whom had passed away, embossed on each of his shoulders for instance), but the vast majority of the Monicamen chose crosses as their permanent skin designs. In addition, the boys wore constantly (compulsively?) the scapular and shirts from the school, inevitably marked with the Augustinian seal. Curious about this devotional[7] turn in religiosity, I pursued it at lunch asking about why there were no students who were "out" (in the sense of being openly gay or openly religious in a strictly catechetical manner actually) at the school, wondering if it had to do with the Catholic character of the place:

Nico: "We're not very welcoming."
Me: "Is that something, like a social thing or because of religion?"
Raff: "No, it's not a religion thing; it's definitely social."
Ray: "We're like cafeteria Catholics. We pick and choose."

Religion was, for the boys, the situation of the school, and it loosely colored (indeed, in indelible ink for some of the boys) discourse in unique ways, yes, but was never used to preempt fag discourse, nor did they see it as outlining it. They were able to pick and choose, as Ray says, and so they inked crosses into their skin without thinking necessarily about the implications. It was ornamental, like the scapular, signatory of their status as cafeteria Catholics, just as their St. Monica shirts made them Monicamen in the public square. Religion was not, at least to the minds of the young men I was surrounded by, the reason they were unwelcoming. Interestingly, though, they didn't have a response when I pushed them further, asking if they really did have a choice regarding religion and specifically prayer, since they were required to pray every morning and afternoon, and further required to attend chapel monthly. It might be we can say that they were affected at least partially by the Church's problematic relationship (or lack of one) with its gay flock, not to mention clergy. But no one, neither the boys nor the teachers, was citing Leviticus. It can be said to be part of an offshoot of the ways that teachers and administrators dealt (or didn't deal) with the situations of masculinities for the boys.

If there was a religion to which the boys actively ascribed, then it would be St. Monica football. Athletics on the whole were intrinsic to the school's identity and sense of self; indeed, the administration walked a razor's edge here, trying to sell academics while maintaining competitive programs, which brought in big money from alumni donors. Participation in sports was not compulsory, but because of the relatively small number of students and the profusion of teams at the place, a significant portion of the population of the school played at least one sport. As such, athletics and particularly football were significant factors in the boys' senses of self, their masculine projects.

Athletics: Pink Jerseys and Other Gay Shit

It's perhaps unfair to pick on the sport of football, as it tends to be easily made totemic of athletics-as-violent-masculinity writ large in America. But football is big business at St. Monica and beyond (even in the midst of a major recession, the National Football League sat on a revenue of somewhere around $8 billion in 2009) and, stuck in a world of fiscal exigencies where the new reality of a contemporary Catholic school requires—this is especially true on the South Side where so many options still exist, each school seeking to carve a specific niche, filling some perceived need—aggressive recruiting of students. There is nothing, then, quite like drawing 12,000[8] fans to a Friday night rivalry game, for revving up eighth graders eager to be a part of something big and exciting and new. This is why the school was raising money for a new—its second—synthetic Fieldturf football field to the tune of something around $800,000.

Such is the milieu that "coach" is an honorarium at the school, one I picked up from a math teacher about a month into the first semester. I felt conferred upon. I mention this because in terms of academics, much of the first semester centered on keeping athletes eligible. Speaking with Tim, the football player who I followed in November, I asked about the cheating I saw as rampant on Wednesdays in an effort to pull grades up for Thursday grade checks, required to play in games on Friday. He replied in an offhand manner, "Well, I mean every teacher's a coach, so they don't care." The point being, athletics matter a great deal in the school, football more than most, and football coaches as much as anyone. [9] So, their—coaches'—influence on the discursive function of masculinity and language, particularly as regarded effeminacy (perceived or enacted) and outlined through an adult version of fagging, inevitably came to trickle down to the boys' attitudes and language, where it was reinterpreted and emplaced in a given day.

It was when Kimani became ineligible for the first of his two games that I found out about the pink jerseys. In Illinois a student with two Fs may still practice with his or her team but may not play in games. As a goad for his failing players, the head football coach at St. Monica had procured pink jerseys that ineligible players were required to wear/endure during their time of ineligibility. They were failing classes and, through the pink jerseys, failing the test of masculinity dictated by cultural messages attached to colors. Pink is feminine, the script reads, and to be ineligible is thus to be made the same. Indirectly, then, came a linkage between stupidity (as tied to bad grades) and failed masculinity inevitably marked as feminine.

When I asked Kimani about the jerseys he didn't want to talk much, either out of embarrassment or frustration, but Qualter, who was a team manager, like a bird always chirping in our ears in first period was more than happy to tell me they looked "really gay" on the field. Indeed.

Messner (2002), in his study of gender and athletics, writes of men and boys who fail at a given masculine project in sport as being made "symbolic women" easy targets as the "pussies and faggots" (p. 35) of the team. From here it wasn't much of a leap to the various instances when teachers/coaches spoke to/of students who were struggling (or complaining) in classes as needing to "man-up." They simply needed to shed their inappropriate failed masculinity; they needed to take off the pink jersey of faggotry. This borderline abusive psychology is part of what Messner calls "a contextual normalization of violence" (p. 50), which leads to the proper hardening of men who are meant to instrumentalize their bodies for the purpose of being punishing (rather than punished). As a pink jersey, one can never punish the opponent because s/he cannot play in the game; the only way to get to that point is to become masculine again, to man up, and pass classes. "This acceptance of body contact and borderline violence seems to be based on the idea that sports is an area of life in which it is permissible to suspend usual moral standards" (Miedzian, 2002, p. 183), which might not be so bad a thing were it not overtly clear how sport and its attendant morality (or lack of it) bleeds into life, school life in this case.[10]

While following Tim, I had the good fortune of sitting in on the head coach's anatomy class. And while Coach Krupke was always gracious in his interactions with me, he—an alum of the school, mind—played into the staff's version of fag discourse which, while more muted than the boys, certainly signaled its presence, acceptability, and malleability at the school. Our first interaction came at faculty orientation when he was told we'd all be required to wear ties, like the boys, to chapel mass throughout the school year. "Well that's frickin' gay," was his response, as offhand as the boys. In the presence of the students, though, he wasn't as blatant in his usage. His discursive forays were more oblique.

Once, after asking Tim to grab a model of a skeleton from a cabinet in the back of the room, he noted in the intervening time as Tim struggled with the fragility of the thing while carrying it to the chalkboard, "You know what? That thing cost about four grand and it didn't look that bad when I got him. But you have things around an all-guys' school and you tend to break things. The thing's totally warped. [Pause] Yeah. He used to be straight." He laughed, catching his unintended double-entendre.

Tim, picking up on it, quickly noted, "Yeah, there's another skeleton in there and they were kissing." This was followed by more or less embarrassed and sidelong laughter from the class. With a wink from the coach we moved on to the details of phalanges and metacarpals. But the precedent was set.

Later in the month, in the midst of the supposed swine flu pandemic, Coach Krupke turned to current events to make a point, asking:

> Coach: "Anyone get the H1N1 shot?" [Hands raised] I would highly suggest it."
>
> Student: "Is that what Tim's sick with?"

Recall for a moment that Tim was in the midst of his senior season and working toward placing himself in a position to garner scholarships to play at the college level. He was, all season long, a starting offensive lineman and integral to the offensive success of the team.

> Coach: "I dunno."
>
> Student: "Is he not gonna play in the playoff game this week?"
>
> Coach: "Yeah, he's gonna play. He's gotta toughen up."

There is an intriguing mix here of health (the coach is a former nurse, incidentally) concern and lack of concern. The vaccine is important and the illness is real and daunting, but the game is paramount. This is, in some ways, understandable considering the pressures of a job where succeeding at a rate of ten wins for every three losses is viewed as mediocrity.

However, what we want to note is a further tagging of weakness to illness and on down the line to an abject version of masculinity. Football is where, for Meidzian (2002) the link to violence and masculinity is welded for boys; even boys sick with pandemic flu must learn "to take unnecessary risks that will endanger their and others' health and lives" (p. 201) where "the language of sport is filled with insults suggesting that a boy who is not tough enough, does not live up to the masculine mystique, is really a girl or homosexual" (p. 202). Not tough enough to play hurt or sick? Then perhaps you are not strong enough to "man-up," and perhaps further, you are then gay or woman, both being abject and undesirable as identities.

We see an example of this compulsory manning-up most strikingly in an exchange that occurred at the end of November, just as I was getting ready to move to a different schedule and leave anatomy for good. In a discussion about skin ailments, Coach, who as you'll note often tied his pedagogy to the real-life situations of the boys, asked:

> "How many of you are wrestlers? [Hands raised] What kinds of skin-diseases have you had?
>
> "Impetigo." "Ringworm." [These shouted from the masses with a certain pride of the survivor, maybe.]

Coach: [Rhetorically] "Why does that happen to wrestlers always? Well, you got guys sweaty rubbing up on each other [here the boys start to snicker at the thought and the possibility of another double entendre] and you got an open wound...[pause, smiling] I mean, I realize we could be describing a lot of things...[The boys start to lose it, the wrestlers are punched in shoulders; they look embarrassed]...but let's not get into that. I mean I don't want to do that to the wrestlers."

What he doesn't want to do to the wrestlers, of course, is make them symbolic fags through their association with a sport that involves a great deal of pseudo-intimate contact. There is a certain embarrassment in Coach's comportment, as he really doesn't mean to call into question the masculinity of the wrestlers through his unintentional fusing of their activities in a sanctioned athletic contest with homosexual sex. No. He doesn't want them to man up in this situation, but only to talk about the skin ailments associated with a sport conducted in close contact in humid spaces, the perfect incubator for staph. These are communicable diseases, yes, but not the ones associated with the feminized gay man. They are more badges of courage and he, attend please, is apologetic at an unintentional fagging. The boys notice, of course.

Another interesting manifestation in terms of athletics and the sacrificial nature of the body for the good of the violent contest came out, pun intended, in a discussion with Kimani before class as the team prepared for a supposedly daunting opponent. As a defensive tackle in a 4–3 defense, Kimani's main role was to take up space in rushing situations so that the middle of the field was, effectively, clogged thus forcing ball-carriers to the outside and into the waiting arms of linebackers holding their contain. The strategy of it is less important than the understanding that in most situations, Kimani was asked to dive into legs in the interest of creating a pileup. Relaying some coaching in anticipation of a mythic (they turned out not to be much of a team in the end) opponent and their granite and monolithic offensive line, he told us, "Coach told me, you have to grab ankles. These are some big, fat fuckers."

The euphemism alludes to a derogatory term for gay male "bottoms" in a sexual position, who are said to grab their ankles in the process of being penetrated. What's interesting, of course, is that Kimani is being asked to take on the passive sexual role in a gay, phantasmic coaching allegory. Bersani (1987) suggests that in the pantheon of structured male sexual behavior, "in terms of activity and passivity," we see "a correlative rejection of the so-called passive role in sex," both hetero and homosexual. So it is interesting that Kimani must now man-up by, to borrow from a baseball maxim, taking one (well, many over the course of a game, really) for the team. This suggests a confused rhetorical imposition of the fag, which occurred occasionally in classes in ways similar to this:

> Student: [Talking about the chapel shirt, required for Mass days] "I don't like wearing these things. I feel gay."
> Student 2: "You look gay. If it helps, I'm gay too."

Here we find an empathic gayness, or a voluntary passivity, perhaps. This is not a rhetorical challenge for either student: they both must suffer the gayness together; they are both made gay in service to the Mass; they are tagged until they can each shed the chapel uniform so why not take it together? And why not preempt others' labeling by taking the passive role, actively, first. Kimani is cloaked in a team ethos where he must sacrifice his body for the team in a way only a gay man (supposedly) gives up his power, voluntarily feminizing himself through actively taking the passive role in sex (I know, I know, such paradoxes). In a different scene, we see a student ribbing another for his gayness, but reassuring him that it's ok, because they will suffer the indignity together.

Both situations, Kimani's and that of the students in chapel ties, are instances where school-sponsored discourses called into question masculine ideals in ways that invoked or allowed students to invoke gayness as a coping strategy. The school required a certain mode of dress that the boys found inconvenient or offensive to their independence (preferring the slouchy style of polos-not-quite-tucked-into-khakis); it also required that Kimani subvert his individual desire for statistics, say, for the good of the team. Both situations, again, played upon a need for the student to subvert independence (of dress, or creative athletic play) for the monolith of a school discourse that dictated what was appropriate on the field or in the chapel. Boys coped by becoming gay together in service of (for Kimani) or resistance to (the chapel ties) the requirements placed on them by representatives of the school.

One final instantiation to indicate just how embedded fag discourse had become in the flow of the school comes from a first-period history class in December. From across the room, as the teacher Mr. Creighton walks towards them, we hear an exchange between a senior football player, Johnny, and his friend, a basketball player named Hanns:

> Johnny: [Talking about a student at another school] "That kid is such a faggot."
> Mr. Creighton [overhearing]: "Whoa!" [In disbelief]

Hanns: "You can't say faggot?" [Genuinely baffled]
Mr. Creighton: "No!" [Emphatic.]

The boys had never, to their knowledge, been corrected by teachers regarding their usage of the gay terminology. And so the slur, faggot, had become so much a part of their lingo that to say it aloud in front of a teacher was not only not taboo, it was indeed shocking to them that such a thing might be verboten. I would suggest that both young men were so much ensconced not only in the fagging of the school, but also of sport, that such terminology became second nature, almost totemic. And speaking of totems...

Dicks, Man

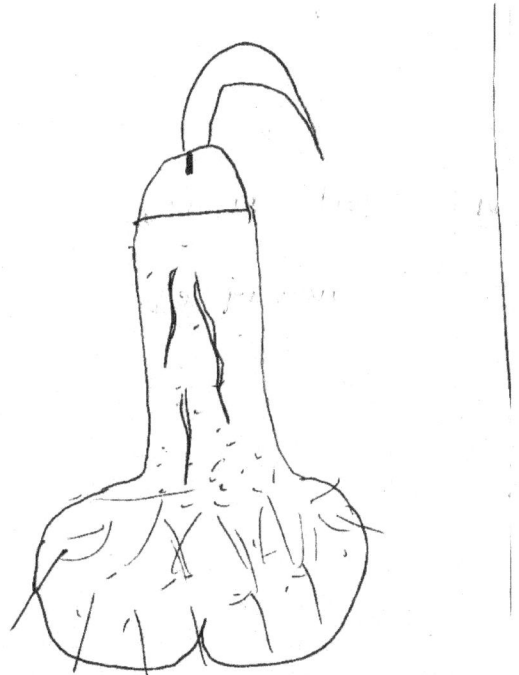

Figure 1: Dicked! (St. Monica Student Drawing):

It was on the first day of new faculty orientation that I initially started hearing about them. We were, the seven of us coming into the school as newbies, gathered in the ad hoc conference room of St. Monica, seated in the midst of late August humid-heat wondering just how much of the daunting week-long agenda laid out in bullet point on papers in front of us could possibly come to fruition. A few of the first-year teachers itched visibly to set up their classrooms; the basketball and wrestling coaches traded barbs on their Blackberrys. In the end, we spent the morning shuffled through successive presentations and welcomes from various dignitaries of the place. Here we got much of the party line on the history of the school as well as details about grade submission and contract expectations. The minutia.

Exiting lunch on that Monday, though, and speaking in an offhand manner to a female Spanish teacher who asked about the dynamics of an all-boys school, Mika a veteran of 30-plus years, and a mother of two alumni, asked Julie, another longtime vet helping with orientation, "Where to even begin?"

> Mika: "It's scary; it's frightening. Teenage boys looking at women of all ages. And, oh, Julie, should we talk about their fetish? [Conspiratorially, complete with cartoon shifty eyes to make sure no one in the empty halls might be listening in] They will draw penises. They will attach them to each other."
> Julie: "You don't want to react to this. I would suggest just tearing them up and throwing them away."
> Mika: "It's a guy thing and ignore the smells, the farting in class."

It may well be a guy thing.[11] It may well, further, be a guy thing in an all-guys school. What I found, actually, was that the discourse of it just being a part of the school came to constitute A) why the issue was never addressed by the faculty and B) why the boys continued drawing away. This was a continuance of the unspoken policy regarding the profusion of fag discourse: it's just how they are/talk/draw and how they always will be. Tradition, recall, one that will never undo itself because it's not engaged critically by faculty; one that will never undo itself because the boys view the penises as a chance for play in what they see as the rigid structure of a school; one that is viewed as generally harmless precisely because the boys never take sharpies to pictures of saints. Paradoxically, the impermanence of fag discourse—affixed to nothing but the ethos of the boys and the teachers and their coaches—allows its permanent status. None of this is written in a text, or on a wall and so it is perpetuated through the discursive flow of the classrooms full of boys. Were someone to scrawl "fag" on a classroom door, things might change but for now it's just boys being boys harmlessly in disposable (supposedly) ways.

And then, tipped off, I started to see them everywhere. Once while sitting just off of the altar after a Kairos event, I caught sight of a small, crudely rendered penis on a strip of tape in the middle of the chair in front of me. It seemed, after a full semester in the school, oddly apropos. Boys cribbed them into my notebook when I wasn't looking, they showed up on the spines of textbooks, on crumpled looseleaf littering the floors of classrooms, and drawn in pen in the middle of polo-shirted backs (this was rare; mostly they were temporary and disposable). They were the cave paintings of the place and it was a constant low-level source of anxiety for students, whenever touched on the shoulder or the back, as to whether someone had hooked a drawing onto them. Interestingly it was extremely rare to find them inked in permanent places. So they were absent from the stalls of the bathrooms—as was all graffiti, actually—and none were etched in desks or on walls in common areas. No, these were fleeting and (re)placeable, pictorial manifestations of the fag discourse out of which, I'd argue, they came to grow. As with the discourse that seems to have birthed them, they were most often attached to a person or his belongings and only for as long as it took him to transfer it to someone else. The chair in the chapel was an anomaly though I suspect it was a way of always placing a penis on the "back" of whoever sat in that chair, in perpetuity. Or at least until faculty or maintenance found it and threw it away.

The construction ranged from a quick scribble on a scrap of paper to the ornate and intricately strategic, as with a young man I sat next to who spent an entire Spanish class crafting a hook out of multiple paperclips. This was his red herring. He then fastened the student in front of him, just as the bell rang, to his chair by a belt loop with the paperclip contraption so that, when the boy was distracted trying to free himself, the target wouldn't notice the penis, cut from notebook paper and with a makeshift hook at the top, being simultaneously clipped to his collar. Mission accomplished: the mark worked at loosing his belt loop and walked out of the room, penis adorning his shirt, like a necktie in reverse.

Similar to the "specter of the fag" (Pascoe, 2007, p. 14), where young men are always attending to the possibility of their own (and others') failed gender, here boys were periodically (spastically and with a certain slapstick quality, really, considering their inability to reach the middle of their own backs) checking their shirts to make sure they hadn't been, well, dicked. The most striking—and comical, actually—that I saw was a case in a physics class where one student mimed with the cap of his pen, drawing a penis on the polo of a classmate who then spent the better part of the next two minutes untucking his shirt and trying to pull it around his body to see if he'd been drawn on, whining all the time, "If there's a wiener on my back, I'm gonna be pissed." There was no wiener, however, just the possibility—the spectered tracings—of it.

I was reminded through all of this of my time in high school. Required to wear one of three colors (white, blue, or yellow) of oxford button down dress shirts, our range of options was fairly limited. I did, however, make it clear to my mother, who was kind enough to buy the things for me throughout my career as a secondary schooler, that on no occasion was there to be a fabric hook on the back of the shirt, above the middle pleat. These, at our school, were called "fag tags" for no discernible reason other than they just were and always had been called that. And anyone who had a shirt with a fag tag was subject to having it (the tag, not the whole shirt) ripped off at any point, leaving twin holes where fabric tore from fabric. This was getting off easy. Leave the fag tag and you were like to get physically hazed, and often guys unlucky enough to have shirts of this kind just tore the fag tag off themselves before wearing them. Once the thing was gone, so was the specter, much like the penis tags I observed at St. Monica.

Psychoanalysis has made a great many claims regarding the status and symbolism of the phallus. Indeed we might argue the entire field was, er, inseminated by a certain Freudian "phallic narcissism" (Corbett, 2009, p. 176). For Lacanians "the phallus is master-signifier, and femininity is symbolically defined by lack" (Connell, 1995, p. 70). Later feminist critiques cited notions of "phallogocentrism" and its role in language and "cultural intelligibility" (Butler, 1990). The initial and flawed distinction between biological sex and socially constructed gender turned upon this assumed (and untroubled) presence and/or its lack. These are battles of identity still being fought around, now, gender testing and hormonal markers meant in the end to clarify and simplify for readers (of culture) categories of "female" and "male," which are always-already presupposed anyway.

Perhaps most striking in popular culture of late, we find the case of Caster Semenya, the South African sprinter who has repeatedly been subject to testing (scientific and in the court of public opinion) to determine if she's lacking enough in the penis department to compete as a woman.[12] The upshot is that Semenya performs too athletically to be "woman" and gives the appearance in her muscularity of being a "man." That s/he has been subject to multiple (humiliating) and intrusive inspections of the genital region as well as blood and hormonal tests and yet results remain inconclusive suggests a betweenness that is only problematic because defined so, externally. Semenya just wants to run;

the world needs young Caster to run with those most like her and can't quite figure out just what that means well enough to soothe the unease of a suddenly fragile gender dichotomy long maintained through sport.

I mention all of this not to engage in a critique of prior treatments of the significance of the phallus in culture or in the development of the psyche. And though the discussion of the phallic did indeed occasionally turn to the abstract notion of "bigness" that Corbett (2009) sees as still emblematic of relevant psychoanalytic work in the development of boys, these rare displays were more meant for comedy, were instances of the carnivalesque say, than as assertions of personal prowess. That is, as with Packer below, the discussion of bigness in reference to the phallus wasn't about claiming masculinity based on size. Rather, it was a way to disrupt expectations of decorum.

Which brings us back to a single-gendered high school, which relies on the convenience of boy-as-not-girl because of the assumed presence of a penis. This was never engaged actively, of course, but we can presume with a modicum of certainty that any boy who took the entrance exam—effeminate though he might be—would be admitted to St. Monica without the reassurance of scientific data affirming the proper amount of testosterone, beyond the assumption that he would wear the same uniform as his future Monica brothers. A girl taking the test, well, wouldn't be allowed to take it.

One particularly striking example from the first semester came as we walked from class to class. Packer, an imp of a kid who reveled in his own laziness, hiding a quick wit from the administration of the school, asked to no one in particular (and because he wanted to get a rise), "You think Jesus had a big dick?" Knowing he'd find a response he then launched, into his prepared riposte, "Oh dude, think about it. God's sending him down here to die? The least he could do is give him a big schlong." Laughter and rolling of eyes from the boys who were very familiar with Packer's schtick as resident pot-stirrer.

Again, I bring this up as a way of saying that, yes, the phallus was important, but most often as an extension of the discursive function of the fag and fagging throughout the school in the form of drawing penises. Talking about them in more than an offhand manner, as with Packer here, was a whole different and difficult ballgame.

When I asked (repeatedly) the boys about why they chose to draw dicks and put them on each other, they tended to answer in two specific ways 1) because it's hilarious and 2) because it was hilarious in *Superbad*.[13] Indeed both sentiments were probably true for the boys. Many of their more meticulous works mirrored phallic characters taken directly from the movie (a penis as head cook at a barbeque, for example, aproned and in a chef hat), in fact. When pressed, though, they got coy:

> Me: "So why draw them?"
> Tim: "They're funny as hell."
> Dan: "It's embarrassing to walk around like that. If they have a dick on them, then they're kind of gay."
> Me: "So but why is it funny to put a dick and balls on someone?"
> Tim: "I dunno, we're just immature?"
> Dan: "Nah. They're easy to draw and we see them every day, I guess."
> Tim: "I mean think of how stupid you look, walking around with a dick on your back."

Later in the semester when I engaged another group of students I tried a different tack:

> Me: "Well, but guys, you say everything is gay, and that's a bad thing, but what's gayer then, than putting a penis that you've created onto someone else?"
> Raff: "No, it's not gay for the guy who draws it."
> Mick: "Also, it wouldn't be funny to draw a vagina."
> Dunbar: "Yeah, they're just not that funny looking."
> Raff: "And it's a little bit embarrassing to have a dick on you, like you can laugh at it, and then if it's in their notebook maybe they're a little gay."

Note, please, as with other linguistic turns in fag discourse, one is not made gay by initiating the sequence. One is, rather, potentially fagged temporarily if he is subject to the hooking of a penis, and he is then impelled to pass that penis along (on)to someone else. Vaginas don't enter the picture as they aren't "funny." This is part and parcel of some of the rhetoric the boys spouted as regarded the shortcomings of women, a topic we'll address in the next chapter and it helps them close their ranks of homosociability under the auspices of brotherhood; a brotherhood formed through the mocking pseudosexual relationships characterized by and carried out through fag discourse.

We might also suggest that the "problem" of the hooking-of-the-phallus is rooted in the homoerotic undercurrent ever-present in the school. To dick someone was to take an active role. The boys, focused as they were on the image of the penis, were still constrained by the notion of gayness that would be implied/indelibly attached were one to actually take his flesh-and-blood dick out and place it on someone in the classroom. This would carry informal social as well as formal disciplinary sanctions in the school. It was not a part of the accepted discourse, in other words. But, turning again to the Greeks and Foucault's (1990b) analysis of the role of mastery/active/passive roles in sexual relationships (homo and hetero), we find the idea that "in sexual behavior there was one role that was intrinsically honorable and valorized without question: the one that consisted in being active, in dominating, in penetrating, in asserting one's superiority" (Foucault, 1990b, p. 215). One way to view the attaching of penises is to think of it as a type of penetration: of making a classmate passive in accepting the phallus; it is in effect a form of domination, a marking of territory, through the claiming of sexual dominance. And again, as with other aspects of fag discourse, it was mobile and remained unchallenged because perceived as somehow impermanent by the administration and teachers.

Vital to the discussion is the understanding that, though the boys were largely unable to find ways of opting out of the discourse, there was never any winner, per say. It was never settled that one or another boy was safe and wholly straight and beyond the reach of the specter of the fag. At any moment he could be brought back into line either with a penis placed on his back or in his notebook, or with a verbal barb thrown from across the table. This led to a constant recycling of discursive sniping that frankly got trite for its sheer repetitiveness. As a result though, the boys found their sexual possibilities within and beyond the school diminished through this regulatory regime, which demanded that they constantly be on guard, policing their own gendered and sexual performances and those of others. Unable to establish a solid ground of dominance or safety among their peers, they turned to women as outlets for (psychic and verbal) aggression, seeking to reestablish a kind of order, that reassured their safety as self-defining sexually. And though faculty didn't engage directly with the students in the recursive labeling and re-labeling they still as in the case of Julie and Mika's dismissiveness and Coach Krupke's overt (on the field) and allusive (in the classroom) deployment, largely condoned the practice. It was a part of the tradition, of the brotherhood, and it bonded all the boys in a bind of the threat of the fag and its creative outlets, such as penile implanting.

All of this, again, was shaped in an environment for and by boys, assuming that the absence of women fostered a constructive (and it was, certainly) presence. That is: the administration and the students set fences at the boundaries of gender. Masculinities flourished in ways, it was assumed, they wouldn't have were there girls wandering the halls during school hours. St. Monica fashioned itself as a place apart from women, laying aside the irony of its name. Let us turn now, to the ways in which masculinities came to be formulated through rhetorical engagement with women and heterosexual relationality.

Notes

1. I was ribbed roundly for eating fruit everyday, even as Nick, who sat next to me, poured electric yellow nacho cheese into a Cheetos bag and squeezed the heart-attack mixture into his mouth.
2. Schools such as St. Monica—and really most any K12 educational institution co-ed or otherwise—operate around the (asserted or subtle) notion of binary and complementary genders. "The claim," Corbett (2009) writes, "of this binary precedes any boy: boys will be boys by not being girls" (p. 91). This is preternaturally enforced by the school in its self-assertion as an all-boys environment, ignoring of course, the presence of female faculty and staff not to mention the "men" who work at the school as well. What's important for us here, though is the idea that "gender is rarely, if ever, totalizing" (p. 15). And though "gender is routinely conflated with anatomy, and gender is routinely conflated with that which produces our desires and personality traits" (p. 91) these are not deterministically limited by the structure of a school and its binary assumptions. There is play for the boys in becoming the Monicamen the school expects and this involves the work of reconstructing masculinities constantly.
3. This has been a subject of recent PSAs from the organization called "ThinkB4YouSpeak" which has enlisted celebrities for ads warning of the unintended effects of saying "that's so gay." One tagline notes, tongue firmly in cheek, "you wouldn't say, 'that's so Mexican.'"
4. It's not that the boys weren't homophobic. They were, though mostly in the abstract as their actual contact with homosexuality remained in the realm of the media where gay is played as camp. No student was "out" at St. Monica, a situation owing to any number of factors, including its location in the largely conservative South Side as well as the Catholic Church's agonistic relationship with homosexuality and homophobia. Interestingly, the only openly gay person at the school was a former priest—and current vice principal. At lunch one day, when the boys told me about Mr. B, they said that it was "fucked up" and "sick" that he was at the school but no one could articulate why that might be the case. They weren't concerned with his sexually approaching them but rather focused on the abjected status of potential male gay sex (Mr. B left the Cloth and currently lives with his partner) which was a way of helping them place him as with Robin Peace's (2001) discussion of cultural dissonance surrounding the reading of lesbians as "matter out of place…an improper body" (p. 50). This is homophobia, yes, and the potentially dangerous mobilization of fag discourse in and out of classes in the school went largely unaddressed but the line where misunderstanding due to a lack of empathy was never in danger of being crossed in favor of physical violence. Were there "out" students at the school, the situation might have been very different.

5   In a conversation at lunch one day, Johnny, a football player, was catching flak for leaving a party to "hook up" with a girl. In an attempt to point to the boys that they were, essentially by attacking him for leaving them to spend time with someone else, the jealous girlfriends they warned each other about avoiding, a conversation about friendship ensued:
Me: "So when is Johnny, or anyone, supposed to hang out with girls? Like you guys are in school together all day, and then you play sports, and then you're supposed to hang out with your boys at parties, so when is there time?"
Villa: [Who had a longtime girlfriend himself] "You can do it on Sunday."
Me: [Playing with fire, but still within the rules because I'm laughing as I ask in exasperation] "Well, I mean you guys are always trying to avoid this 'gay' tag, but isn't it kinda gay to only always hang out with guys?"
At this point the entire table breaks down and Villa, in his default rage mode, laughing dismisses me with a "Who the fuck are you, Burke? Whatever, you fag."
We'll return to this scene in-depth in a later section regarding relationships in a larger sense.

6   "Squish" is a term used to refer to women, or rather girls usually of a certain sexually targeted age. The principal of the school, a married grandmother was never referred to as a squish, but my girlfriend and most of the girls that the boys referred to carried the name. I'll get deeper into the etymology of the term in a later chapter, but feel free to use your imagination regarding its origins as well as what 'posting up' might mean for now.

7   Also known as "Paraliturgical devotions" these are actions and modes of worship that exist outside of the traditional liturgy (or Mass) of the Church and are at times, often even, in contradiction to Church teachings. The Catholic Church is most noticeably accused of such heresy as "Mary" worship for its intensive focus on the story and symbol of the mother of Christ. In reference to this manner of concern, Fr. Tom was always careful to let us know at Novena that the cross containing a portion of St. Monica's fingerbone, though we were blessed with it and it was considered a first class relic—defined as "the body or a portion of the body of a Saint" ("Information about Holy Relics," n. d.)—was meant as a symbol of St. Monica's faith and devotion and that we weren't praying *to* her, but *with* her to God. And so it is that Catholics in particular are always asking for intercession through patron saints. It might be worth noting at this point that St. Monica is the patroness of hopeless causes. I might have uttered a few devotional prayers to her on the sly myself in the process of writing this.

8   Parking for the game against despised and despicable—to hear the students and even the administration tell—Brother Field Crusaders spread miles into adjacent neighborhoods. Monica won the game and bragging rights for the year in front of one of the largest high school football crowds this side of small-town Texas.

9   After a three-loss 2010 campaign, in spite of winning the city championship and four years removed from a state title, the head coach (an alum, even) found himself dealing with—largely anonymous—calls for his removal.

10 I'm reminded of Mr. Paterno, in his opening address to students on the first day of computer science class, talking about how much he preferred teaching in an all-boys' school to his

prior work in co-ed environments. "It's great. If you guys are pissed, you just get in a fight, throw some punches and it's done." Girls, in contrast, were prone to gossip and backbiting, by his measure. Boys, the message clearly went, don't gossip and they solve things by physical contact/contest. A little blood or a split lip would solve most everything. Another young male teacher often forced boys who got too mouthy in class to hug each other as a way of mitigating conflict. Joe, embarrassed and unwilling to hug his rival, whined, "Why can't we just be men and box or something."

11 I am reminded here of Nespor's (1997) discussion of socialization in schools in reference to the "hiding away of natural functions (as in the example of farting...)" in favor of "a socialized an rationalized body" (p. 127) the purpose of which is meant to define "the inappropriateness of farting in public" as "so basic that it doesn't rate mention" (p. 129). In a sense, the boys and faculty both conspired to laughingly (in the case of the students) and disgustedly/dismissively (in the case of the faculty) flout social rules of propriety which functioned outside the walls of the school. This was part of the "grotesque" if you will, of the all boys high school, where bodily functions particularly in their "dirty aspects, should become means of evading, resisting, and scandalizing normative social power" (Fiske, 1989, p. 97). This sentiment became most prevalent in discussions about students' decisions to attend an single gendered school:

> Nico: "I like to fart."
> Dunbar: "That's not why you went to Monica, not to fart."
> Nico: "No, it kind of is. Like I couldn't do that with girls around."
> Cody: "You also don't have to worry about showering in the morning."

So the boys were able to construct an ethos of grotesqueness in the absence of same-aged (and thus sexually available) females who, as we'll see in the next chapter, were often manifest/idealized/dehumanized in their minds as outside of the dirty aspects of the physical shitting and pissing that remained the realm of boys.

12 For a wonderfully engaging discussion of Semenya's case and the human cost of the fiercely guarded dichotomous gender regime, see Levy (2009).

13 A teen comedy released in 2009 that featured a character who became "addicted" in middle school to drawing penises in various (and voluminous) detail, personifying them in myriad ways. When he is caught by a teacher drawing "a big, veiny, triumphant bastard," he is sent to counseling and becomes, we assume, reformed. The film ends with a montage of the character's more creative and detailed works of art. Interestingly, he never places them on anyone else, instead hiding them in a secret notebook.

Chapter 5

Squishes: The Abjectified

> Boys and men are left to traffic in women, construct them outside of mutual recognition with little to no acknowledgment of the dynamics of separation and dependence that color, construct, and embroider men's and boys sexualized love relations.
>
> Ken Corbett, "Boyhoods"

> It was an ethics for men: an ethics thought, written, and taught by men, and addressed to men—to free men, obviously. A male ethics consequently, in which women figured only as objects.
>
> Michel Foucault, "The History of Sexuality: An Introduction"

> Women suffer because both men and women alike have trouble seeing women as fully human, autonomous subjects; instead they remain closer to objects.
>
> Catherine Roach, "Mother/Nature"

One of the ways that St. Monica High School, as a single-gendered and Catholic institution, affected the discourses around masculinities came in the form of relationality to women. The boys worked within the constraints of an artificially constructed "male" world in the school where, their contact with the women-made-other by their absence in student desks was limited to interaction with faculty as well as the religious iconography of the school. This made for unique points of departure in gender relations as the young men asserted masculine poses when contact with, or conversation about women occurred. I'll argue that the masculinities, the possibility of masculinity occurred in much the same way as with fag discourse: the school provided a loose frame of restrictive disciplinary gazing and the boys willingly pushed at its edges at every turn.

Hockey

This is my first hockey game. We've plunged headlong into a Chicago winter characterized most strikingly by its sleepy gray days, which give way too quickly to the howling cold of pitch black nights. Tonight, Saturday, St. Monica is playing my alma mater at a rink in the far southwestern suburbs. For a moment as I ready myself for the drive I am torn as to who to root for, but recalling that I never made it to a hockey game in my first go-round in high school, I settle on the team full of students that I know as opposed to the name on a jersey that used to mean a great deal more to me than it does now.¹

Walking in, I find a rink abutted by cold—everything is cold this December—metal stands backing up to the concrete outer wall of the arena. Across from where we (the fans of both teams, split down the middle by allegiance, roughly separated at the midline of the ice) sit, the two teams shuttle back and forth over bench boards, preparing for the start of the game. I have to walk past the Marist faithful to get to the St. Monica side, feeling an odd twinge of guilt as I do. Those ties run deeper than I supposed. This has much to do with tradition.

A good portion of the senior class and some few juniors who pal around with the various senior groups (and who most likely provided rides as payment for their passage) mill behind the far goal or stack themselves eight deep up in the stands, from the Plexiglas boards to the low steel support girders which sweep from the pitched ceiling above the ice on down to the low-hanging lode-bearing walls against which the collapsible benches come to rest. The Dean of Men,² a hulking mass of a being—there are well-founded concerns for his health; New Balance outfits the football coaches and had to make a special warm-up for the Dean as their largest size, as a 4XL was too small—has planted himself on the lowest bench of the stands. He is in the section next to the students, such that any of the boys who might want to insinuate themselves into the Marist crowd and cause mischief will have to pass by him first. He cuts an imposing figure; the Monicamen stay out of trouble. Sort of.

I get a number of "hellos" as I sit down and the boys stop by to see how things are or to razz me about Marist's chances in the game. It's always an event seeing an adult from the school outside the confines of the grounds of the place. They ask about my girlfriend in sly and elbowy ways. I am wearing a St. Monica baseball cap to signal my rooting interests to them; they seem to appreciate it. It would seem odd, I decide, to sit in the student section, and so I plant myself three rows back from the Dean and watch, hockey sure, but the stands mostly. Both are fascinating.

Most of the guys are dipping.³ Their costume of choice runs from St. Monica sweatpants to St. Monica sweatshirts and back again through a mess of blue, red, and Augustinian pierced-heart seals. The main variant tends to be gear from college or professional football and basketball teams. Also there is the odd grade-school t-shirt. This is the first time I've seen the full force of the football team at a social event as they are, clearly, limited to the field of play during Friday night gridiron contests. They are a rowdy bunch. I note that, unlike the football stands, which are dotted with parents, yes, but also packs of girls from neighboring high schools, the St. Monica student section at Orland Ice Arena is completely devoid of young women. And then I see and hear why.

During the first period, a group of intrepid girls from Marist makes the trek from left to right, passes by Mr. Dee, the Dean, and with furtive looks begins to walk in front of the seniors. It's a flirtatious move, full of sidelong glances, giggling, and pushing. At that point, as if rehearsed (and I find out later that they've been doing this for years, so I suppose it was rehearsed), Luke, a wide receiver on the football team, jumps up and starts chanting:

"GIRL. GIRL. GIRL. GIRL!"

Within seconds the entire section is on its feet, pointing at the young women as they walk by, shouting in unison:

"GIRL! GIRL! GIRL! GIRL!"

Abashed, the interlopers make a quick turn and beat a hasty retreat to the safety of their own side of the stands. The boys break into high fives and laughter, settling back into the hockey game, which has become suddenly incidental. I'm a bit stunned. Coach Dee shakes his head. Play on the ice (and in the stands, I find) goes on. The scene as above repeats itself each time a high-school-aged female comes through the human barrier of the Dean of Men. By the end of the game, various girls are used to the treatment and venture over just to test for the reaction. The boys remain dedicated to the trope, however, and each time the girls are driven back to the safety of the gender heterogeneity offered by the Marist side of the stands.

The next day, considering the experience and admittedly a little exasperated by the whole thing, I ask Mr. Paterno, a veteran of co-educational alternative and Catholic secondary schools, if he's experienced anything like it elsewhere. He says that he's not seen it anywhere he's worked. As he walks away toward his classroom he laughs, "Yeah, it's like Thunderdome."

This is a reference to the gladiatorial arena from the third and perhaps most famous film in the dystopian *Mad Max* series, where Mel Gibson and Tina Turner clash amidst the wreckage of a violent and dying world. Dramatic, perhaps, but I get what he's saying: it's loud, intimidating, and scarily baffling in the moment. Later, I ask Luke, the ringleader, about what I'd seen. He chortles,

"It's just a joke. Like, it's not a pick-up or anything. You just don't bring girls to hockey games."

Right. The list of places you don't bring girls, of course, begins with school for these boys and extends like foreboding tentacles to a great number of places, I've found. The fundamental split in gender relations sold and constantly reinforced by the notion and practice of single-sex education has served to gird troubling—even if presented as trifling at times—assumptions of physical and emotional differences between boys and girls, men and women; such that separation is seen as, and becomes, natural and even necessary.[4] At the hockey game, indeed at all hockey games, the boys take glee in raucously labeling young women "girl" from the safety of their crowd. This functions both to keep her away from the safety of the male space that is the stands at a contest, but it serves also to extend the gender-limited context of St. Monica High School beyond the schoolday. In effect it makes all school events, all-boy events. And while girls were present in numbers at basketball and football games, they were most often clustered in groups separate from pods of boys who stood and half-watched games and half-watched them. I'll suggest, further, that the presence of Mr. Dee, who presents a significant physical barrier, serves as semi-official sanction for the kind of shouting-down of women that happens. As long as the boys maintain their language in a clean way (there were no "fuck you's", though the tone could have been interpreted that way), they were within the sanction of the school. Though they might wield the term *girl* like a cudgel, it was indeed accurate and unoffensive in form, if frightening in function. The school observed as the boys self-segregated, and even provided the gatekeeper to make things official.

Pollut/ed/ing Women

Cut to a moment in class in December when Mr. Paterno, looking for a student who had been absent for the better part of the week, asked, "What's wrong with Keck?" The response, given with equal parts gravity and sarcasm, was, "He's got a girlfriend."

This offhanded tethering of boy-to-girl-to-trouble is the crux of the issue for the school. Boys are the business of the place. And they will be boys, in all of their expectant and self-fulfilling differentness from girls. Such is the condition of setting, well, conditions that include only the bodies of boys (and older women, who are assumed to be sexually unavailable to them) in an educational environment. The single-gendered school inherently relies on certain assumptions about what maleness includes (and excludes of course). In the case of St. Monica, as with fag discourse, the self-evidential separation between boy (gendered and sexed) and girl (gendered and sexed) became the excuse for not addressing discursive elements, which shaped masculine possibility and impossibility. That is: if we rely on the fact that boys will be boys by not being girls, then we don't have to deal with a great many problems because they won't exist (like sexual contact within school, for example, or the danger of teen pregnancy because, well, boys don't get pregnant).[5]

In essence, the school provides the a priori frame: you are boy, which in turn then means "rationality with absence of emotion" (Miedzian, 2002, p. 32) (except on Kairos, which we'll discuss in the next chapter) and the veneer of "hard[ness], tough[ness]…ruthless[ness], and competitive[ness]" (p. 37) traded in throughout social media and in pop psychological texts, which assume, most famously, different planets for men and women. The school provided light surveillance and kept a semblance of order, as with Mr. Dee at the game, who would have jumped at the appearance of vulgar words, say, but chose to ignore the functional and verbal bludgeoning of young women daring to pass through the senior section. The boys, knowing this, worked within the frame through discursive traditions, pushing at the edges of acceptability, manufacturing and repacking difference that had already been sold to them through the very separatist structure of the school. And in the process *girl* became a dirty word.

As long as the boys fell within acceptable—read: traditional—limits of gendered expectation, then they were free to play with masculinity however they saw fit granted it confirmed the school's sense of public decorum (at events such as the hockey game) and didn't challenge staid notions of dress code or hair. So it was that hair had to be shorter than the collar. It could grow out as wide and up as far as the boys liked, but once it hit the collar of the polo shirt, it became a sanctionable offense. Women wore their hair long, boys, Monicamen didn't. The uniform was part of the bringing into line of the school. Wearing the "SM" outside of the walls required that a Monicaman act with a certain sense of decorum, which meant, seemingly, not throwing a bottle of discarded spit at a woman, but throwing her gender at her in loud and crowd-backed frenzy was fully acceptable.

GIRL! it is, then, and she is certainly not boy, nor is there much of any overlap. Keep her away from the school so that the boys will learn to keep her away from their section one supposes. I am reminded of a presenter—during professional development in summer orientation—who, with all of the faculty present, launched into an odd, unbalanced diatribe. He was an alumnus of St.

Monica, a former teacher, and some sort of retired CIA operative, a self fashioned Jason Bourne. His lack of usable pedagogical content aside—the presentation was more a series of tales of his exploits in assassination plots he "couldn't go into details about"—there were moments when he encapsulated the sentiment of much of the faculty, which came to rest in the minds of the students as well: "What is it about boys? There's something wrong; we're not right. We're wired different—we know this—than girls; girls'll just sit and listen. Boys won't. They'll just smell and push limits."

Though teachers approached me after (I, the guest, recall) and told me that they weren't on board with much of what special-ops-guy said, they were apt to turn around and shake their heads at the "knuckleheads" in the school when it was brought to light that penises kept appearing on walls, or girls were fended off through chants confirming their girl-ness. That's just how they, these predictably unpredictable creatures, are. Boys will be boys, wired weird and all. The boys, sensing complicity, ran with it most blatantly in the case of fagging each other, but also as outlined in their approaches to women.

Anxiety, Sickness, and Crap (Literally)

Mac an Ghaill (1994) in *The Making of Men: Masculinities, Sexualities, and Schooling* suggests that there is a certain sexual anxiety for heterosexual boys at the high school level due to their own self-assessed lack of acuity with women as measured against the suggested sexual ferociousness attributed to masculinity in social messages. He notes that in his study boys "preferred to talk *about* [women] rather than spending time *with* them" (p. 104) citing further, Connell's argument that this "male heterosexual ambivalence towards women should not be read as an aberration, but rather as an intrinsic aspect of" what ze calls "hegemonic masculinity" (p. 105).

I've asserted before that I don't support the notion of a largely static hegemonic masculinity in the sense that I feel Connell utilizes it. Rather, I see more play in the power and resistance present. I will, though, support the notion of heterosexual ambivalence. Note that Keck is sickened by the act of having a girlfriend; he is literally made unhealthy by spending time with (sexually available) women; he's not missing school to be with her, he's missing school because he's been contaminated by his connection with her. In a sense he has become less of a man by engaging in the trappings of heterosexuality. And while this sort of thing could be seen as functioning as an extension of fag discourse—

Keck is emasculated by the contaminating women around him—seen in the conversation with Anthony here:

> Me: "How do you know if people are gay, Ant?"
> Anthony: "Like, if they're really feminine. Or if they hang out with just girls."
> Me: "Well isn't that the straightest thing you can do?"
> Anthony: "Not if you're not in it to get some."
> Me: "So you can't be friends with girls? Aren't you supposed to be friends with a girl you're dating?"
> Anthony: "Yeah, like, I'm dating my girlfriend and she's my best friend, but it's different. And besides, like I have guy friends and I'll go over to their houses and it's just guys then my girlfriend is for later."
> Me: "Isn't that first part kind of gay? I mean it's all guys."
> Anthony: "No. [frustrated] Now you're messing with me."

Of course he's right, I was just messing with him at that point, but the information seemed vital. Notice he has to walk the line between heterosexual and homosocial relationships, all outlined by the possibility of being made gay should he become too attached to his girlfriend. It's a fine line to walk.

What the rhetoric at the school (at lunch, in hallways, in classes, on the field; really everywhere and most visible, of course, at the altar populated exclusively by men) became about, though, was the fundamental differences on a biological and social level between boys and girls. Something consistently reinforced through media messages, yes, but also through the very structure of a school that excludes women pupils on basis of their being, well, not men.

Daly (1973) furthers her point that women are treated as impossibilities in Christian contexts most notably through the exclusivity of the clergy." Non-Semites or persons over, say, thirty-three, have not been universally excluded from the priesthood on the basis that they do not belong to the same ethnic group or age group as Jesus" (p. 79). Women, of course, and especially in the Catholic Church, have been limited to roles as "brides of Christ" (used most often in reference to religious vocations) specifically because they are said to lack the "particularity" of Jesus, the fundamental assumption of which lies in his gender, his sex, which separated him from the women in his life and in our modern lives still.

In a physical sense, at St. Monica it came down to, often enough, the boys drawing a strict distinction between their own humanity and the questionable nature of the embodied humanity of women. Two exchanges highlighted this most notably. Once, in Campus Ministry I heard a student between classes as he made an offhand comment about women and defecation. Mike notes jokingly, when I question him on it that, "yeah, they're not human. No I'm kidding. But I just don't want to think about them pooping. It's just gross."

> Me: "Why?"
> Mike: "Because it's a playground right near a sewage plant."
> Me: "But isn't that the same for guys too?"
> Mike: "Yeah, but I don't care about that 'cause I'm not gay."
> Me: "You don't really believe that women don't poop, though, right?
> Mike: "No, but I don't want to talk about it, necessarily."
> Me: "But you brought it up."

The lesson here seems to be that women are just fundamentally different beings whose bodily processes separate them in the sense that what makes them sexually attractive also makes their necessary functions as humans (defecation, menstruation, and so on) repulsive and fascinating, in a gawker-at-a-car-crash sort of way. This is some of the ambivalence Mac an Ghail makes reference to: Mike doesn't want to talk about it, yet he broached the topic to no one in particular in a more or less public space in Campus Ministry. It was my probing on the topic that he wasn't used to.

My presence makes critical engagement with the topic possible. This is not a conversation that Mike can have with a teacher, subject to the disciplinary constraints of the school as he would be. And he'll not get pushback from his schoolmates. My betweenness (not student/not teacher) allows him to test his hypothesis of dehumanization to see if I'll agree with him. I don't, and things get dicey. I would suggest that some of unraveling the troubling rhetoric of gendered difference would come from spaces where boys could try out and undo these women-are-different-and-less-than strains of talk. The school, though, has no space for this aside from Kairos, which ultimately, we'll find, functions as a conservative institution for re-instantiating traditions.

Later in class, I caught the tail end of a discussion between three boys who all had girlfriends and were engaged in a tête-à-tête about them:

> Petrbach: "Girls just don't fart or poop."
> Anthony: "That's a lie."
> Toth: "Maybe yours does, Ant."

Anthony: "No seriously. I walked into a single bathroom after a chick and it stunk and she hadn't flushed. She was a MILF[6] though."

In the end, the boys know that women both fart and poop. The point, though, is that they are not supposed to do either in the presence of men, for it will call into question their sexual availability/attractiveness as well as the strict boundary lines demarcated between maleness and femaleness. It's a study in the breaking down of fragile borders, which Longhurst (2001) discusses in terms of the abject, and the notion that difference, especially those differences around which the gender binary is constructed, might just rely on artificial assumptions that become more threatening the closer they come to melting away through critical examination.

Thus the boys get to revel in their own "'grotesque bod[ies]'" and their requisite "'earthy realism'" (recall their discussions of farting in class) characterized by being "intransigently, obstinately dirty" (Fiske, 1989, p. 99). Here we see very clearly where notions of "the body" as "the power-bearing definitions of social and sexual normality [is], literally embodied, and [it] is consequently the site of discipline and punishment for deviation from those norms" (p. 90). To be masculine, in this sense then, is to revel in not being woman. It is to be loud and to yell and to point out that women are different, either by literally pointing them out as they walk by at a sporting contest or by taking away their ability to deal with and process human waste. It might be worth noting that there is a general dearth of women's bathrooms at the school. Go figure.

Your Boys

At lunch again. Johnny is, as I approach the table, catching grief from Huey. Late, I settle as quietly as possible into the flow of the conversation. They are talking about the weekend, when Johnny left a party full of his friends, his Boys, to spend time/hook up with a girl he's been seeing. As noted in the previous chapter above, Huey is pissed—though not truly angry; this is rather a way of ribbing Johnny for being under the sway of a girl—that his friend has broken the brotherhood code and eschewed party time for intimate moments with a girl. He is, as Huey says, to do that sort of thing on his own time, on Sunday, if anything. I try to probe for a rationalization here:

Me: "But Huey, all you guys talk about is girls or being gay. Why is he getting shit for hooking up with a girl? Shouldn't that, then, prove he's not gay, and make you happy?"

Huey: "He ditched his Boys for a girl. That's fucking gay. You gotta do that shit on the side, Burke."

Two things to attend to first. At this point I was versed enough in the fag discourse of the school to understand that this wasn't really about Johnny's heterosexuality being called into question, but I wanted to hear how Huey would work out the problem. He drew, by the way, knowing nods of agreement from the eight or so other boys at the table as he talked. This was really about the bonds of homosociality formed in the school being extended beyond its tiled and worn walls and into social lives. Monica brothers were Monica brothers even in a basement in Bridgeport drinking clandestine beers, and the bond forged on the athletic field or in Mr. Latke's class extended outside the brick and mortar of 77th and Western. The common terminology would be, though the guys used it wryly, "bros before hos."

Further it seems that girls are at best side projects to the work of being with one's Boys. They are entities—largely amorphous and interchangeable in the way they're discussed (or more often, *not* discussed*)* by the young men—serving the practice of heterosexuality and assertive heterosexual public masculinity, but always they were secondary to one's Boys. Cross that line and a student in the school risked being called "whipped" and losing his friends; many was the case that a guy got heavily involved with a girlfriend, broke up with her, and had to try to reestablish himself with his Boys at the school. In essence, there was a choice to break up with the girl or with the Boys, unless he could work out a way to accommodate both, in which case the girlfriend was always the side project, the Boys the main show. Is this any real surprise, though, considering that girls have been excluded from the main socializing element (the school) of the boys' lives?

This affinity for male companions runs in direct contrast to the work of Harris (1995), whose survey research relied on assumed dominant male messages and asked men to rate their perceived correlation with various social roles expected of men. Some of the contrast might be attributed to age difference (he used 560 males of various ages, but did ask them to answer first how they felt at age 18, so the results are at least loosely related in chronology) and methodology, of course. But note that Harris found that men "do not make male friendship a priority in their lives" and have intimacy patterns determined at a young age by "mothers" who "teach adult men to turn to women for emotional support" (p. 107). Now, granted, we might not call the Monicamen "adult men" yet, but if alumni speakers at monthly masses are to be believed, then the bonds of friendship and emotional support established at the school extend well beyond the years of matriculation. And they inevitably rely on the mythical ideal of the Monicaman, who is tied to school and current and former students through the bonds of brotherhood (again, mythic) forged in years playing at, with, and for the school.

This is, I would argue, characteristic of the work of a single-gendered context necessarily invested in tradition and Catholic messages for the purpose of selling a notion of brotherhood—as a pedagogical tool and team bonding activity, yes, but also as a way to foster a closeness with the organization which relies heavily on donations from alums for its survival. The Boys become lifelong friends and women, outside of the officially Church-sanctioned sacrament of marriage, remain(ed) incidental to this. Friendship, in essence, becomes intertwined with allegiance to the school, as well as the tradition of the Church and the disentanglement of the three through lifetimes becomes unnecessary: a number of alums from the 1940s and 1950s were waked in the chapel over the span of my time there, carried out by their Monica brothers on the way to their final resting place. Wives, if still alive, walked behind the casket, disconnected from the act of the Mass and the physical act of the final passage from school to ground.

The lessons of the school are lifelong. They begin and end with tight homosocial bonds that are fiercely protected institutionally (women are allowed into very few spaces within the building of the school and only at dances and sporting events which are heavily surveilled; their role is further diminished in a funeral mass where they are, at most, escorted in and out by men who run the ceremony, and provide the escort to the final resting place). Women have, at best, an ancillary role to the main project of masculine bonding. Or they are totemic of the religiously aspirational which we'll see evidence of momentarily. Regardless the Monicaman from cradle to grave becomes more and more powerful in service to the tradition of the school. The boys mock this openly as seniors (in high school) and pine for it as seniors (aged) at their alumni gatherings. The loop gets closed largely in the making-strange of the creature that is woman.

Tradition and (Un)Available Women

As a product and producer of tradition, we find that each year the school fabricates a promotional poster full-up with photos from the previous year, overlaying the Augustinian seal and outlined by a unique slogan. This is used for recruiting's sake, but it also comes to shape the ethos of the students—and eventual alumni—as each poster, after it is retired, comes to rest on a wall of honor, blown up to billboard proportions, in the dining hall. Similarly, every classroom is adorned with multiple pieces of propaganda. Slogans always begin with "The St. Monica Family" and are then followed by the year's tagline. Near the end of the first semester one showed up taped to the outside of my office door reading: "The St. Monica Family: A Timeless Tradition." Others around the school include "The St. Monica Family: A Bond That Never Breaks," as well as "Remembering Our Past, As We Work in the Present, to Build for the Future." Of themselves, these might be little more than collages, condensed yearbooks adorning the school and bringing some color to otherwise drab 1960s era school construction, all seafoam tiling and re-re-re-painted stand-alone knocky radiators. But this is about consistency of message; it's about building tradition (107 years of it and counting) to the point that the main foyer of the school houses a mini-museum commemorating the centennial of the place.[7]

When an individual receives the Baptismal rite, he or she is told by the celebrant, a male priest or deacon, "I claim you for Christ by the sign of the cross." This is for life, recall, as one cannot be un-baptized in, or rather out of, Catholicism, leaving aside excommunication, which serves a different and drastic function and is outside of the sacrament.

In a similar way, then, these boys are being constantly claimed in the name of St. Monica High School for life. It begins with their opening first-year retreat when they are all handed buttons with the acronym IALAC (I Am Loveable And Capable, by special dint of their status as new members of the community) and their first t-shirt. For a great many of them, their induction begins before that with (grand)parents and uncles schooling them in the gospel of Mustang football and baseball from the time they can walk, and from what I saw in the football stands, even earlier than that. Beyond this, they become members of a century-old brotherhood, the institution of which only recently allowed for its first female principal. That brotherhood, I found, left little room for women, particularly those of sexually desirable ages. The boys had to find ways to accommodate for their physical urges, yes, but also for their need to play out the scripts of socially accepted dating rituals. This led to a strained relationship between the rhetoric of brotherhood and its attendant homosocial ideal, and the budding relations with women that some of the boys found beyond the school walls. Loyalty was required, but exceptions could be made. On Sundays. For squishes.

What to do, then, with women and the constant bombardment of media messages and gendered expectations[8] that dictated a certain amount of interest in and desire for sexual attention from attractive and attracted girls? Because even an all-boys school, if it's to become a "family" with a century's worth of existence to trumpet, requires women, if only as props in support of an enacted (and expected) heterosexuality.

Fromm had it that masculinity hung on a specific "contempt for women" (as cited in Connell, 1995, p. 18). Not wholly outside of the purview of an all-boys school, certainly, but this misses an important point of departure: the boys at St. Monica didn't feel contempt for women on the whole, but rather women of a certain age rooted in their sexual desirability, the taproot of which I sensed came from a fear that the brotherhood might be disturbed by the intensive work of heterosexual coupling (and eventually) marriage. That is, they didn't feel contempt for mothers or even older female teachers. In fact they often became quite closely bonded with the older women who ran the attendance office as well as the dedicated teachers who remained at the school well past the age at which the boys' eyes might linger on sexualized body parts. The distinction, of course, came in the sense that these women were largely de-gendered, unsexed, by their implied loss of sexual desirability. Problematic, certainly, and I don't mean to draw away from the misogyny that I did see and hear from the boys, but there was a certain skewed logic to it that struck me as more complex—and discursively constructed of course—than might otherwise be assumed.

I'm reminded of two different exchanges with Kobe in reference to Mrs. Daley, the principal and his calculus teacher and more importantly a grandmother in the final year before her retirement, as contrasted with his interactions with and feelings about Ms. Garcia, a Spanish teacher in her late twenties.

> Me: "Kobe, how come you guys are silent in Mrs. Daley's class? Is it because she's principal?"
> Kobe: "I dunno. It might be because of that, but it could be that the stuff is so hard."
> Me: "But you always complain about how hard Spanish is, and you guys are all over the place in Ms. Garcia's class. Do you take advantage of Ms. Garcia 'cause she's young?"

Kobe: "I try not to because I'm doing pretty well in her class and I want her to treat me like a student. But I think other guys do it 'cause she's younger."
Me: "But you guys flirt with Ms. Garcia."
Kobe: "She flirts with us!" [Indignant, and actually he wasn't completely in the wrong here]
Me: "Why don't you flirt with Mrs. Daley?"
Kobe: "Sick. 'Cause she's old and she looks like Chicken Little."

The boys, it seems, saw Ms. Garcia (who was unmarried) as a challenge because she was still in a range of sexual possibility for them. They saw her, in essence, as sexually possible, probable even for the more cocksure. She was, thus, treated far differently and with much less diffidence or deference, really, than the older and sexually unavailable Mrs. Daley. Mrs. Daley, in effect, didn't represent a threat to their homosocial relationships because she was beyond their purview of attraction and thus would never "steal" one of their boys from them. Ms. Garcia, well, she just might. It wasn't, again, that the young men of my experience viewed all women with contempt;[9] this turned on the specifics of their age and potential for stealing away the attention of their Boys.

Squishes

Ruhlman (1996), on returning to his own all-male secondary school, felt an odd aura in the air of the place, which he could only suss out by suggesting that "while girls [were] not physically present, their influence [was] always in effect" (p. 48). I found out some of how this echoed at St. Monica relatively early on, as I sat in on a history class and overheard some of the boys planning a weekend trip to a college in Michigan. Packer, our imp, was asking a few of his friends if they were "going up to Squishigan." Sleepy, a fellow football player, replied:

> "No way, man. We can't call it that. Cause there's no girls there. Dude, we went to a bonfire at my cottage and every night we put up a bedsheet toward the water that said 'Bitches wanted,' on the pier and shined a flashlight on it and no one even showed up."

Romantic, eh? And shocking that women could resist such an eloquent siren song. This, though, prompted me to try to turn around a discussion with Nico and Chunk about the terminology after Nico asked "Do you have a squish, Burke?"

> Me: "What does that mean, Nico?"
> Nico: "Well, it's kind of awkward to talk about…."
> Me: "Why, Nico?"
> Scott: (always tired of my questioning) "It's sex. He means sex."
> Me: "But it can't just be sex, though. Do you mean the woman and the act of fucking with the woman?"
> Nico: [Brightly] "Yeah, it's the total package."
> Me: "So why that word?"
> Nico: [Stammering now] "Well, you know, it's like…if you think about the sound…and they, well…[He halfheartedly mimes grabbing breasts]…squish."

The word, we find, means a sexually attractive girl, and it comes out of sounds presumably attributed to the sexual act, but also to the feel of a woman when she is grabbed in various sexually coded bodily places (the breasts and the rear end, primarily). It came to be used as a fairly versatile and comedic term for its onomatopoeic qualities, as when Packer asked me if I was taking my "squishy, squishy squish" to the Homecoming dance.

Squishes, it turns out, were quite the topic. This isn't highly surprising considering Ruhlman's assertion about the always-present-absence. The dialectic at St. Monica manifested itself in unique ways and I think this has much to do with the single-gendered context and specifically the onus on brotherhood. In contrast to the ways in which Pascoe (2007) found her subjects constructing masculinity through tales of sexual conquests most especially as rooted in the grosser details of sexual acts characterized by "farts, feces, and blood" (p. 104), the Monica students were, as mentioned earlier, more likely to build a masculinity around one's Boys first and then his squish second. The details of the sexual act were largely absent from discussion.[10]

Rather, the sense was that engagement with and commitment to a squish meant a certain weakness ,as noted earlier with Keck and his sickening girlfriend. Trumpeting attachment, a way to garner masculine footing in Pascoe's coeducational study, meant certain mockery in the groups I came to run with.

Token, a widely recruited basketball player, was roundly mocked for a keychain he first (accidentally) brought out of his backpack in Physics class. It was simple enough, just leather strings holding in descending order his girlfriend's name in block letters. A teammate, frowning at Token and looking to me mournfully sighed, "She cut up his playa card with them scissors, Burke." To be playa, of course, is to be potentially sexually promiscuous. Turning in one's playa card meant tethering to a girlfriend. A dangerous act in the school. Still, boys, in the face of a heavily disappointed crew of Boys, committed constantly but not, as it turned out, continuously. This was easy to monitor through Facebook, where relationship statuses changed from "single" to "in a relationship" seemingly on a rotating basis. In the end, though, the larger rhetoric focused on staying as far away from squishes for as long as possible. One, in effect, had to commit to the relationship with the school, with the Boys, and to sports and even academics; squishes came last.

The Buffer of School or School as Buffer

School was a haven from girls. It was not, however, a space devoid of very specific and telling imaginings of women. Which is perhaps why young female teachers caught so much flak in classes: they were invading in their corporeality what was to be an exclusively male space. Mr. Latke, who considered himself "old school" (and he'd been there for 51 years, as student first, and teacher after, so I suppose if anyone could take that label, it would be him), recalled a young female teacher who left the year prior to my coming:

> "They ate her up; there was a fight and she just had to leave the next period 'cause she was so upset."

He rolls his eyes.

> "See, when I was hired there weren't any women on faculty and I thought it would be that way always. But they hired the first woman teacher and the boys, I mean I felt bad for her, were just brutal. The things they did were just terrible. The boys put pictures of naked women on her charts so when she pulled them down, there they'd be. The boys know that wouldn't bug me. Plus I speak their language, so we have an understandin'."

The idea being that the school ought to be a protected space from the invading forces of the abject other: girls/women. The boys picked up on this discursive element.

Me: "But you guys like girls, right? Why wouldn't you want to be around them?"
Mick: "Sometimes we just need a break from them."
Raff: "Yeah, like, we like 'em, but we don't really want to spend time with them."

Funny to think about the break that Mick speaks of, considering the fact that the worlds of these boys were so heavily male: they went to school with boys, played sports with them, and constructed social spaces outside of school where they hung out exclusively with their Boys. I wondered intermittently what it was exactly they needed a break from.

They need a break, it turns out, not from persons in the specifics, but rather from their expected stereotypes. Or, put another way, they needed to be away from the one-dimensional image of girls: dramatic, emotional, disruptive, and always reveling in their not-maleness. In the world of St. Monica, mutually constructed by the school, teachers, and students alike, women would only bring complication to a simple environment where guys can just be guys (to say nothing of the creative work they do navigating what kind of "guys" to be, of course).

Luke: "I wouldn't want to go to a co-ed school."
Me: "Why?"
Luke: "Girls ruin school. 'Cause here we can just do whatever we want and not worry about it."

The question, of course, is what specifically that vague "whatever" to which Luke alludes means and, further, what exactly girls would be ruining, something Dunbar, Nico, and Matt helped me figure out:

Dunbar: "Guys'd act differently [with girls around] and guys would be all distracted, and guys would show off and change how they act to impress them."
Nico: "Yeah, like I wouldn't have the GPA I have now and I wouldn't be sleeping in class, that's for sure. I mean, you've seen me when I wake up [sadly from a pedagogical standpoint I had; the seniors spent a great deal of class time napping] and it's not pretty."

Hanns: "I think it would be stricter with girls. Like we wouldn't be able to be ourselves and teachers wouldn't let us get away with as much as we can get away with now."

Gone would be, in effect, the farting with impunity, and the fagging, and the space apart and more importantly, gone would be the bond of brotherhood and a century of tradition in the face of potential heterosexual hazards, those great pregnancy liabilities from Mr. Latke's worldview: women. The school is a place, as constructed by faculty and students, for boys to be boys in the most stereotypical ways, away from girls. It's a place where Mrs. Byrne can tell me that "our young men are very territorial" in the same sentence that she worries if they will be offended by the potpourri ("too girly?") masking the backed-up sinks in her science classroom. It's a place where Mrs. Marks sarcastically refers to *Macbeth* as confirming that "women are the root of evil, the downfall of man twenty-five years of teaching and not an argument against that" and Nico quietly in the back of the room can mutter in sardonic response, "Do my laundry," and face no challenge as he garners nodding snickers; it's a place crafted by faculty who say "this is a place that's full of opportunity with room for professional and spiritual growth" and then, as an aside when speaking of losing a contest chide, "well, I'm not holding any grudges, just because I'm a girl"; it is a place where Raff, finally, can tell me that he is "ripshit" about being ratted out for some disciplinary failing, spitting, "You don't tell on someone at an all-guys school. Seriously, you just don't." Because that is a flouting of the rules of brotherhood, which are inevitably defined by the fact that only brothers can exist safely in the school. To "tell" is to become the mythical girl, the gossip, the weak link. This girlness (femininity), as we've seen, is unacceptable on the football field, as much as it's impossible for young female teachers in the classroom. And so: Man up.

Where This (Almost) Breaks Down

Bishop John Shelby Spong (1992) made a literary career out of trying to reappropriate the Bible and its corresponding meaning from what he perceived as the very real danger of literalism (religious fundamentalism, if you prefer). Of the Virgin Birth, and in reference to the birth narratives of Christ in general, he writes, "the myths and folk wisdom of a particular day always shape the understanding the people have of their intense experiences" (p. 35). His argument turns on the Apostles' gradual literary reconceptualization of Jesus the Christ after his crucifixion. He first analyzes the increased focus on the birth narrative of Jesus from non-existent, "Mark, the first Gospel, wrote his story of Jesus' life with no allusion whatsoever to Jesus' birth or origins" (p. 42) to mythically prominent in later tales of the writers (or their composites, more probably) Luke and Matthew.[11] This he sees as the alteration in the function of the Jesus-story for early followers as they transitioned from thinking of themselves as Jews to Christians. As the text is centered on a feminist critique meaning to re-assert the Gospels' status as Midrash (a composite of mythic tales, carrying social context and thus contextualized social meaning) Spong turns the headlight of his work onto the increasingly narrow role played by Mary (the Mother and Magdalene, both) as the Gospels were developed.

The fulcrum of Spong's argument lies in "the figure of the virgin...employed as a male weapon to repress women by defining them...to be less human than males, to be the source of a sexual desire that was thought to be evil, and therefore to be guilty just for being women" (p. 198). His exegesis of the re-creation of Mary both born of virgin herself and birthing God virginally focuses on the crafting of her as a character "who was hailed as the ideal model" of womanhood while covering up the fact that she was, discursively, "totally defined by men" (p. 214): the men who wrote of her, the men who preached her impossible virtue, the men who grew up praying for her grace. This is much in keeping with Mary Daly's (1973) early work, which excavated the two essential Biblical models for women in Christianity: the fallen Eve, who tempted Adam (read: as all women are viewed as coming to tempt men, inevitably) into his own—and our great—fall, and the virginal and thus impossible Mary. For though a woman might remain chaste and embrace marriage with God through religious vocation—a recreation of the heterosexual cultural model—she, unlike Mary, was not of a virgin born herself, mind. The neat trick tying up the loose ends, of course, is the presence of Original Sin from which Mary was exempted. The final say being that "the inimitability of 'Mary conceived without sin' ensures that all women as women are in the caste with Eve" (p. 82) and to blame for being, first and foremost, and for being so audacious as to not be Mary in the process.

The fact remains: my subjects and I attend(ed) a school for boys, named after a woman. Odd, that. These Monica boys are schooled in a context, that consistently reinforces the message of mythical and chaste and impossible women. Faced with a decision as to how to handle their own hormones, but also the general need to interact with women in their lives, they turn to the models provided them. The girls in their lives, flush with their own sexuality and a sexuality foisted on them by social messages, confronted as well by the boys' desire of course, face impossible ideals. Or rather, the boys, in figuring out how to interact (or deal) with the women who inevitably come to invade their boyspace at St. Monica High School, return in ways knowing and unknowing, to their tradition and their faith. Or said more accurately: The traditions of their faith which dictate prescribed and circumscribed roles to its liturgical women.

In the chapel of the school during new faculty orientation, Mika faced us as we sat in the pews awaiting the arrival of Father Tim, who was to give us a tour of the significant iconography of the place. She quipped darkly, "This is the only time you'll see me standing up and speaking in front of church." Too true. Had we looked behind us on our progression into the chapel, we'd have noticed above the central nave, banners listing the many roles of St. Monica in her lifetime: Mother, Widow, Wife, Nun, and Saint. If we were then to take a walk to the small shrine to St. Monica set to the side of the liturgical space, we'd find a statue imagining her bodily. At her forehead is a telltale drop of blood, a sign of the stigmata.[12] In full habit, she holds a rose aloft in prayer pleading to and bleeding with Christ. Across the church, on a diagonal opposite is a shrine to Mary, the mother of Christ who was raised bodily into heaven upon her death. On the altar is a picture of the mother of St. Augustine. These three, Mary, St. Monica, and Monica the Mother of Good Counsel compose the female trinity of the school. Students on any given day will ask Mary, St. Monica, and Monica to pray for them multiple times. They pass in the hallways and particularly in classrooms, pictures, mosaics, and various other guesses at the bodily manifestation of the patronesses in their lives. They are, in effect, surrounded by indelible imagery of women who are sainted, mothered/mothering, virginal, and so devoted to God as to become afflicted with the nail and thorn marks of Christ or to have given birth to Him.

The point is that, indeed, Mika will only ever very rarely speak from the front of the chapel because her story has not yet been written by the Church. It may yet get written; we don't know. But the women the boys see, pray to, and come to admire are always mothers, wives, ethereal, saintly, desexualized, and, quite frankly, dead. I would suggest that the gap in treatment between young female (and mostly single) teachers and those older married and grandmotherly women in the school turns on this discursive element. Monicamen have models of respect in their faith tradition—one hammered home for the vast majority of them from the time they entered Catholic school in kindergarten—for mothers and for those women seen as sexually undesirable for the very impossibility that they might have ever had sex. Younger teachers face impossible odds because the only other group into which the boys can hope to lump them is with the young women in their lives outside of school who certainly don't fill the bill as chaste or motherly or saintly simply because they exist in the world in the only ways open to them as yet. They are fallen in the rhetorical tradition of the Church, Eves all, and the only way the boys know to interact with them is through the ongoing discourses of sexual conquering and punitive disrespect. They are, most importantly of course, not male either.

The school, in essence, functions as an arm of the Church in limiting the lived possibilities of women and men through religious iconography of impossible models. The boys, working to reconcile this with cultural messages of sexuality and desirability, settle on a compromise, which suggests that a school for boys would be ruined by the presence of "real" girls though it is protected by, and named after, mythic ones. Their space apart is a space away from all those fallen tempting Eves who would draw them away from their Boys and further from the theological ideal of a carefully crafted narrativized saint and mother and wife. This, however, is not universally true. It takes, though, a space apart for the boys to open up to different possibilities of humanity for women and themselves; it is on Kairos that these discourses change and the boundary between masculinity and the emotionality of femininity are openly played with and examined.

Notes

1. As an educator, and a teacher educator further, it intrigues me that there seems to be so little research on teachers who return to their former schools (or rival schools) and how this might affect pedagogy, as well as educational outlook. I would suggest it as fertile ground for further research, most especially as schools seek ways to hook into the affinity of alumni by differentiating their institutions from surrounding rivals.

2. Monica's name for what would probably pass as the Dean of Discipline at other schools. Coach Dee ran JUG and was in charge of parking and uniform issues as well.

3. This is a form of chewing tobacco. It's the vice of choice for a number of the boys because, unlike smoking, they can hide that they're dipping in school, in class even. Also, it doesn't make their clothes smell and so parents can retain a certain plausibility to their willful ignorance of it if they want to. Something like chewing gum, one puts it between the front lower lip and the bottom teeth and sucks the juice. I have heard of guys who cut the inside of their mouths so that the tobacco gets to the bloodstream more quickly. Often the football players will "throw in a pinch" during lunch, or at least they would until it was explicitly banned after a bottle full of discarded chaw spit (a 'spitter') was thrown in the stands at a football game, hitting a mother who in turn wrote a letter to Father Tim. Shit, as they say, hit the fan.

However, because a number of the football coaches chew, they tend to be more lenient in allowing the boys leeway as with Coach Dee at the hockey game who looked the other way while boys spit into cups, bottles, really any receptacle available.

4 This was—and perhaps still is—rooted in assumptions about sexual appetites and their need for control. It's a sentiment echoed by a math teacher, Mr. Latke, who told me that:

> The original reasoning [for single sex Catholic schools], and let me think how to say this, was to keep the boys away from sex and inappropriate things until they were old enough to handle it. Like now you got girls pregnant in grade school. That didn't used to happen.

The homage to the halcyon days of moral certitude aside, we see this concern with preserving the sexual austerity of boys in its original (and largely unaltered by time really) form in Foucault (1990c), who noted that "virginity [was] not simply abstention" for the Stoics, but was rather "a choice, a style of life, a lofty form of existence that the hero chooses out of the regard that he has for himself" (p. 230). Thus, the choice for boys to attend an all-boys high school is one supported by the twin regulatory gazes in society: one that sees them as too uninformed to avoid sexual promiscuity in coeducational environments and one that celebrates them as heroic (as special) for "choosing" the austerity of a single-gendered context. Note, of course, that the (assumed) absence of a possible homosexual desire here. Foucault spends a great deal of time explicating the complexities of "boy-love" for the Greeks and Romans who saw the practice as natural, but one to be controlled as a measure of manhood, in favor of, but also silent partner to the more dominant and (re)productive heterosexual bond. Boy-love in this Catholic school might best be referred to as "brotherhood" a phrase foisted on the boys from the first day of orientation. They leave, upon graduation, with Monica brothers, entering a brotherhood of countless alums. Note above, too, that Mr. Latke cites teen pregnancy as problematic and places the trouble solely on the girl who has somehow gotten pregnant. The trouble, it seems, is that girls get pregnant and this somehow vaguely implicates boys, but essentially in the sense that they will then become tied down by the consequence of sex, bonded to a girl before having the chance to find brotherhood.

5 In October an Augustinian priest visited the school to give an anti-abortion presentation. The slide show, displayed to the entire school (in four shifts) in the auditorium was produced in the early 1990s and relied on slippery statistics to "prove" that abortion was always regrettable and that human life existed from conception. These are not unusual arguments considering the Catholic Church's ongoing crusades against, say, condom use in African nations ravaged by AIDS. However, throughout the entire presentation, all examples were rooted in the feminine. Women got into trouble and made bad decisions and that led to abortions which were forbidden by God. Only at the very end was there a single summative statement made by Fr. Tim, who said, "Gentlemen, we're men, and these are important issues that we need to think about." That was it: back to class with images of aborted fetuses and fallen women on the mind.

6   Similar to the term "Cougar," which indicates an older woman on the prowl for younger male sexual partners, MILF is an acronym that stands for Mother I'd Like to Fuck. It's used fairly liberally at the school and came most prominently from movies targeted at the age group, particularly *American Pie*.

7   The school has only existed in its current spatial form since 1990. Before that, it was emplaced at 63rd and Claremont, two miles north and east. This is an interesting study in the ideas of theoretical space and place in the sense that the St. Monica High School to which older alums hold, no longer exists in the same space but it remains emplaced for them as a combination of "lived space" and "concreteness, immediacy, and cultural affect" (Soja, 1996, p. 40). It is not the building, the place of 7740 S. Western that means St. Monica to them, but rather the history, the memory, the brothers of the old space that remains at the fore of their loyalties. The implications for my "returning" to home to do the study resonates with these fluid spaces. My high school has changed a great deal over the years, but its name is fixed in amber in my consciousness, even as I adopt more malleable notions of historical discourses in relation to St. Monica.

8   Connell (2002) gives a nice synopsis of studies that examine the formation of gendered expectations through mass media (p. 11, 37).

9   Ms. Garcia dealt with waves of young men who tested her constantly. She was also the recipient of numerous romantic overtures from the seniors. Her willingness to reject their advances—none of these notes and Valentines made their way to the older Mrs. Daley—led to a defensive and recriminatory "hatred" for her. She was caught in a bind of flirting with the boys to keep them interested or shooting down their hopeless mooning, and losing them to weeks of bitter disappointment.

10 There were exceptions. Packer was holding court in the hallway as I walked by once surrounded by listeners who had become, over the years, careful about parsing his truth from bombast. Most people saw him as an exaggerator if not a flat-out liar. Regardless, like a clown he was entertaining. He was telling, in this instance, a story about his girlfriend: "Dude, she sent me a text. It was hilarious. It said 'don't give me any more jizz [slang for semen] showers. ' I fucking busted all over her back Friday night. And she was chasing me around 'cause she was pissed." This is Pascoe's graphic bragging in stereo. But the accepted notion after Parker left was that he was just telling stories to be heard. Truth was another notion. Still, that he felt the need to entertain or brag in this way does bespeak a certain masculinity constructed through grossness and demeaning sexual interaction with women. This was an exception to the rule, as I found it however.

11 John, the fourth Gospel (excepting those many companion stories considered apocryphal by the Church), is not part of the Synoptic tradition and thus begs a different analysis, he argues.

12 Emblematic of the five wounds of Christ from the crucifixion, the stigmata was often "awarded" to especially devoted followers who suffered with Him as a symbol of their synchronicity with holiness. They appear at the wrists, the ankles, and the forehead in statuary and pictography.

Chapter 6

Kairos

Space and Time Apart

Heterotopias are…fleeting, transitory, precarious spaces of time [that] Foucault sees [as] increasingly converging in compressed, packaged, 'invented' environments that seem both to abolish and preserve time and culture, that appear somehow to be both temporary and permanent.

Edward Soja, "Thirdspace"

What is an ideology without a space to which it refers, a space which it describes, whose vocabulary and links it makes use of, and whose code it embodies? What would remain of religious ideology—the Judeo-Christian one, say—if it were not based on places and their names: church, confessional, altar, sanctuary, tabernacle? What would remain of the Church if there were not churches? The Christian ideology, carrier of a recognizable if disregarded Judaism (God the Father, etc.), has created the spaces which guarantee that it endures.

Henri Lefebvre, "The Production of Space"

I want therefore to reflect for a moment on this space and the opportunity it provides us in reconsidering the scope and sense of cultural analysis today.

Ian Chambers, "Cities Without Maps"

Until this point I have attempted to illustrate the effects a school, an all-boys Catholic school, has on the gendered (and masculine) possibilities of the students it enrolls. Further, I have tried to delineate ways in which the boys are creative in resisting, reappropriating, resenting, and reasserting the discourses of the school (and the culture at large that defines its possibilities) as their own in a swirl of becoming probable beings.

Thus, we have discussed the swarming discursive functions of fagging and the ways the school shelters boys from certain difficulties in navigating the dialectic (present as it may be in society at large) by its formation as a single-gendered space. In another manner, we have examined the ways that the school's construction of mythical women enables students' feelings of entitlement as part of the process of separating themselves from the sort of "female pollution" that Thorne (1993, p. 83) encountered in her observation of differently gendered spaces in coeducational schools. Both of these strains of analysis required a familiarity and at the very least a limited engagement with the religiosity of St. Monica High School. We have touched upon the charism of the Augustinians and taken a critical view of the stories, or Catholic wonder tales, through which much of what passes for religious faith for the boys comes to take form. This is, notably, braided with the tradition of the place, which takes on a pseudo-religious role as a way of ensuring that brotherhood is what the boys learn, affixing their loyalty to the school, with the gender, and with the Catholic faith. The school essentially presents itself as a place special in the world, and in many ways separate from it. This is the school as shelter from women and proving ground for the heteronormativity of conservative religious ideology. At this point it makes sense to dig into where much of this cathexis for St. Monica (the school, the woman, the tradition of brotherhood) as a space apart from and important in the world comes from: Kairos.

To be becoming a man, a Monicaman, is to navigate the streams of fag discourse on a daily basis. It is to be made not-woman in the halls of the school (or pseudo-woman on the football field, perhaps), and it is to constantly reform oneself in relation and service to the evolving tradition of the place, to "Conquer today; prepare for tomorrow," as one popular wall sign entreats. What the school wants, recall, is a Monicaman. What *he* is the faculty and students can't quite describe. Such was the diversity of answers around the term that I stopped asking after the first month because there was no anchor to the responses. Well, that's not entirely true. There were many forms of platitude, t-shirt slogans and all a bit banal to be honest: he respects the "SM"; he acts as a gentleman; he tucks his shirt in; he has his brothers' backs, and so forth. It's not that these answers are untrue; it's that they're largely un(der)considered. One becomes a Monicaman by going to Monica, they mean. Which is true.

The phantom ideal served as both disciplinary mechanism (a Monicaman wouldn't do that) and filial tie (there are Monicamen in all fifty states; we are nationwide) utilized to claim everyone from the school for the purpose of continuing its legacy. The Monicaman is an everyman as long as he's an alumnus. Under that umbrella, well, the boys worked at shaping a self. The only mandatories in a boy's time at the school were fag discourse, a negotiation of women mythical and real (and their reconciliation into a decision to respect one and debase the other), a negotiation of the will of one's "Boys," and the senior

Kairos trip where the first three prerequisites found their undoing (or a reordering, perhaps), at least temporarily, in a lodge in the middle of Illinois cornfields.

Prayer

Prayer, outside of the Kairos experience, was most often utilized within the school as a classroom management strategy. Think of it as Catholic bellwork, if you please. Each class was to start with some manner of religious invocation and for the most part teachers were accommodating of the administration's request. These were not, however, deep treatises on personal faith (though they could have been, internally) but by and large were rote prayers repeated en masse (a Hail Mary, an Our Father; less often the Glory Be, but as often as not, the Prayer of the Peacemaker,[1] an evocation of and homage to, St. Monica). It was religion functioning on a microlevel as control. Talking during class was disrespectful to teachers and students; screwing around during prayer was disrespectful to God (and do you think you're more important than God, young man?). Still, to appear respectful during prayer is different from actively engaging in a deeper process of spiritual reflection. It, this appearance, requires only a tucked-in shirt and the mouthing of words. Religious devotion wasn't gradable, and it would be difficult to give a JUG for a boy's mumbling through. As long as he was in line, that's all that mattered.

The boys read this fairly adeptly and used the nonchalant nature of the practice as well as its repetition to blunt the spear of evangelism into a persistent buzzing of religion necessarily present in a Catholic school attached to a chapel, mazed with hallways full of iconography. This strategy of passive resistance is perhaps best exemplified by the following discussions, both from stolen moments in Campus Ministry. The first occurred upon the visit of my colleague and advisor, a cultural Jew, who delights in questioning (on any number of levels). He began:

Avner: "What does it mean to be Catholic?"
Nico: "It's just the same as every religion to me. Maybe because I've never studied any other religion."
Avner: "What about your kids, will you raise them Catholic?"
Nico: "I think it's important. You decide that you want to be Catholic at confirmation. And it's a healthy lifestyle to me because it doesn't limit you too much. Then I can send him here."

What followed was a spirited discussion among a number of the boys and Avner about the workings of sexual release and sacramental confessional forgiveness in the Church. Most memorable (and the exchange above illustrates it well) was the notion that religion, for Nico, is so much regurgitated prayer that doesn't get in the way of the life of a high school boy, nor the life of his imagined parental self. Like the school itself, it provides the loose limits of how one will raise his children, say, but doesn't require much application or sacrifice of the self in the process.

To a man (loaded term, I realize), each student professed his hope that his sons, should he have them, would attend the school, presumably as Catholics. Lost in these daydreams is the whole process of getting to the point of having children (with a woman, always). But it bespeaks the importance of continuing the tradition of the school and its brotherhood, as well as the handing down of the Catholic faith in preference over the assumed engagement with a partner in the creating and raising of a child. In some ways we can forgive the young men, at ages 16 and 17 for not knowing the workings, nor really considering the ramification, of siring children beyond deciding prematurely that they will raise them in familiar environments (Catholic faith and St. Monica). But the idea is to highlight the notion that religion and the school, in essence, become naturalized choices for Nico and others. Becoming a man is having a son who goes to St. Monica.[2] The boys either aren't giving themselves up in the process or don't realize how much they're being molded through years of Catholic school. I would suggest it's a little bit of both as they mold the faith into their self-asserted Cafeteria (pick and choose) Catholicism, characterized most starkly by the paraliturgical devotions they settle on over, say, older doctrines of celibacy, weekly fasting, or attendance in mass on holy days of obligation.

Later in the semester when I'd been asked to read the morning prayer over the PA, I stumbled a bit over the wording and discussed my embarrassment with students during a break in periods after the event. Mike reassured me that it was fine: "Don't worry about it. Nobody cares." This fed into a conversation about the upcoming all-school Mass the next day.

Rob: "You can write down all the people who are sleeping."
Hanns: "I take pieces of paper out and see how many times I can fold them before it gets impossible."
Me: "I don't get it. You're at a Catholic school, but you guys ignore everything the administration does in terms of religion."

Rob: "Well, like I believe in God, but we only have Mass once a month and it's, like three hours long, so I sleep."

Of course, the boys didn't ignore everything the administration did regarding religion in the school. They couldn't, subject as they were to walking by imagery of Sts. Monica and Augustine throughout the place, and covered in Augustinian seals as they were no matter what they wore from the school. And they couldn't abstain from attending mass or praying at the start of class. However, their attendance never presupposed an active participation. The school wanted future priests; the boys wanted to sleep.

Religion, through all their years of Catholic schooling (and Rob, Hanns, and Nico were all parochial lifers), had become a functionary of discipline and surveillance. If they were in danger of being scolded for prayer in the chapel (with heads down) in the same way they were being scolded for sleeping in chapel (again, with heads down), then they were going to resist passively this extended form of classroom management in the same way they embroiled themselves in schoolroom battles about seating arrangements and pop quizzes. Scapulars and tattoos were choices, masses and prayer were requirements, and inconvenient ones. The school could require them to be there, and some of them might even serve as acolytes at the altar, but they would still find modes of non-participation like, say, placing a piece of tape on a folding chair, ripe with a newly inked penis. Having a presence does not always denote that one is present, in other words.

The Kairos retreat, however, represented something very different for the boys. It was in this space that they were able to transgress the rules of discourse surrounding fagging and women without fear of recrimination or social sanction. It was here, in the space apart from school,[3] that they were able/forced to come to an extended religious encounter and it was on the retreats that the senior class, without fail and to a (Monica)man, flouted traditional masculine tropes of emotional distance, demonstrative loving physicality, and religious indifference. They became evangelical Catholics, if very briefly. The Kairos experience was manufactured as a heterotopia, in effect which for Foucault "begins to function at full capacity when men arrive at a sort of absolute break with their traditional time" (as cited in Soja, 1996, p. 194). And Kairos is most certainly all about time.

God's Time

The term *Kairos* wends from two origins. The first derives from early Greek orientations to time, the sense of which later generations of Christians appropriated for the sake of grafting on God. Chronos is, in its modern interpretation of the ancient ideal, lived linear (see: chronological) time and Kairos is felt time; it is contemplative time—it is time apart: God's time. The offshoot, in the field of Rhetoric, has Kairos as "the opportune moment," or the point at which action and creativity occur. It is creation. This is easily enough, for the faith-filled, brought back into the fold of theology in the form of God as prime mover, or the manifestation of action itself: God as the moment. Also, similar in form and pronunciation comes the earliest Christogram, which is essentially a monogram or a mash-up of letters used to signify the Christ. The conflation of the Greek letters "chi" and "rho" forms the ChiRho, seen here: Before and concurrent with its adoption by early Christians as a symbol of their faith (twin to the simple line-drawn fish, often used to mark early secret gatherings of believers in those legendary catacombs) the roughly juxtaposed letters had been used by scribes to mark passages of particular value or relevance, where the symbol stood for *chreston*, meaning "good" (Grant, 1993, p. 42). This manner of religiously vital marginalia continued well into the monastic era of Europe, in fact. So there's a history here, and it's been tapped into for interpretive purposes.

This playfulness with time (good and God's) is something very much a part of an individual's Kairos experience, as the first thing that the Campus Ministry staff and student leaders (drawn from former retreatants) do upon arrival is collect candidates' cell phones and watches. The idea being that they are to leave chronos behind and give themselves up to God's time. They are to become disconnected from the world of school and settle into the hard work of retreating from what they'd known. From there, ironically, the lead team[4] is heavily scheduled and immersed in the details of the newly abandoned chronos as a way of exhausting the possibilities of the compact three day retreat; the point is also to physically, mentally, and emotionally (as well as religiously, as a result) exhaust the candidates as a way of breaking down their inhibitions. Avner was kind enough to point out that this separation from time and its attendant sleep deprivation is the same tactic used in interrogation programs (torture?) for the purpose of disorienting victims in an attempt to solicit information. Fair enough. We might think of Kairos the retreat as a bit of torture, considering Church history (read: The Spanish Inquisition for starters), and the assumption still written into the sacrament of confirmation that men and women entering the

Church as adults are to become soldiers for Christ. There were absolutely moments of immense pain on the retreats.

The larger point for now, though, is that the school places great value on the Kairos retreats. Every senior is encouraged to attend. Every senior goes. This is a mix of coercion (the alternative is a mandatory one day encounter with Father Tim; a senior retreat *will* be made, Kairos is the preferred mode of delivery) and the mythic lore that is built up around the experience. When the retreats occur—six times throughout the school year—teachers of upperclassmen are requested to make accommodations to the instructional schedule so that candidates and leaders don't miss vital information. This means that from Tuesday to Friday over six weeks out of the school year, the entire senior class—with a few rare exceptions when teachers find creative ways to deal with the inconvenience—is sidetracked wholly from the work of scaffolded content. Those left behind on chronos end up marking linear time with a whole lot of movies. The interruption of classes amounts to almost an entire quarter, mind.

In addition, teachers who wish to help in planning and attending the retreat are welcome, indeed encouraged, to volunteer (and they do, fairly readily) and since candidates receive letters from past retreatants as a major part of the mystique, all members of the school (including boys who have not yet gone and aren't supposed to know about the letters, but inevitably find out) engage in a frenzy of surreptitious epistolary affirmation in the weeks before a send-off. Each team of leaders and candidates, at the conclusion of the retreat, is given a hooded sweatshirt that reads "St. Monica Kairos" on its front with the unique number of the retreat, preceded by the letter "K" to denote when they've attended on the obverse side. This is a convenient way of cataloging the school's ongoing belief in the power and influence of the thing. I was fortunate to lead K96 and K97, so this is a long-standing tradition and one that heavily influences the ways the school thinks about itself. It also affects the ways students think about and come to connect with the school. The sweatshirt, much like the tattoos that came later, becomes totemic of a Monicaman's having passed through the vision quest that was Kairos. He was a different man on that retreat; the sweatshirt is a ready reminder that he is part of an exclusive club.

To assume that a retreat sponsored and run by the school, designed by its leadership, and shaped by its religious ideals is actually a retreat from the tendrils of the place would be naïve. What I will suggest, though, is that the actual move in physical space, shifted from 77th and Western to Plano, Illinois, allows the boys latitude in their masculine projects. The administration at St. Monica looked to (and talked about) the retreat in terms of lasting religious formation.

Fr. Tim is director of vocations for the Augustinian friars; the hope is something so vital would bring boys to the old model of the ultimate male in the Church: the priesthood. The school would settle, of course for renewed religious devotion and Monicamen leading a spiritual community among themselves. This was their ideal, their masculine model. The boys reflected back a very different picture.

Soja (1996) ciphers for Baudrillard in writing of simulacra, by noting that "as our ability to tell the difference between what is real and what is imagined weakens, another kind of reality—a hyperreality—flourishes" (p. 238). The Kairotic, for these St. Monica seniors, is a hyperreality of interconnectedness, furious prayerfulness, and emotive bombast. It is where their discursive masculinity within St. Monica the school meets and clashes with the intensive heterotopia that is a retreat into another, smaller and differently delineated St. Monica: that of the idealized, open, and uncloaked Monicaman who willingly espouses his belief in Christ, his respect for women, and his love for his brothers. And no one calls him a fag for this loving, though it may be the closest to an erotic/spiritual homosociality that he approaches out in the open in his time in high school. There is still a level of trepidation regarding the experience regardless of the legend.

In early September, while sitting in history class not learning about Teddy Roosevelt, I overheard Jack and Chunk talking about Kairos. It was my first encounter with students that dealt with the retreat. This is understandable since only a small percentage of the senior class had yet attended the week away. Of necessity, as a way to maintain a candidate count of roughly thirty per Kairos retreat, Campus Ministry holds five senior retreats a year, and the sixth is exclusively for juniors so that there will be leaders available for the first retreat of the next school year when the junior class has moved into their end-of-days at the school. The scuttlebutt around Kairos hadn't reached the fever pitch resultant from the initial October candidates' ebullient return. One of the rumors that has always surrounded the experience is that there exists a naked mass.[5] This is one of the "surprises" of the retreat and its aura of mystery hangs over the candidates. In the context of St. Monica High School, the marked queerness that was the possibility of a naked Mass served as a frightening force; while on the retreat, this notion of fear would have felt just as absurd. I realize more and more just how odd a concept this is.

What actually occurs is "Mass as they've never experienced it before," where in a bit of comic theater, the leaders of the trip confront the candidates in the chapel wearing only towels and ask if there is trust in the room. Two long days deep into the timelessness that is Kairos, the candidates inevitably say "yes" and are then told (because they know the rumor of "naked Mass") to start to strip. There is some mumbling and worried laughter, but they were asked/ordered to trust and so they do. Socks first. They are stopped before they get completely naked—though on K96 we did have boys in boxers and nothing else—and told that the Mass will actually be a teaching Mass. This is an informative, though torturous because it is at the end of two sleepless days, three-hour affair where Fr. Tim explains all the symbolism and history behind the ritual of Catholic services. That the boys on the retreat are so willing to be naked in the presence of others bespeaks the odd absence of fag discourse on the retreat. This bears further examination,[6] but let us return to the classroom and Chunk and Jack:

> Chunk: [who later led K96 after attending K95] "I heard there was a naked mass."
> Jack: [who later led K98 after attending K96] With a bit of bravado mixed with nerves. He wants to be right, here." They don't do that; it's just to scare you."
> Chunk: "My brother told me, like five people were sitting around all just crying on it. That's so gay."

And of course, in the realm of the school this emotional breakdown would be quickly reigned in by the rigors of fag discourse. It would, indeed, be gay. Prior to their retreat, both boys were certain that they would at best endure the experience (this was the tenor of the remainder of the conversation as I heard it) and certainly not cry—nor, gasp, get naked—rooted as they were in the spliced notions that to emote in such a way was abnormal and feminine, thus made gay. Their tune after the retreat changed. As did mine after my first foray into God's time. In a sense, we were all very much laid bare.

My Kairos

I was a senior in college and had been on the waiting list for the Kairos retreats presented under the auspices of the Ignatian Society (a collection of alums from Jesuit high schools who incorporated their experience into both club and continuation of their own fondness for their secondary schools at the college level; we all found it sort of annoying and cliquey, but they ran Kairos, so…) from the beginning of my first year in Boston. I'd waited and been wicked impatient about it. But in October of 2001 I had finally gotten the nod. It was, you'll recall, a tumultuous time.

Beyond the rhetoric of a united front and the calls of "we will never forget," the United States was in economic freefall and New York was still under what we might best call martial law in the wake of 9/11 and the subsequent anthrax mail scares. Bombings had begun in Afghanistan and between classes we roommates of four years paired in half dozens in adjoining suites in Rubenstein Hall, spent hours glued to CNN. There were whispers of a revived draft. Lost in my own father's military shadow, I had inklings of enlisting. As well, I had a scheduled interview with General Mills, but no suit to complete the picture of corporate aspiration. All was a-muddled, in other words and life seemed huge; graduation loomed. It felt like the right time to step away. God, they always said, called you to Kairos when you were supposed to go.

Seven of the twelve of our suitemates had attended all-boys Catholic high schools. Nine of the twelve had by this point made a Kairos retreat, half had subsequently returned to lead them. Omar, a practicing Muslim of Palestinian origins, had politely passed; Mikulitz just didn't give a shit. Which meant that I was the last one and after all of the build-up from eight years of legend (high school *and* college), it was pure relief to finally step on the bus and head to the bucolic Green Mountains to find God.

I narrate this not to speak of religious revelation, though it may well have occurred on my part (or behalf). Rather, I write it as a bit of confession. Apropos, I suppose, given that word's religious connotations and Foucault's enduring critique of its function, as well as its clear influence on the structure of the retreat. This research has felt, all year, very much like a visitation to avatars of past selves; nowhere more so than on Kairos. And so to see the seniors sob their way through their candidacy—especially as their world degraded into the tumult of recession and war, even as they thought about endeavoring into a big and wide and confusing universe beyond St. Monica—felt hard. It was, in essence, a challenge to get distance which is why I became increasingly enamored of the closeness built into autoethnography. Distance is impossible. It punctures me to critique the experience.

The details of my moments on God's time in college are mostly moot here. Suffice to say I cried a great deal and felt religiously convicted (in both senses of the word) and skipped my General Mills interview to take on the challenge of a teaching life. I made peace with the memory of my father, his twenty-one-gun salute, the horse-drawn caisson, the monochromatic grave marker overlooking the Pentagon at Arlington National Cemetery. I didn't enlist. Or rather I enlisted in a different kind of service.

I also started wearing the scapular again; later, at twenty-seven, I got the Jerusalem Cross (symbol of the Kairos retreat at Boston College) tattooed at the base of my neck, a reminder of a passage from Thomas Merton that begs us to attend to the fact that "we do not exist for ourselves." But I didn't start going to Mass regularly, I still prayed half-heartedly: At most, I reengaged with the paraliturgical and began a journey of teaching religion with my fingers crossed behind my back. Some of my motivation for entering into this research project, if I'm to be honest, was to try to make sense of this hypocrisy: I don't believe in the story behind the scapular, though I will always wear it because its tradition is part of who I was growing up.[7] I am increasingly aware that the cross on a whole—but particularly the one at my back, for its second name is the "Crusader's Cross," given as it was to those misguided and murderous knights who hacked their way to Jerusalem in red rage against a dehumanized other— as symbol can rightly mean "two millennia of bloody crusades and pogroms" (Carroll, 2001, p. 15) but there it remains, buried in pigment below my agnostic skin. So I got that the boys were devastated on their retreat, and I got that they wore scapulars and had the Augustinian crucifix needled into arms and legs, but I needed more: to understand, to survive my own contradictions, masculine and spiritual.

Plano, Illinois: Off the Bus

Halting time, God or no God, takes quite a bit of work. After ninety plus retreats, however, St. Monica has it down pretty well. From the moment the candidates step off of the bus in Plano they are regimented to the minute, from Tuesday's opening until Friday evening's closing back at the school in the chapel. The overall structure of the retreat involves talks, given by adult and student leaders, followed by small-group discussions co-facilitated by peers meant to allow or force candidates to deal with the topics of the preceding talk.

Each day involves a Mass of the Eucharist, prayer is led by students at each meal, and there is about as much free time over the course of the days as there is sleep. Neither exceeds ten hours. The constant movement, the lack of a discernible schedule, and the missing watches and cell phones (and computers and video game equipment) build a relationship of dependence in the candidates: they are to follow the orders of the leaders and, as they no longer have time, their orientation to themselves begins to break down. New ways of being, of relating, of discussing become rapidly possible. Small groups, further, are decided upon before the retreat occurs and are organized to separate close friends and to account for ethnic diversity (race and grammar school being a strong determining factor for who hangs out with whom back at Monica).

The onus of the retreat is on the individual: what will you do differently? How will you reflect? How are you neglecting God and your self? The talks are harangues disguised as personal testimonials. Because they are dressed with filigreed care in the confessional mode, candidates are trained from the first "share" that they are to disclose. Nightly leader meetings function as check-ins to ensure that people are sharing. If they aren't, they may be pulled aside by a leader to "see what is wrong," which is really a way of forcing dissidents into line. All of this is coded in the language of attending to the self. A hyperreality of (solicited) openness and emotion necessarily occurs. Both are manufactured by the format of the retreat, or by God, depending on how you choose to believe.

It is worth revisiting the purpose of mining Kairos here. Seniors who have gone, as well as alums who return to the school, speak of the experience as the time when they were most or first cauterized to St. Monica High School. More than anything, it is when they come to think of themselves finally as Monicamen, and that this occurs in a space that is outside of the schoolday and beyond athletics is intriguing. In a great many ways, also, Kairos is the capstone of the experience of what could be called mission and ministry at the school.

The retreat from chronos, from school, is what ends up linking them indelibly with the place of St. Monica High School. This occurs as they, seniors, prepare to move into, society tells them, the real world and it is in this Kairos space, too, that they are able to try on roles and friendships and emotions absent from/otherwise articulate in the discourses of all-maleness of their high school experience. They are changed by the heterotopia of a time without time where they are compelled to encounter Christ as within themselves and within others. That this—the retreat as a space apart, embraced by the boys—occurs suggests to me that alternative spaces could be set up within the school itself where students might engage in thoughtful discussions about the function of and issues surrounding, for example the regulatory function of fag discourse and its attendant resulting limitations for/on masculinities. Similarly, it provides a window into the kind of discursive possibilities regarding women and gender expectations on the whole, should the school wish to pursue such ends outside of the Kairos retreat. In other words, the Kairos experience is viewed as an interruption of the real life of the school. It might be leveraged to interrupt in more fruitful ways, more often, and at the building of the school itself.

Kergyma: A Conservative Project

What I will choose to argue, though, is that Kairos is the school's way of not dealing with these things—the messiness of boys-emotional, the dehumanization of racism and gender discrimination, all topics spoken of and cried over on Kairos—on an extended level. Or rather, it's a convenient mode of replicating the kind of sexism and homophobia present in chronos by encasing in amber forays into liberality of feeling and expression on the Kairos weekend. It is a convenient space for ghettoizing emotional openness, engagement with critical gender work, and personal religious revelation. The boys continually and violently cry thinking about the ways that their mothers and fathers love them. Or fail to. They talk about how much they care for their girlfriends. They hug each other and hold hands. All of this goes back underground upon return to the school. As it was the only curricular space in which students were compelled to discuss issues such as masculine expectations placed upon them by society, or their treatment of the women in their lives, or even their faith as a personal journey over the course of their four years, we find that the retreat is really a way to engage issues in an alternative space (and reality) and then to leave them there. Because we always have to return to chromos, and this clever splitting of time makes it very easy for kids to come back from Kairos (the term is Kai-high), leaving all the discursive openness of their moments away within the vortex of timelessness that was three days apart. God's time, in essence, where they find themselves, exists apart from the school and from life at home, and to talk and hug and sob like a being on a Kairos retreat would mean serious social sanction back at St. Monica.

The cathexis of the weekend ends up becoming reintegrated into a loyalty to the school and to the Monica brothers encountered differently in Plano. The love of brotherhood and school comes back from the retreat on the bus with the boys, in effect; the crying, hugging, prayerful openness does not. Why, though?

It begins with the student leaders. Each leader is assigned a talk of approximately fifteen minutes or so. Each talk is bracketed by two songs chosen by the student as an intro and outro. This is a meme repeated throughout the week, to the point where candidates know to become silent the moment the first song plays, as it means the leader is descending the stairs into the basement room used for group gatherings, to share. The second song signals the end of the talk and a collective deep breath at the close of an emotional rollercoaster.

From the first talk, candidates are taught by the example of the leaders that they are to all get up and give the leader who has just spoken a hug for sharing. It's a form of release and a way to thank them for opening up to the voyeurism in the room. Awkward at first, the mass hugs get more and more teary as the days melt into each other. This is, ultimately, about creating a pattern and a disciplinary structure. After the talk, small groups are formed as a way for students to share their stories in relation to the one told by the leader, who has primed the emotional pump. Once this is complete, there is a short break to refill on food and have a smoke, and then reload: new leader, new talk, same song structure, same hugs, and the repetition begins to wear them down. They share.[8]

And the leaders bear/bare their souls. On the retreats I attended one boy spoke of losing his father and then his stepfather before the age of fourteen. Another talked of his elder brother's death by heroin overdose; one admitted to failing his friends in the room when they needed him most because of his own arrogance, still others mourn their own addictions to alcohol or other drugs, some even lamented their own lack of respect for their girlfriends and mothers. One boy spoke of his role in an almost-race-riot and the humanizing intervention of a counseling program that brokered peace between black and white participants. These are deep-set secrets. None of these tales are discussed in the course of the school day at St. Monica. The leaders cry as they talk, their audience sobs; the small groups begin to bond. It's a process of wearing down wariness at first, and from there it's almost necessary to reign in the sharing as boys pour out all of their concerns, and fears, and deaths, injuries, shortcomings. No one sleeps because they are furiously journaling or communing in late-night ad hoc gatherings. This is the only place they find where that kind of sharing has been made possible. There is snot everywhere. Boys pray voluntarily and in groups and they start to try to figure out what they're feeling.

All is in the confessional mode, understandable when considering Foucault's (1990a) historical view that "the confession became one of the West's most highly valued techniques for producing truth" (p. 59). There is, repeated by the boys, the compulsion to judge Kairos as the time when they finally realized who they really were. This would not occur, they insist, were it not for the Monica brothers who accompanied them on the journey; they are brothers who shared openly of themselves and in the end confessed to major shortcomings. Their truth has been produced.

At the outset, candidates are prompted as they listen to "Be open. Be Honest. Let Go." and "Let God." The rest takes care of itself.[9] To a (wo)man, each leader speaks about his or her (female faculty attend) story—tragic tales mostly, but not always—and the way that they realized who they really were and how they were failing themselves/their parents/their God on their own Kairos retreat. It's a nice little tautological argument for the effectiveness of Kairos: Kairos was where I found myself; if you follow the directives we've given you, you will find yourself as well; if you don't, well, you didn't open up enough to God on Kairos. Surrounded by the messiness of the confessional mode, boys come to share and to rethink their orientations to people around them. It's all a bit of clever manipulation, which isn't to belittle the intensity of the experience for the students: this is where they find a space to share in ways they couldn't at home, at school, in the world. No one ever asks why this level of emoting happens only on retreat, though, because Kairos is God's time and we're outside of chronos and so things are easier here. "One confesses," Foucault (1990a) insists:

> In public and in private...in pleasure and pain, things it would be impossible to tell to anyone else...One confesses—or is forced to confess. When it is not spontaneous or dictated by some internal imperative, the confession is wrung from a person by...threat. (p. 59)

Familiar with the confessional from their lifelong engagement with the sacramentality within the Church—confession is offered in the chapel at Advent and Lent; students miss gym to attend, whether they confess with a priest or not—the boys are well-exposed to the form. They are also familiar with the absolution that comes with the sharing of hidden sins. Kairos, by modeling through leadership the kind of confessional it requires and then producing small-group situations where boys are compelled to confess of their own darkest regions, is essentially an orgy of reparative talk. It is confession writ large and primed by four years of hearing about the life-changing process of Kairos, so the boys take the moment and run with it. Their stories are unique and their emotions are real, but the space is carefully manufactured precisely to avoid any genuine spontaneity. Indeed, a boy on the second retreat, told the leaders on the second day that "it fucking sucked" being there. He was told to get in line or to call his mother to pick him up. He did neither, and on the final day, thanked his parents and his Monica brothers for the experience. His confession came. It was demanded.

The "counter-site" of Kairos has to end in its physical reality for the boys after their Tuesday to Friday journey, however. They cannot exist in the heterotopic space anymore. Soja (1996), cribbing from Foucault writes of the heterotopic as various spaces beyond time "in which all other real sites within...culture are 'simultaneously represented contested, and inverted'" (p. 195). The senior Kairos retreat represents the school and is fostered by its Campus Ministry, and yet the work of the week is an inversion of the traditional discourses present in the school and at school-sponsored events. All is in relation and opposition to regular time. The idea that they are on Kairos and not at school is hammered home every time the students pray together and sing openly, or almost get naked, or try to look at a watch that isn't there.

This is not forever though because, well, Plano isn't home and it's too expensive to house students out there. Chronos beckons, as does the school and the life the discourses of which the boys have subverted over the course of three days (no one has been fagged, no penises are drawn, no women belittled in public spaces). Which of course means that the problem of stepping back into chronos must be addressed. The retreat accounts for it this way: there are three days of the experience filled with leader talks. The final talk is entitled *The Fourth Day*. It is during this leader's confession that we are told that the fourth day of Kairos is the rest of our lives. It is up to us, it turns out, to recreate Kairos in our world back at school, at home, on the playing field, in life at large. The fourth day, we are told, exists as long as we want it to. Or as briefly. It is on the individual. We are already moving away from the collective, the reformation of new friendships, new religious discourses, a hugging, crying masculinity is rendered immediately fragile. The improbability of "living the 4th" weighs on us suddenly.

On Friday, candidates and leaders are greeted in a secret closing ceremony back at St. Monica in the chapel. Here, parents and family of the students are present as well as Monicamen who have made the retreat in the past. When candidates enter they are cheered first, as heroes returning. From there, team leaders present them with wooden crucifixes symbolic of the weekend. Before everyone is free to leave and collapse into sleep, all the candidates are compelled to speak, from the altar, about their experiences. One final confession. They are told that all of the love that has been given to them by the community, in letters most especially ought to be reciprocated. A compulsion to tell parents they are loved is conveyed.

They inevitably thank their parents for the letters[10] that were sent, and for the opportunity to attend the retreat and St. Monica High School, but what most prominently comes out of this final fitful bit of openness is a need to talk about their new Monica brothers, gathered at the foot of the altar, in the shadow of the Augustinian cross hanging behind them, who have helped them through this harrowing reckoning with their own shortcomings and the difficulties of their coming-to-be on Kairos. Then that's it. They are sent home.

Fr. Tim reminds the parents that "if you sent a slob, you'll be getting a slob back," and he's right. The lessons of Kairos, all that openness, all that crying and hugging, and all those entreaties to live the Christian life in community by and large end there. Students might return to lead the retreat, and a surprising percentage of them most certainly will get tattoos of crosses to indicate their loyalty to the personal relationship with Jesus, but come Monday they are back in the space of fagging, the space of school and the space of symbolic women who are impossible. The inversion on return to 77th and Western, is neatly undone and it begins as we disperse for home when the boys are handed back their watches and their cell phones. Chronos and its discourses come with the trappings of linear time.

The neat trick is that much of Kairos is a secret. This means that the letters written to candidates from parents and family and friends who have attended the retreat are revealed on the second day of the experience. Too, the shared prayer and reconciliation as well as the Friday closing are explicitly kept from non-candidates. Leaders remain a mystery until the bus arrives in Plano. This builds the mystique of the retreat for younger students, certainly, but it also ensures that all that happens on Kairos cannot be discussed openly after the retreat, in the school. So any attempt to build frank conversations about religion or gender or sexism, which are engaged with constantly on the retreat, has no space in the school because the secret is paramount: it makes the retreat explosive for new candidates. The 4th day becomes a personal journey at best. Which is ok, but it bespeaks the school's usage of the retreat as an essentially conservative project. The secret of the retreat limits its scope in potentially reforming spaces in the school.

At the closing, Fr. Tim describes to the parents a bit of what occurs from Tuesday until early Friday. He suggests that for those few three days the boys lived together in genuine Christian community "perhaps for the first time in their lives." Two points of note: first that the Christian community is, just like the school, an exclusively male space[11] and second that it occurs on Kairos but not in chronos. As they leave the retreat the boys are being trained already to know that they are to contain much of what they encountered in the remembered space that was the retreat itself. They are, in essence, done retreating and now must move forward back into the discourses of a world that will have little patience for the emotion, the honesty, or the confession of the retreat. They were different kinds of Christian men on Kairos, and their, OUR, tattoos are desperate grasps at a remembered heterotopia where masculinity takes on a very different discursive function. It is no wonder, then, that candidates eagerly apply to lead (to go back to timelessness!) and write letters for their friends with such verve.

In Christian theological studies, the Kerygma is the "basic story of Jesus" as it "took shape in the first months and years after his death" (Carroll, 2001, p. 25). This is one way to account for the different versions of the Gospels—both sanctioned and apocryphal—which are best considered Carroll argues "history remembered" or "prophecy historicized" (p. 129). This is one way, in other words, that the birth narratives of Jesus came to be. The first Gospel authors didn't find the story of the birth compelling (or necessary), but as the discursive function of the Christ came to be shaped in history, the tale of the birth (the census, the shepherds, the guiding star, all of it) bubbled up from the surface borrowed in bits from other legends and religious traditions as a way to comment on his adult meaning. This is mythology. Just as I believe the tale of St. Simon Stock seeing the Virgin at Mt. Carmel is mythology; just as I believe the historical woman St. Monica's stigmata is mythical." But to assign the birth narratives" or any religious wonder tale, I'd say, "to mythology is not to dismiss them as untrue" (Spong, 1992, p. 45).

In the lives of the Monicamen, and in my life as well, Kairos becomes integrated into our own humble kergyma. It is part of how our history is remembered by us and it suffuses the basic outlines of our faiths (lapsing, vibrant, or otherwise). Beyond that, it's mythic and impossible for its fleeting heterotopic inversion of the discourses we navigate daily, weekly, in life at large. That it's impossible and mythic, though, doesn't mean that the confessional space was invalid. No. Instead, we might think of the process and experience of Kairos as more of the Carnivalesque, as "a pageant without footlights and without a division into performers and spectators" where "everyone is an active participant, everyone communes in the carnival act," which is "not even performed; [rather] its participants *live* in it, they live by its laws as long as those laws are in effect" (Bakhtin, 1998, p. 250). We all were complicit, were alive in Kairos, in the writing of letters, in the setting aside time, in the demands of confession and emotion and then, poof, with the reintroduction of chronological reality again, the laws fell away.

I'm intending, in other words, to call to light the ways that the school manipulates the concept of split systems of time—the *carnivalistic life*— to isolate certain more or less unsanctioned or undesirable masculine traits/failings to a space beyond the school. This is the opportune moment for the maintenance of the patriarchal: Kairos as Carnival, as a heterotopic space, fleeting and very much unreal upon reflection.

Kairos, I think, is a conservative project for St. Monica High School. It is a week that unintentionally, in its earliest iterations at least, came to bond the young men of the school with the tradition of the place. It is a way to engage in theology in a different space and it's part of selling vocational formation to the young men. The boys read this. What they miss most, though, after their time in leaving Kairos—and this is the continual bond rooted in paraliturgical devotion—is the open community where it is finally safe to be vulnerable, to be effeminate in the sense of being emotionally available, and to "find" oneself. They come to tether the school with the opportunity to attend (to) this new and fleeting discourse and much of their religious faith stems from a desire to be back in the heterotopia of Kairos. Tattoos, like Kairos, are timeless. Scapulars don't end. They are not classroom management. Individual masses end and sleeping (or praying in a sleeping pose) still gets them scolded. To be a Monicaman finishing up after four years, we find, is to pine for the space apart where the "true" person, the man they could be, is revealed—vulnerable, open, religious, confessional, and awash with emotion—ironic in its/his careful construction by the school.

Notes

[1] The legend of St. Monica relies heavily on her initial rejection from the convent after the gangland deaths of her husband and sons. The Mothers superior feared an invasion of secular violence into the Pax Christi of the religious sanctuary. Troubled by the impression of her family, Monica had a vision while praying that her "three heavenly patrons" told her "there was but one more thing to do" and the "gift of peace…would unlock the doors of Saint Mary Magdalene Convent" (Di Gregorio, 2003, p. 30-31). Emerging from her trance, she sought her extended family and brokered a peace with the neighboring Mancini family, bringing an end to generations of sabotage and murder on par with, one presumes, the Hatfields and the McCoys. Sufficiently appeased, the leaders of the convent allowed Monica entry to the novitiate and she became the peacemaker evermore.

[2] This is of particular interest to me as a pedagogue and nascent scholar in teacher education because the boys provide a trenchant analysis of the quality (or rather its lack) of the curricu-

lum they endure at Monica, most particularly in the senior year. Josh, a student in e-music class with me told me from the start that I "should write about how St. Monica is the worst school around." Kimani mimicked a popular platitude among the students when I began following him, smiling, "Welcome to daycare, Mr. Burke." And, finally, as Scott settled in for a nap during one of the many movies shown in his history class, he was told, "Hey, this isn't the Holiday Inn." Gallows humor to a T, he shrugged, "It's the St. Monica Inn. We're getting serious value for education here." Why send your son to St. Monica, then, knowing this? So he can continue the tradition.

3   A space one might presume to find in the sacred space of the chapel, say. But fagging and dicking and women-debasing were all constantly in play at the fringe of the pews, though quietly. These were not discourses that could be checked at the doors, even while dipping a familiar hand in holy water and sanctifying oneself with the sign of the cross. Nope, this was still part of school, no matter how much the administration tried to jazz up the practice with modern music and guest speakers. Kairos allowed them to leave behind the discursive traditions that limited bodily and spiritual familiarity back at the school in ways that church never did.

4   Student leaders for the Kairos retreats are chosen by Campus Ministry from applicants who have already attended the experience themselves. Students, and adults, actually, who are attending Kairos for the first time are called "candidates."

5   Though I will go further into my own extensive history with the Kairos experience momentarily, it is worth noting here that the naked mass rumor existed when I was in high school myself—though my high school didn't hold the retreats—and floated too through the buildings of my Jesuit university as well.

6   Why a naked Mass? I assume it has origins in the beginnings of the Kairos retreat and may have something to do with the early Disciples of Christ being fully submerged, naked, for their Baptism as they "died," shedding their old life, to emerge from the pool into new life as Christians. But it takes on a different significance at an all-boys' school of course, because all nakedness as I found, was especially charged. That the event was really no big deal while it occurred struck me as emblematic of the temporary out-of-timeness that they boys were experiencing.

7   Men in the Beverly neighborhood start wearing their scapulars, rolled up in a style I've not seen replicated elsewhere, from early grammar school. This enables them to last long after the pictures on lithographed paper inside have disintegrated through the sweat and showers of countless nights. I have had them rolled for me by my father, my brother, my friends. I have rolled them for my nephews and my male students. It's a bit like the laying on of a mantle; a symbol of maleness handed down through the ranks. It will always remind me of home, and the men in my life who I have loved. Occasionally it reminds me to pray, to whom I do not know, but still the words come.

8   It's important for me to assert that I do think that Kairos is an important experience for the seniors. They do speak in subtle and wrenching ways about the pressures and failures (and successes and dreams) in their lives. There is an odd community of sharing that's formed

and I was proud of the leaders and the candidates on their time away. Clearly, as evidenced by my tattoo and continuing will to help out on the retreat (I gave one of those talks I'm analyzing here), I'm of a mind to believe that something important occurs. That doesn't mean, however, that I'm not struck now by how carefully managed and manipulated the emotion and soul-baring really is. Nor does it mean that I'm not deeply troubled that what feels very possible for young men on Kairos is immediately impossible again once they step back into "chronos."

9   Not really, of course. The week is heavily planned and the product of ninety-plus trial and errors before it. It appears natural to the candidates, though, particularly because time has been taken away.

10 We might call Kairos an epistolary retreat. A month before a given retreat occurs, the Campus Minister sends out missives to families of candidates requesting that parents, siblings, extended family, and friends write letters about their love for their son/brother, etc. They come in piles and one of the big reveals of the retreat is this packet of letters showing the boys just how important they are to the people back on chronos. It's a beautiful moment, actually. But the form also ensures that the conversations that might happen upon return, are first fixed in writing, which, to my mind, makes them more difficult to talk about because the template has been set. Parents and friends write what they cannot say aloud. Kairos both encourages and entombs the conversation in script. Krondorfer (2010) writes of "confessiographies" that "mediate intimacies…the written from…transforms inarticulate experiences into speech, body into voice."

11 Spong (1992) writes of the erasure of women from the Gospels over the course of their development. In Paul's letter to the Corinthians he asks, "Do we not have the right to be accompanied by a wife, as the other apostles and the brothers of the Lord and [Peter]?" (p. 189). The idea being that women were present, of course, but remain nameless, subjugated for the purpose of building a narrative about the male bond of Jesus and the Apostles. One of those bonds, recall, led to perhaps the most famous denial in history, not to mention the betrayal that caused it. Friends like these…

Chapter 7

Make Me a Fucking Sandwich

Making Sense of the Research(er)

The sights and sounds of boys at play have correlated with my efforts to capture the lives of boys, in particular the movement, the aggression, the competition, the rivalries, the friendships, and the muscular eroticism that inform boys' lives.

Ken Corbett, "Boyhoods"

We've got to develop relationships with these kids, and relationships involve feelings, not simply content or information.

Peter McLaren, "Cries From the Corridor"

We must not look for who has the power in the order of sexuality (men, adults, parents, doctors) and who is deprived of it (women, adolescents, children, patients); nor for who has the right to know and who is forced to remain ignorant. We must seek rather the pattern of the modifications which the relationships of force imply by the very nature of their process.

Michel Foucault, "Method"

I suppose it's fair to say that I had, in spite of myself, liberatory ideals coming into this project. As much as I'm of a mind that research such as this is really about exposing the workings of dialogism and its effects in the lived and breathed masculinities and religions of the boys at the school, still I pretended to (hide my) emancipatory claims. I couldn't help it; I've years of liberation theology encoded in me. To this end, I will suggest a call for the usage of "flash interviews" as minimally invasive instruments for helping subjects engage with their own voices and knowledges within research contexts. First, though, I need to deal with the interruption that was me.

This means, really, that I got heavily involved in the world (their homes, their loves, their spiritual struggles, their mistakes and triumphs) of the students at St. Monica. It was inevitable. They adopted me (and I, them; perhaps too uncritically on both sides). I became a curiosity for the faculty, but most particularly for the students as they jostled to read my notes, to laugh at their being quoted, and to figure out how I felt about them. I identified with their struggles, gave them my phone number to catch up on athletic updates, became a target of their late-night-drunken-reveries, and begged them not to drive in altered/drunken states. I worried. They came to feel like younger siblings—there was one exception and I'll take time in a moment to deal with his case—and it was often difficult to parse my developing emotional connection to their battle to thrive in an increasingly complex world from a need to be critical in my data creation. Theoretical frameworks, fortunately, account for messiness and this messiness, I suppose, became my data.

What follows here is a brief look at the ways the boys negotiated the presence of a researcher in their social and schooled lives. I will propose that, in the end, their making sense of me—and my coming to establish myself in the school and with them as subjects/friends/students—had a great deal to do with (the pursuit of/the clash for) mastery. Foucault (1990b) makes a great deal of the Greeks and the valuation of a masculinity of moderation. The highest order of a man, in effect, was one who could take what and all that he wanted (sexually or otherwise; with boys and women or both) but chose instead the self-controlled middle road of ethical restraint. He was, in the view of Isocrates, "capable of moderating the power he exercises over others by means of the mastery he establishes over himself" (p. 174). Power, in this theory, equals the possibility of domination as well as the benevolent (mostly) employment of its tendrils, beginning with domination of self and desire and extending outward to peers. We were all seeking to lead in some way at the school, and some of what fag discourse and the sublimation of real women (in service of their Mythical mothers and sisters, frozen in amber by tales easily controlled and edited by administration and utilized in prayer and devotion constantly by the boys) helped us to do was show that we were "completely in command of [our]selves" (p. 81), just as we affected and de/limited the actions of those around us at the lunch table, in the classroom or through the hallways.

The purpose is to illustrate, as thoroughly as possible in a very brief space, how much a researcher such as myself came to matter to and have an effect on the data presented. I became, in no small way, some part of how they developed their masculine selves. As an agent both of the school and of an indeterminate origin beyond it—most of the Monicamen couldn't figure out how I was surviving if not employed by the school, no matter how many times I explained my situation to them—I was a liminal agent through which the boys might reimagine the possibilities of masculine adulthood. I hope not to overstate this but I do feel I was read uniquely and my embeddedness helped the boys consider me (and themselves) possible in different ways. That I had no disciplinary role in their lives was confusing and freeing and that I was willing to engage in conversations that challenged or questioned those discourses that felt normalized (fagging, dicking, distancing from women) opened up a unique opportunity for them to examine and become meta-cognitive about their development as men. Flash interviews amidst the flow of their days were vital for this. They became, in essence, willing characters in the dissertation-that-was-their-lives. My intervention was not necessarily intentional and I have no measure to suggest that I've "altered" their masculine and spiritual development beyond the conversations I will examine here.

Still, as research, just like teaching, involves a certain manner of seduction in order to exist, I will look at ways in which the boys were seduced by the presence of a researcher. Further, I will have to, then, take up the case of one student who resisted this seduction and how that affected my status in the school as I became a victim of bullying and what that meant for my own masculinity and the way power was given meaning in my life. I want to delve into three specific realms of making sense here which all have to do with the negotiation of multiplicities of power relations. The first begins with a picture.

Shalom!

In my third month, while following Tim, I spent my 6th and final period each day seated next to a young man named Murph. Later, I would come to know Murph very well through Kairos and lacrosse[1] but on this sleepy day in November I knew little about him aside from his penchant for needling teachers with an elusive sense of humor. Perhaps he liked me because I laughed at his jokes; maybe he was just bored; I suspect though that it was something more. At any rate, in the midst of a discussion about the context under which the novel *Frankenstein* was written, he turned to me and said below the drone of the teacher he was ignoring, "Mr. Burke. I'm gonna draw you a picture."

And he did. For the better part of the period. In some ways I felt guilty that he wasn't catching the import of Mary Shelley's formation as a Romanticist and the specific situations of her cautionary tale about blind scientific ambition. But really I was curious about the picture.

Figure 2: BFFL (Courtesy Tom Murphy)

He handed it to me on our way out of class and I ended up taping it up on the wall of my office, amidst the other detritus passed to me throughout the year. It wasn't rare in its being given to me by the students—they were constantly passing me notes or leaving them in my bag. The following is more or less representative of the message I'd get:

Figure 3: Grammar! (Courtesy Tom Riordan):

What was unique, though, about what Murph handed me was the detail. It's not my intention to do a full visual analysis of the contents of the piece, though there is rich ground to be tilled there (from our muscularity and the homosociality of a shared waterski line, to the bikini-clad girls waving from the desert island, not to mention poor Matt Moss who is being devoured by a wayward shark). Rather, I want to use this picture and the note from Chunk—its unused contraction, grating to my English teacher eyes, still—to stand in for all of the materials handed me by the young men of St. Monica over the course of this year in the school. The function of these pieces of looseleaf folk art, different in kind and form from the other art prevalent among students (penises mostly, but also crosses on paper and skin) was to remind me that they—the students I wasn't explicitly following—were present and worthy of inclusion in the text I was composing. Also, it was a way of confirming for the students that I was different from a teacher, but also not-quite-a-student. I never saw notes nor pictures passed between students and never, certainly, saw them passed between students to teachers. For some reason I filled that space. And much of that had to do with the fact that the boys liked the attention. These notes and drawings were, in a sense, a form of courting me.

These were spaces that the boys were able to examine and try on seductive homoerotic roles: to find love, sex, even if only the prurient elusive possibility of either or both. It's probably telling that of all of the notes and pictures that I received, all but one came from a student with whom I'd experience/d Kairos. And of course Kairos is (made to be) all about (the fleeting expression of) love. Plato uses the character Xenophon to aid Socrates in elaborating a dual notion of true love, which turns upon the difference between "love of the soul and love of the body" (Foucault, 1990b, p. 233). What Murph mixes in his display of "full-bodied muscular eroticism colored by vigorous exhibitionism" (Corbett, 2009, p. 14), his peers like O'Dea, Dunbar, and Chunk further plumb with their brief and variously un/ambiguous love notes. Couched in a debate about the relative social value of "boy" love, "Plato puts this question aside [and] raises the question of what it means to love" (Foucault, 1990b, p. 236). This is some of what the boys are trying to figure out, through the researcher who presents a unique situation at the school: an outsider with insider knowledge who readily engages them at the level of their own productive realities and presents no readily available sanctions when they speak of their own selves, in vernaculars, as characters willing to seduce and be seduced.

I don't mean to suggest that the boys were or weren't looking for some manner of actual physical romantic connection with the researcher—though that certainly might have been the case for some students; recall that no one was "out" at the school and so there was no venue for expressing that sentiment. Rather, I mean to put forth the notion that the boys at the school were very comfortable with performing for an audience and I was a differently captive one. That they were so fascinated by the field notes I took, constantly searching for their own role in the text, suggests that they valued the opportunity to be seduced into the role of character just as they sensed that they were shaping the narrative through specific interventions, like the notes and pictures handed to me or slipped under my office door.

The notes and pictures served as reminders that they, the students, still existed should I not have seen them in a while (for the first semester, when I'd return to school on Tuesdays, I was subject to persistent questioning as to why I'd not been present in class on Friday and Monday; I was perpetually explaining that I taught elsewhere on those days. This never seemed to fully register.) and further that they were available and willing to be intextuated. They were, in effect, performing in order to be connected to "the book" but perhaps also more closely connected with me.

Knowing, as they did, that I was writing—and this was my stock answer when asked—about "the development of masculinities and spiritualities" at an all-boys school, they readily played into the language of the examination. This is partly because of the conversations we continually engaged in around the usage of "fagging" and "dicking" in the school. Also, though, it was some of their wanting to remind me that they knew I was still there and to suggest that they were, too.

Once, on picking up my computer bag from the Campus Ministry office after a day at school, I had a note that read, "O, I Burke. I type things! I gay. Love, Dunbar." Signed in his pseudonym, Dunbar was checking in and performing in a way to reconnect with my work as we often had discussions about the genesis of fag discourse and the creative usage of the term *gay* in the school.

The punctuation is ambiguous in the note, though. It's unclear whether Dunbar is suggesting that he is gay, or that I am. Probably it's both since, in the ubiquity of fag discourse, we were all gay at some point. Corbett (2009) plays with this, noting that "Faggot = anything. Faggot = everything. The ubiquity of faggot [and 'gay'] redoubles its meanings, and at the same time diminishes its meanings, or at the very least blunts them through sheer repetition" (p. 173). *Gay*, as with *faggot* for Corbett, is a rich and generative term here, bespeaking Dunbar's willful condensing of my gendered possibility, say, but also exploring as, with Murph and the others, the homoerotic possibility of a term and a love, let's say, that has found a soulful outlet colored by a certain anxiety that my disappearing might mean the window has closed just a bit. This anxiety about inclusion extended to my monthly shuffling of schedules.

Seduction, or Burke! Where You Been?

There was a certain in-built disorientation to the rhythm of my observations. The constant, of course, was the time at lunch with what came to be two calcified groups (two lunches, recall) of seven or so students. Also, there came to be a consistent stream of boys who passed through Campus Ministry during fourth period, particularly immediately following Kairos retreats. Otherwise, though, on the first of each month I managed to throw my own little universe in the school completely off-kilter. The benefits of following a new student each month—a reduction in boredom at largely underengaging classroom content; new encounters with different classmates; wider exposure to differing teaching styles and teaching spaces—far outweighed the drawbacks. Still, the first week of any given month was more than a little like beginning anew: finding a desk and then an informant group around that location, navigating suspicious teachers, cataloging wall-art and back-of-the-shirt art, mapping new hallway routes...all of the mundanities of initiating research in a school. These changes I figured on. The reaction of the boys, I hadn't anticipated.

Because my new schedule often took me on altered routes through the hallways as I tried to find my way between classes in the four minutes allotted, I often lost touch with the "friends" I'd made over the previous months. These were the casual contacts, the soft-sells in e-music or English 4 who moved slowly from stolen looks back in the direction of the mysterious "writer" at the rear of their class, to asking me what I'd written during a given period, to a level of comfort where they began doodling in my notebook as they walked by, often pausing to ask me about my squish. Always, these minor informants, though important in my adjusting to the rhythm of what could be an incredibly boring day—I gave up coffee in solidarity with the students who weren't allowed to carry any liquids into their classes and often I paid for it with lethargy and slight withdrawal headaches—lost touch.[2]

Eventually, though, we would meet again. This was usually through some glitch in a route I'd taken and then, there they'd be. It's really not a large school, but somehow it was possible to lose people for a week or two. And they'd greet me with a mix of relief (that I'd not left) but more strikingly, anger. Always it was the same: wondering where I'd gone ("I switched schedules. I'm following someone new.") and then recrimination at my betrayal for leaving them. I had become a part of their day and that I was exercising my right/privilege as an adult by choosing to alter my own schedule was an affront to the rapport we'd developed. It was a stark reminder for both of us that I wasn't really a classmate; I was a researcher and our relationship had been based on inherently false pretenses on my part. Jake, encountering me in the hall outside of lunch, put it best:

Jake: "Where you been, Dr. Burke?"
Me: "I switched schedules. I'm following Tim now."
Jake: Walking away, sort of laughing but with an edge in his voice: "Fuck that. You're a traitor."

Once, after seeing Packer for the first time in weeks, he looked at me with faux-crazed eyes and mimed slitting his throat saying, "You're dead to me." Like so many interactions with the boys, I knew he was kidding, but not. In a sense this betrayal came to feel very much how they reacted when someone was spending too much time with their girlfriend. I had, in essence, betrayed the Boys for the mistress that was my research.

I suppose I don't blame them. The seductive part of my research was the possibility that I might just be genuinely like them. Or, further, that I might genuinely like (love?) them. I was interested in their inner lives and I asked questions that empowered them as possessing a knowledge that I couldn't possibly conjure myself. In the face of an official curriculum that they viewed as largely oppressive (if not deadening), evoking images of daycare or, worse, the Holiday Inn, they finally had a chance to engage with content in school that was interesting (for them and me): themselves. I'm not intending to suggest that I was interesting to them; rather the possibility that someone was taking a shine to them as valuable founts of knowledge gave them a reason to come to class other than to sleep or to fuck around with their friends. We shared intensive months, moving through a kind of accelerated courtship from doubt to the embrace of trust, and then I'd disappear, revealing myself once again, not as fellow student but as adult who could readily transgress the hard and fast rules of restrictive scheduling. In a way, I used them for their data and got out for selfish reasons: more and different dialogic situations and the desire to stay awake in the face of stifling quizzes and repetitive lectures.

It's not a huge stretch, then, to liken our relationships with small courtships throughout the year. As there was a persistent homoerotic element floating through the school centered quite often on the casual grabbing of crotches, or the occasional mock arm-in-arm skipping of friends in hallways, but always (all ways) rooted in some sort of slightly taboo physical contact, their losing me from sight (and schedule) carried real weight. I was no longer present, physically. I couldn't be groped. Nor could I provide spaces in the middle of class for them to, in turn, provide the knowledge I lacked (or projected to lack). They were always asking to be interviewed, but rarely seemed to realize that we were constantly interviewing each other in classes, in moments when I'd stop the flow of a conversation to ask for clarification as to why someone might be called "gay" for having a drawn penis hooked on his belt, but not so when he reached around a classmate to rub pectoral muscles in the midst of a Physics lecture. When I left them, we broke up; our dialogic space disappeared and their fag discursive days lost those interruptive/interpretive possibilities. They could no longer share knowledge, coo, and woo me with what they came to think I needed to know.

So of course they drew me pictures. Of course they left me notes in my bag and of course they added me as a friend on Facebook and occasionally flamed my page. This was their way of being remembered—it was an attempt to remain connected with the character that they saw themselves becoming in the imaginary text of my "book." Is it possible that they exaggerated their usage of fag discourse and their penis regalia in my presence as a way to better place themselves in my hallowed notebook? Absolutely. That magnification, though, doesn't to my mind negate the data we created, it only bespeaks their incorporation of my presence into the life of the school. I was another way to be masculine; I was another way to be masculine *around*; I was a validation of their resident knowledges even as I challenged them on why they did things. They welcomed that challenge and it changed everything I wrote down in the first semester and come to write here. They were always searching for ways to make sense of me, to reign me into an intelligible form.

The phone calls began around Thanksgiving. It was by this time that the majority of the core group (again, something around fifteen or so students mostly from lunch and then radiating outward through athletic and parish ties) had decided that I wasn't intending on ratting them out to either the administration or their parents. They began prodding me, insisting that the "real book" would be written on weekends, if I'd only hang out with them. This was part of the bravado of being 17 and convinced that the art of rebellion, that specific instantiation they'd chosen, was the most original and unique way to flout the establishment's rules ever in the history of human creation.[3] Which is to say that the boys were really enamored of how much alcohol they drank and how awesome it was to be drunk.

They were right in a sense about the "real" book: I could have written much, I'm sure, about the function of partying and alcohol(ism) in the lives and development of these young men, most particularly as it related to masculinity—how much you drank was important, for example, as was how little you showed that you had consumed Herculean amounts; the point was volume measured in pyramids of empty cans, not sloppiness. But the legal ramifications of being present and party to minors and controlled substances felt huge and the rigors of research, luckily, in this case gave me an easy out as I insisted that I was beholden to the project as it tied to the school. True or not, it worked and they backed off, choosing another route to keep me abreast of their exploits.

Anyways. They started calling me at all hours. I wasn't particularly inclined to pick up at 2am when I saw one of the boys' numbers illuminated in the fog of interrupted REM sleep and so I let them go to voice mail, always. Which was perfect for the sake of transcription. What I got from those phone calls was another example of the boys' need for validation and their consistent seeking to remain a part of the project. They were, again, in character and reminding me that they knew I existed beyond the school. This was another way of encountering me in the hallway, of insisting on mattering as material for the text. Here's a sample of one of the longer exchanges from early January. I'm including the message in its entirety for the sake of presenting the complexity of the different relations to me that each student had taken for himself. Note, please, that the form consistent in each voice mail was a compulsion to shout a message and then hand the phone off. These were always communal displays of "affection":

Music and voices both blasting in the background
Raff: "Shut up. Shut the fuck up. Don't say a word. Kevin? (With an uptick and lilting, almost. He's delighted to call me by my first name), It's your friend Raff from Kairos. I'd just like to say that you're mine and Huey's bitch and we fucking killed you. Motherfucker. And now, here's Packer…"
Packer: "Hi, Mr. Burke, it's your favorite: Packer. I just called you to tell you that you know this is my world and you're just livin' in it…and…ah, we're having a good time right now but I assume you're not cause you're a coward and all you do is just write your little gay book that nobody's gonna read and it's not gonna get published and you're gonna fail your assignment 'cause I said you will and now I'm passing the phone to Murph…"

A brief note before proceeding. These soliloquies, I realize, appear quite harsh. When I showed the transcribed exchange to a teacher at the school who'd become a friend, he laughed a bit, saying, "You know, the weird thing is this is their way of showing affection." Which is exactly how I read it. There was a certain code to these manners of interactions; it's those closest to the heart that earn the right to be put down. Fag discourse alights at the outlines of it. This affection is more apparent—and less coded in standoffish masculine posturing—in the next few monologues:

Murph (of waterskiing picture fame): "Mr. Burke. Shalom! Um, just chillin'. Shut up, shut up. Alright, no, but Mr. Burke, I love ya and I'm kinda disappointed you didn't answer, wait dude you guys got to talk already, well, love ya. We all do. We were talking about oh remember that picture I drew you? Yeah, that was good shit. And, ah, can't wait for the book. I'm gonna buy it and have you sign it. I can't read though. Help me read? Here's Donnie..."

Donnie: "Mr. Burke, I missed you the past few days motherfucker on Kairos and on Monday, I mean Tuesday you better come to the aquatic center and watch us play water polo cause my team is unreal [this is the swimming pool and he's talking about gym class]. I really did miss you on Kairos and sorry I didn't write you a letter. I wrote 21 letters but, love you; I'm gonna call you later. You better answer. Here's Raff again..."

Raff: "Hey Burke. I was gonna tell you that: how's it feel all those years of college mean nothing 'cause your book's gonna suck! Have a good night."

Click.

This was how the calls always ended, abruptly as, presumably, the boys got back to the busy life of cheap beer and swilled inhibitions. The above is representative, though, of the compulsion for outreach into my life beyond the school. My Monica "friends" were eager for me to exist beyond the purview of the lunchroom and hallways and had a hunch that I might just be interested in their habits as young men finding themselves, not just at Monica, but in their homes and relationships, beery or otherwise. Once a call was made, there always ensued a certain battle for phone time as each character took his place on the message. Raff played the role of "bully" as he did at the lunch table, and Donnie settled into his place as my kindly initial contact. This was how they were willing to be written and how they started to, in a sense, construct a masculinity for me the author, as well as me, the adult-who-paid-attention to them as more than athletes or JUG dwellers, as failures or successes of GPA. Ultimately, there was always a tenor of affection; this was nearly universal even when I'd been accused of abandoning schedules and thus cadres of classmates each month. It's not a stretch, however, to imagine how these forms of affection can/do become extended to the kind of discourse of physical, emotional, and mental (most often, gendered) violence that relies on an "I hit you because I love you" line of reasoning/abuse to justify itself. It is perhaps the best measure of what I "could not see" as an insider that this only occurred to me through the ministrations and urgings of a trusted reader of mine. And of course it brings to relief, the character/experience of Scotty.

Bullied

My intention is not to make a caricature out of Scotty. He was by accounts from friends, actually a kind and giving guy ("He only hits me when I deserve it," perhaps). I only saw evidence of that when I was finally out of his sway. From the first week of school he decided that I was vulnerable—and I had the misfortune of watching him exploit vulnerability constantly in his classmates in cruel ways that required a kind of intelligence turned toward willful emotional abuse that made me particularly worried for/about/around him…and me—and made me feel ill at ease at every turn. This was in direct contrast to literally every other student I encountered, who moved perhaps from suspicion initially to, at the very least, acceptance of and interest in my project. Scotty, I realized later, was pissed I'd not picked him to follow and took every chance he could to let me know I was thus unwelcome in his world. And St. Monica was *his* world. I'd not been bullied in a decade but I very quickly felt as small as 14-year-old me, chasing my books down the hallway as the varsity soccer team took to practicing touch-passes with my vocabulary and algebra texts.

Let us return to Foucault (1990b) and the Greeks for help here. Always with the Greeks. Foucault puts an onus on the "moral reflection of the Greeks" as related to sexual behavior, yes, "but" also "to stylize a freedom which the 'free' man exercised in his activity" (p. 97). The problem, of course, was that no man was/is truly free in a society that dictates expectations around sexual activity and so the paradox of the freedom of a free man meant that his ultimate freedom was manifest in control, of his desires, yes, but also of the objects of his desire. This led to the codification of "regimen" which was seen as "a whole art of living" (p. 101) focused most particularly on mastery of self (and thus others) and the exercise of free will for "encompassing all of a man's activities[; it] problematized the relation to the body and called for" (p. 102), to steal from *Harry Potter*, constant "vigilance" in the policing of the self and others. I became subject to Scotty's need to extend his control, to consolidate his schooled regimen by engaging in a mastery of the new element: the writer in the room. This, in turn, would allow him to control my narrative. It's telling, we'll see, that his first foray feminizes me but his picture aims at the destruction of my written project. He sensed the totemic power of the text and sought to control it in a test of masculinity and will.

Again, I write about this here not so much for my own ego—though that is so much, inevitably of the research and I suppose I was hurt in a way that I couldn't "get to" Scotty as I'd have liked—but to illustrate the extent to which I became a cipher through which the boys performed masculinity, yes, but as characters for a text on masculinity. It matters not so much that the boys called me or drew me pictures or that I was bullied as much as it matters that these things would not have occurred in quite the same way in my absence. I was in some small way a nexus through which the Monicamen chose to express themselves and their own unique masculine and religious characters. Some embraced me as a loving brother and coach, others embraced me as a rhetorical foil (Huey and Raff particularly), and Scotty, well, Scotty resisted seduction in his own way and constantly.

The trope that Scotty adopted, much like Huey and Raff (though his tack felt harder, embittered and even a bit dangerous; certainly enough to make me feel vulnerable) lay in making me his bitch. There is much to mine in terms of symbolic effeminacy or even the abjected role of passivity in a homosexual partnership, both of which we've touched on earlier in this text. For now, though, I want to provide a different contextual basis because Scotty, like his classmates, drew me a picture. He wanted to be a character, too, but his way of going about it involved subjugation rather than adoption. This was a very different and creative move and one that left me uncomfortable for reasons I can't fully explain. The other boys called me a bitch all the time; when Scotty did it, well, it stung. As much as this project is about making sense of the masculinities of the boys in the school, it is, too, much of my own coming to a fuller or alternative sense of my experience in the school and in Marist High School years before. As with Murph, our relationship turned on an illustration:

Figure 4: Make Me a Sandwich (Courtesy Scott Smolik)

This was handed to me in the middle of my third week in the school. I was still as yet underestablished among most of the senior class and at best a benignity for the faculty. I had yet to find my office, nor was my anchor dropped yet in Campus Ministry. I felt, in essence, placeless.

The text is difficult to read, but it's Scott telling me, "I own you, Burke. Go make me a sandwich." He is also ripping up my notebook while I plead with him, "No! You own me. Just don't rip my book up." The crudity of the artwork aside, the message is fairly clear. Part of his ownership lies in his dominance through the violent act of destroying my research, but it also relies on a sort of servitude represented in my preparing food for him. I am slave, but also woman, this connection wrought through the use of the term *bitch*. In fact, as I looked up from the picture, handed across rows of desks from Scotty in the middle of the room, he stared me down and mouthed, "I own you, bitch." For how much his case weighed on my mind for the first month and a half of school, I suppose he wasn't wholly wrong.

This went on for the rest of September. At lunch he tried to cow me: "Burke! You're my bitch. Where's my sandwich?" On subsequent days in math class, he traipsed in announcing, "Burke's my bitch." Later in the month when talking about Homecoming, he turned to me and asked, "Burke, what're you gonna do when I fuck your girlfriend?" Contradicting himself in that same week, he elbowed Packer so that I could hear him, asking, "Hey, Packer, you know Burke has a boyfriend? He's a HOMOsexual. Isn't that right, Burkey boy?" He then launched into a brief campaign questioning my legitimacy at the school, asking all of the lunch group and the entire math class by turns, "Who the fuck is this guy? Who do you think you are? Why are you even here?" These last three were honest questions, I suppose, and I answered some version of them constantly and willingly throughout my time at the school. But Scotty, well, he was disconcerting. He often spent class periods just staring me down. It was, to borrow the language of a contemporary comedy news show, a "threatdown."

This stuff was fairly tame, to be honest. It's more or less all of the same verbiage that the other boys used, but from Scotty it felt dangerous, pointed, more serious. Even one day in lunch when he caught me by surprise, after he assured the table that my girlfriend's name was "Frank," by telling me that he was just messing with me, still then I couldn't find comfort, or distance.

It might have been that I couldn't read him or that I was just beginning to believe he hated me. What frightened me is that it started to feel important. I had lost my ability to step outside of the discourse of the school; I wasn't above it and I had lost the ability to master the situation. I was made, in a Greek sense, less masculine due to my inability to get control. I really, for the month of September, couldn't get a purchase on the kid. Then he called me, in October after I'd been out of his class for two weeks, when I passed him in the hallway, "a fucking traitor," and I started to be able to make some sense of things. What mattered in the end for Scotty was much the same as with his classmates: it was the attention, the wrangling of the situation to get it under control. His caustic reaction to my presence didn't necessarily bespeak a more trenchant need to marginalize me in his classes or his lunchroom spaces, rather, it was his desire to be included of his own accord, on his own terms, that led him to the bullying. He stood out in a text about masculinity as a stereotype of violent and abusive masculinity. It was a master performance. This was his way of ensuring a space for a character in the text. After a number of weeks, as I continually asked the boys in my immediate surround, how I should read Scotty and his claiming me as his "bitch," he ramped up the abuse. They were, no doubt, relaying my queries. He began to relish acting the part of tormentor.

And then, at the end of September, I disappeared to another schedule (a higher track, actually), losing touch with him until that day he called me a traitor with a certain measure of hate and fear in his eyes. He'd lost his daily sway over me, by that point, and in that moment became much more like his classmates who reacted similarly to my abandoning them for greener pastures, newer data fields, temporarily interesting classes. Scotty, in that brief moment, found himself reconnected and pissed that he'd lost his role and found his sway unsubstantiated. He'd lost his bitch, his role, his character. The picture, though, remained.

(En)Title(d)

To be etched in text was vital for the boys. They acted as characters for me and I reacted accordingly with a mix of trepidation, joy, fear, disgust, and utmost respect. Their masculinities were myriad and they were ever filtered through the ideologies of the school that helped them produce themselves as their own version of a Monicaman. I became a part of that picture for one brief moment. And it was an honor to come to think of myself, in some small way, as a Monicaman as well.

Always—without fail, and this is not hyperbole—after a student found out I was writing a "book" about them—they asked about the title. This happened from the first days of data creation on through lacrosse practices in April, and my answer was always the same: "I don't know yet. What should it be?" An old teaching trick, that: bounce it back at the student and see what brilliance they come up with that's worth stealing. But it was an honest sentiment as I really still don't know that I have a title for all of this messy work of research.

The importance of the title, to the boys though, seems significant. I attribute it back to their coming to sense that they could be characters in a text. This started with their meticulous selection of pseudonyms, continued through their combing of my notes to find quotes and jottings from/on them, on through their later reminders by phone call and drawings that they still existed in the world, in my world, even though I'd abandoned the desk next to them for an office down the hall. Their acting for me, their performance, was in need of a venue to make it significant and that venue, which came to be this text, had to have a good title because that title would, in turn, make them significant again. Part of this work, then, has been about elucidating the ways that these boys acted in the great dance of gender creation under the restrictive—but still generative—auspices of St. Monica, the saint for sure, but more prominently the all-boys Catholic school on the South Side of Chicago. St. Monica made them feel vital (and they performed accordingly) by bringing them into the folds of the great brotherhood—to the exclusion of women not sainted or virginal—of the Catholic Church, certainly, but moreso into the great tradition of the alumni of the school.

Butler (1990) reminds that because "the gendered body is performative [this] suggests that it has no ontological status apart from the various acts which constitute its reality" (p. 185). So too with masculinity, and masculinities more to the point, as well as religiosities. The lesson to remember, then, is that St. Monica High School has no status apart from the Monicamen it creates. So too with the Catholic Church and her much malingered clergy. Gender and religion and schools and churches are constructed through the repeated stylizations of this world. Writing about them, becoming a character in one's own text is one way to look critically at the way these acts are misconstrued, through the repetition of tradition, as ontological and a priori. The point is that the boys could be the undoing of a gendered system—and a school—through the same process that they become its reification embodied, dialoged, remembered. But they need chances to (re)create. Which is a roundabout way of saying that though I've written their and my story here, I remain troubled by the title of this piece. They were not hopeless causes, but defining their masculinities in a text such as this carries problems of representation and construction. "Construction," Butler asserts, "is not opposed to agency; it is the necessary scene of agency, the very terms in which agency is articulated and become culturally intelligible" (p. 201).

My tentative liberatory critical-theoretical roots tell me that this means part of the making of this text was the making of new and altered characters of masculine and spiritual possibility. I'm not a flashpoint, but maybe the text, retitled someday, serves that purpose.

Implications

I had brunch with some nomadic friends on a rare day in February when we'd all landed back in Chicago simultaneously. It was pleasant to reconnect with travelers who have radiated outward from the Midwest and then headed back for the lovely biting wind of mid-winter. While there, I had a brief conversation with a friend of theirs who was seated next to me. He, too, had read Pascoe's text for a course he was taking at a local Catholic university. He said that his sociology professor commented at the end of the class-offhandedly-that the two most homophobic organizations were fraternities and all-boys schools.

This makes sense in a commonsense, anecdotal sort of way. It also whitewashes the complexities of some fairly diverse institutions. That's troubling. As troubling as the homophobia that is no doubt rampant in certain spaces authorized (and created) by some fraternities and some all-boys schools? Perhaps not. But to dismiss them in kind does not eliminate them, or their influence, from existence. A more productive tack, I think, is engaging with and closely examining the discursive function of this uncomplicated homophobia for the sake of complexity and context and perhaps with an eye toward intervention.

Research into the complexities of the formulation of genders as affected and effected by single gendered schooling contexts bears fleshing out. Further study ought be pursued into what self-consciously single-gendered schools do to and with the boys and girls they enroll and seek to encode through their structure of/and curriculum. Much work could be done with the ways that students creatively engage the rhetorical strategies of their schools once they become a part of them.

Too, as many of these schools are private and rely on a strong base of alums for their fiscal survival, longitudinal work in relationality between and among students such as those at St. Monica as regards the link to brotherhood and tradition after years of what might be called indoctrination might carry value. There are ready rolls of these alums and constant reunions meant to reconnect them, but also to draw funds. They are, in essence, a fairly captive and well-documented population. Research into the lasting effects of single-gendered schools particularly in terms of the continuing role of fag discourse as well as homosocial bonding, would be well worth examination if we're to measure some of the true effects of a system of schooling.

"Flash" Interviews

I hesitate, in some ways, to claim credit for the idea of a flash interview. I am familiar with the methodological traditions of semi-structured interviewing that allows for a great deal of latitude in service to the whims of a meandering and pseudo-organic conversation. But this, often enough, occurs in a prescribed environment with parameters agreed upon between subject(s) and researcher(s) and bespeaks a kind of forethought and planning. What flash interviews allowed in this context was the ability to interrupt, in the midst of discursive elements that occurred (as they occurred) to attempt to bring context for the author. Always the boys were free to move in and out of the situation (physically) and conversationally. At times these encounters lasted for one question and often enough they extended through class periods as we all ignored the pick-up basketball games surrounding us in gym class. The point is that these moments of inquiry allowed the students not only to reflect on their situation (while still in the situation itself) but also to bring a meta-cognitive awareness and insider knowledge that the researcher (they saw) valued and required. As the data was then immediately encoded into the notebook they had daily access to, they could drive later interviews and initiate them as they came across the streams of conversation/consciousness of peers or younger/previous selves. It may be that flash interviewing is not wholly groundbreaking methodologically, but it certainly was helpful in accessing a discourse-about-the-discourse in the midst of the researched situation that otherwise might have been impossible to uncover had we all taken time to prepare to perform as interviewer and interviewee in a sequestered room.

The Field of Catholic Education

In 2007, the University of Notre Dame hosted the launch of an initiative facilitated by Lee Shulman at Stanford University aimed at discussing the unique situation of Catholic education in the United States. This initial "Carnegie Conversation on Catholic Education" cited a general profusion and tradition of empirical/theoretical research on and in public schools, but a dearth of work of the same breadth and character as regards Catholic (and parochial in general) schooling. As a means of remedying this perceived gap in the field of educational research, Shulman (2008) suggested the need to build a "field of Catholic research" that "is [in] some sense" its own "body of knowledge" bringing with it "processes needed to critique knowledge claims....and [seeking] to connect knowledge to other bodies of understanding and to domains of practice" (p. 2). Further, he cautioned that "if Catholic education is to become a robust field, it must become a robust field of scholarship" that is of interest outside of "the club" of "Catholic educational institutions" (p. 4).

In support of this new conversation and its ensuing calls for more and broader research on, in, and about Catholic schooling those universities participating in the initial proceedings have begun a series of biannual national conferences (the first of their kind in Catholic Education aimed specifically at producing research) looking at the unique theoretical possibilities of scholarship in and building of the field. Notre Dame, in the intervening years, has opened a publishing house (ACE Press) and Boston College currently houses *Catholic Education: A Journal of Inquiry and Practice,* both specifically charged with disseminating the work spurred by the Carnegie Conversation. Also, I am now a member of a

Special Interest Group for Catholic Education that has just been formed under the auspices of the American Educational Research Association.

This book hopefully contributes to a nascent field of Catholic educational scholarship at a time when the character of the work done in such a field is particularly malleable. And so early work in critical and post-modern autoethnography may just open up more and earlier avenues toward creative conversations about religious ideology and its effects and goals in schooling. This, I believe, is a unique opportunity to bring critical conversations to bear upon the formative stages of a field's development.

Beyond this, though, and thinking about Shulman's insistence that research in and on Catholic schools cannot limit itself in scope and become an insular conversation, my hope is that this study will serve as a critique of the structural limitations of previous notions of multiple masculinities, thus opening possibilities for rethinking the role of discourse and resistive power in the process of the (re)formation of masculinities in schools. That is I think, that the study may just make it more possible to examine the ways that masculinities are (re)formed in schools by actors, in reference to officialized discourses, yes, but also in reference to each other. My hope is that this work will make masculinities as unstable and perpetually reconstitutive in theory as I think they were on a moment-to-moment basis in and around the school.

Further, in light of the legal ramifications of NCLB's allowance for single-sex public education as well as the tendency to rely on un(der)complicated biological understandings that perpetuate binary gender splits, this study may provide an alternative understanding of just what happens (good or bad) in a single gendered school, most particularly as regards the establishment (and undermining) of masculinity for boys. In the process, hopefully, the work offers a more complex view of gender segregated schooling along the lines of Robinson and Smithers (1999), moving the conversation from test scores as a measure of effectiveness to a deeper theoretical discussion about just why gender segregated schools may actually become further constitutive of the exact problems with gender (in both the short and long run) that they propose to ameliorate.

Finally, as I am centered in the field of teacher education, I want to address a common notion among teachers at St. Monica. Continually I heard conveyed a certain sensibility about how the work of a Catholic school was "more than a job; it's ministry." I won't dare refute such an assertion of conviction. I do believe that teachers who enter into parochial schoolwork, quite often do so to the detriment of their retirement and certainly to their fiscal bottom line. This rhetorical move, though, relies on a further claim that "there's something missing" in public schools. Which, again, may well be true. That something missing, though, may just be the invocation of religion as disciplinary, and certainly for its function as crowd control. Ministry in the sense it's invoked, however, bespeaks a deeper engagement with the Catholic/Christian notion of Christ Teacher. And if there were ever a rebel of a teacher, it would have been Christ, man, and/or God. The mission and ministry of Catholic schools, of all-boys Catholic schools, might just serve, created as spaces apart from the world (of public schooling and the ramifications of a purportedly theology-free environment, say) as they indeed are, as radical purveyors of a new kind of Tradition.

Carroll (2001) issues a clarion call for a third Vatican council. The second, called by Pope John the XXIII is often seen as the time when the Church reversed much of its damaging and standoffish policy (moving away from the Tridentine Mass, allowing the laity an expanded role in the Church, among other things). There has been a slow retrenchment of policy over the intervening 50 years or so. Much of that has been written onto the minds and bodies of women. Carroll's insistence is that a New Reformation might just save the Church. We might debate, particularly in light of the latest abuse scandals, which reach to the throne of both John Paul and Benedict, just what is worth saving anyways. Catholic schools, most probably. This is where the newest generations of the faithful might be wrought and the Church and orders such as the Augustinians have incredible autonomy in terms of how their curricular spaces become constructed. What ought occur, first, however, is good and radical and creative research in and on these schools to determine what is done well and/or to the detriment of its students. I would hope that this study, this work here, contributes in some small way to the building of that New Reformation in Catholic schools, certainly, but also of public schools as we sit at the beginning of a new educational era being built beyond NCLB.

Notes

1. I became a junior varsity lacrosse coach despite having never played myself nor really ever having seen the sport played. It was a learning process and I spent the winter running the conditioning program for the varsity team. This was one way as a young male in the school to gain different points of access to the senior students. Because, ultimately, I coached junior varsity, I never ended up having to take on an authoritative role with the boys I'd been following through the year. Murph was a starting middie for an emerging varsity program.
2. As the year went on, the vast majority of the senior (and junior and sophomore) class found my profile on Facebook. I was added nearly universally as a "friend" which gave me a presence in their lives in cyberspace (so often differently represented than their lives in real-time) but that "add" didn't denote any substantive contact necessarily. This was really just a way of collecting friends in numbers. I became another chit mark on their way up the ladder, which was fine. I mention this, though, to say that unlike teachers and administrators at the school, I had access to the profiles of most of the seniors and was privy to the groups they created and joined and could comment on some of what I saw posted on various pages. They did not hold back at all in terms of what might be called "foul" language and "inappropriate" content. At one point, Packer went through an album of mine and captioned a number of my pictures. This led to a frenzy of commenting back and forth among the boys in which they wrote things they perhaps ought not have. But these were things that they put on each others' pages and so I was, in essence, more student in cyberspace than even at school.
3. Everything is always in superlatives at 17, no?

Bibliography

Adams, J. R. (2008). *Male armor: The soldier-hero in contemporary american culture*. Charlottesville: University of Virginia Press.
The Augustinians. Retrieved April 20th, 2009, from http://www.augustinian.org/whoweare.htm.
Austin, J., & Hickey, A. (2008). Critical pedagogical practice through cultural studies. *The International Journal of the Humanities, 6*(1), 133-139.
Bakhtin, M. (1998). Carnival and the carnivalesque. In J. Storey (Ed.), *Cultural theory and popular culture* (pp. 250–258). Athens: University of Georgia Press.
Bakhuizen Van Den Brink, J. N. (1974). *Ratramnus, de corpore at sanguine domini*. Maryland Heights, MO: Elsevier Science & Technology.
Baudrillard, J. (1994). *Simulacra and simulation* (S. F. Glaser, Trans.). Ann Arbor: University of Michigan Press.
Bersani, L. (1987). Is the rectum a grave? *October, 43*, 197–222.
Biesta, G. J. (1998). Foucault and the subject of education. *Interchange, 29*(1), 1-16.
Bourdieu, P. & Wacquant, L. (1992). *An invitation to reflexive sociology*. Chicago: University of Chicago Press.
Britzman, D. P. (2000). "The question of belief": Writing poststructural ethnography. In E. S. Pierre & W. Pillow (Eds.), *Feminist poststructural theory and methods in education* (pp. 27–40). New York: Routledge.
Brown, S. (2003). Desire in ethnography: Discovering meaning in the social sciences. In M. Tamboukou & S. J. Ball (Eds.), *Dangerous encounters: Geneology and ethnography* (pp. 69-88). New York: Peter Lang.
The brown scapular. (1999). Retrieved April 17, 2009, from http://carmelnet.org/scapular/scapular.htm.
Bryk, A. , Lee, V. , & Holland, P. (1993). *Catholic schools and the common good*. Cambridge: Harvard University Press.
Burke, K. (1966). *Language as symbolic action: Essays on life, literature, and method*. Berkeley: University of California Press.
Butler, J. (1990). Subjects of sex/gender/desire. In *Gender trouble: Feminism & the subversion of identity* (pp. 3–44). New York: Routledge.
___ (2008). *Gender trouble*. New York: Routledge Classics.
Cameron, D. (2006). *On language and sexual politics*. New York: Routledge.
Carper, J. C. (1998). History, religion, and schooling: A context for conversation. In J. T. Sears & J. C. Carper (Eds.), *Curriculum, religion, and public education: Conversations for an enlarging public square*. New York: Teachers College Press.
Carroll, J. (2001). *Constantine's sword:The church and the jews*. New York: Mariner Books.
___ (2004). *Crusade: Chronicles of an unjust war*. New York: Metropolitan Books.
Chabon, M. (2009). *Manhood for amateurs: The pleasures and regrets of a husband, father, and son*. New York: Harper.

Chambers, I. (1993). Cities without maps. In J. Bird (Ed.), *Mapping the futures: Local cultures, global change* (pp. 92–114). New York: Routledge.

Chernin, K. (1987). *Reinventing eve: Modern woman in search of herself.* New York: Harper Perennial.

Cherryholmes, C. H. (1988). Thinking about education structurally. In *Poststructual investigations in education* (pp. 16–48). New York: Teachers College Press.

Chevalier, J. (Ed.) (1994) A dictionary of symbols. Oxford: Blackwell Reference.

Clark, B. L. (2003). *Kiddie lit: The cultural construction of children's literature in America.* Baltimore: Johns Hopkins University Press.

Connell, R. W. (1987). *Gender and power: Society, the person, and sexual politics.* Palo Alto: Stanford University Press.

Connell, R. W. (1995). *Masculinities.* Oxford: Blackwell Publishers.

___(2002). *Gender.* Polity Press.

Corbett, K. (2009). *Boyhoods: Rethinking masculinities.* New Haven: Yale University Press.

Cupane, A. F., & Taylor, P. C. (2007). *African culture in the science classroom.* Paper presented at the Australian Association for Research in Education, Canberra, AU.

Daly, M. (1973). *Beyond god the father: Toward a philosophy of women's liberation.* Boston: Beacon Press.

Denzin, N., & Lincoln, Y. S. (2000). Introduction: The discipline and practice of qualitative research. In N. Denzin & Y. S. Lincoln (Eds.), *Handbook of qualitative research* (2nd ed., pp. 1-28). Thousand Oaks: Sage Publications.

Digest of education statistics. (2009). from National Center for Education Statistics http://nces.ed.gov/programs/digest/d09/tables/dt09_059.asp

Di Gregorio, M. (2003). *The precious pearl: The story of saint rita of cascia.* New York: Society of St. Paul.

Epstein, D., & Johnson, R. (1998). *Schooling sexualities.* New York: Open University Press.

Fendler, L. (2010). *Michel Foucault* (Vol. 22). New York: Continuum.

Fine, M. , Weis, L. , Weseen, S. , & Wong, L. (2003). For whom? Qualitative research, representations, and social responsibilities. In N. K. Denzin & Y. S. Lincoln (Eds.), *The landscape of qualititative research: Theories and issues* (pp. 107–129). New York: Sage Publications.

Fiske, J. (1989). Offensive bodies and carnival pleasures. In *Understanding popular culture* (pp. 69-101). New York: Routledge.

Foucault, M. (1980). *Power/knowledge: Selected interviews and other writings, 1972–1977.* New York: Pantheon.

___ (1989). Talk show (P. Aronov & D. McGrawth, Trans.). In S. Lotringer (Ed.), *Foucault live: Interviews, 1961–1984* (pp. 133–145): Semiotext(e).

___ (1990a). *The history of sexuality: An introduction* (R. Hurley, Trans. Vol. 1). New York: Vintage Books.

___ (1990b). *The use of pleasure: The history of sexuality* (R. Hurley, Trans. Vol. 2). New York: Vintage Books.

___ (1990c). *The care of the self: The history of sexuality* (R. Hurley, Trans. Vol. 3). New York: Vintage Books.

___ (1998). Method. In J. Storey (Ed.), *Cultural theory and popular culture* (pp. 165–171). Athens: University of Georgia Press.

Gee, J. P. (1996). *Social linguistics and literacies: Ideology in discourses.* London: Taylor & Francis.

Geertz, C. (1973). Thick description: Toward an interpretive theory of culture. In *The interpretation of cultures.* New York: Basic Books.

Grace, G. (2002). *Catholic schools: Mission, markets, and morality*. New York: RoutledgeFalmer.

Grant, M. (1993). *The emperor constantine*. London: Weidenfeld and Nicolson.

Grossman, J. R., Keating, A. D., & Reiff, J. L. (Eds.). (2004). *The encyclopedia of Chicago*. Chicago: University of Chicago.

Harper, P. B. (1996). *Are we not men? Masculine anxiety and the problem of african-american identity*. New York: Oxford University Press.

Harris, I. M. (1995). *Messages men hear: Constructing masculinities*. London: Taylor & Francis Ltd.

Hartsock, N. (1987). The feminist standpoint: Developing the ground for a specifically feminist historical materialism. In S. Harding (Ed.), *Feminism and methodology* (pp. 157–180). Bloomington: Indiana University Press.

Hawhee, D. (2002). Bodily pedagogies: Rhetoric, athletics, and the sophists' three rs. *College English, 65*(2), 142–160.

___ (2006). Rhetorics, bodies and everyday life. *Rhetoric Society Quarterly, 36*, 155–164.

Hoffer, T., Greeley, A. M., & Coleman, J. S. (1985). Achievement growth in public and catholic schools. *Sociology of Education, 58*, 74-97.

Holstein, J. A., & Gubrium, J. F. (2002). Active interviewing. In D. Wienberg (Ed.), *Qualitative research methods* (pp. 112–125). Malden: Blackwell.

hooks, b. (2002). *Communion: The female search for love*. New York: Harper.

Information about holy relics. Retrieved March 2nd, 2010, from www.ecrosaries.com/site/601007/page/453613.

Iversen, J. (2007). *High school confidential: Secrets of an undercover student*. New York: Simon and Schuster Adult.

Jepson, J. J. (2008). *St. Augustine: The lord's sermon on the mount*. Mahwah, NJ: Gardiner Press.

Kearney, G. R. (2008). *More than a dream: How one school's vision is changing the world*. Chicago Loyola.

Krondorfer, B. (2010). *Male confessions: Intimate revelations and the religious imagination*. Stanford: Stanford University Press.

Lazerson, M. (1977). Understanding american catholic educational history. *History of Education Quarterly, 17*(3), 297-317.

Lefebvre, H. (1991). *The production of space* (D. Nicholson-Smith, Trans.). Malden: Blackwell Publishing.

Lesko, N. (1988). *Symbolizing society: Stories rites and structure in a catholic high school*. New York: Falmer Press.

Levy, A. (2009, November 30). Either/or. *The New Yorker*, 46-59.

Lorde, A. (1984). *Sister Outsider*. Berkeley: Crossing Press.

Mac An Ghaill, M. (1994). *The making of men: Masculinities, sexualities, and schooling*. Philadelphia: Open University Press.

Martin, J. R. (1985). *Reclaiming a conversation: The ideal of the educated woman*. New Haven: Yale University Press.

McCall, L. (2005). The complexity of intersectionality. *Signs: Journal of Women in Culture and Society, 30*(3), 1771-1800.

McCloskey, P. J. (2009). *The street stops here: A year at a catholic high school in harlem*. Berkeley: University of California Press.

McDonald, D. & Schultz, M. (2009). *United states catholic elementary and secondary schools 2008–2009: The annual statistical report on schools, enrollment and staffing.* National catholic educational association.

McLaren, P. (1980). *Cries from the corridor: The new suburban ghettos.* New York: Methuen.

Merton, T. (2003). *No man is an island.* Garden City, NY: Doubleday & Company.

Messner, M. (2002). *Taking the field: Women, men, and sports.* Minneapolis: University of Minnesota Press.

Michael Di Gregorio, O. (2003). *The precious pearl: The story of saint Monica of cascia.* New York: Society of St. Paul.

Miedzian, M. (2002). *Boys will be boys: Breaking the link between masculinity and violence.* New York: Lantern Books.

Nathan, R. (2005). *My freshman year: What a professor learned by becoming a student.* New York: Penguin Books.

National Association for Single Sex Public Education. Retrieved April 27th, 2009, from http://www. singlesexschools. org/research-brain. htm.

National center for education statistics. (2009). Retrieved April 12, 2009, from http://nces. ed. gov/fastfacts/display. asp?id=65.

Nespor, J. (1997). *Tangled up in school: Politics, space, bodies, and signs in the educational process.* Mahwah: Lawrence Erlbaum.

Nodelman, P. (2008). *The hidden adult: Defining children's literature.* Baltimore: Johns Hopkins University Press.

Nord, W. A. (1995). *Religion and american education: Rethinking a national dilemma.* Chapel Hill: University of North Carolina Press.

Olivas, M. R. (2009). Negotiating identity while scaling the walls of the ivory tower: Too brown to be white and too white to be brown. *International Review of Qualitative Research, 2*(3), 385-406.

Oswald, J. C. (2001). *Beverly hills: A brief history of the village in the city.* Chicago: Threshold Publishing.

Pascoe, C. J. (2007). *Dude, you're a fag: Masculinity and sexuality in high school.* Berkeley: University of California Press.

Peace, R. (2001). Producing lesbians: Canonical proprieties. In D. Bell, J. Binnie, R. Holliday, R. Longhurst & R. Peace (Eds.), *Pleasure zones: Bodies, cities, spaces* (pp. 29-54). Syracuse: Syracuse University Press.

Pennycook, A. (2001). *Critical applied linguistics: A critical introduction.* Mahwah: Lawrence Erlbaum Associates.

Philpott, T. L. (1978). *The slum and the ghetto:Neighborhood deterioration and middle class reform, Chicago 1880–1930.* Oxford: Oxford University Press.

Pinar, W. (2006). *Race, religion, and a curriculum of reparation: Teacher education for a multicultural society* New York: Palgrave Macmillan.

Rich, A. (1980). Compulsory heterosexuality and lesbian experience. *Signs, 5*(4), 631–660.

Roach, C. M. (2003). *Mother/nature: Popular culture and environmental ethics.* Bloomington: Indiana University Press.

Robinson, P. , & Smithers, A. (1999). Should the sexes be separated for secondary education?: Comparisons of single-sex and co-educational schools. *Research Papers in Education, 14*(1), 23–49.

Rose, M. (1989). *Lives on the boundary: A moving account of the struggles and achievements of america's educationally underprepared.* New York: Penguin.

Royko, M. (1971). *Boss: Richard j. daley of chicago.* Charlottesville, VA: Dutton.

Ruhlman, M. (1996). *Boys themselves: A return to single-sex education.* New York: Henry Holt.

Salzman, T. A. , & Lawler, M. G. (2008). *The sexual person: Toward a renewed catholic anthropology.* Washington, DC: Georgetown University Press.

Schein, R. (Ed.). (2006). *Landscape and race in the United States.* New York: Routledge.

Scott, J. W. (1986). Gender: A useful category of historical analysis. *The American Historical Review, 91*(5), 1053–1075.

Segall, A. (2001). Critical ethnography and the invocation of voice: From the field/in the field--single exposure, double standard. *Qualitative Studies in Education, 14*(4), 579–592.

Shulman, L. (2008). Preliminary thoughts on creating a field as it might apply to catholic education. In J. Staud (Ed.), *The Carnegie Conversation on Catholic Education* (pp. 12–14). Notre Dame: Alliance for Catholic Education Press.

Soja, E. W. (1996). *Thirdspace: Journeys to Los Angeles and other real-and-imagined places.* Cambridge: Blackwell Publishers.

Spong, J. S. (1992). *Born of a woman: A bishop rethinks the virgin birth and the treatment of women by a male-dominated church.* New York: HarperCollins.

St. Christopher. Retrieved April, 17 2009, from http://www. catholic. org/saints/saint. php?saint_id=36.

Steinem, G. (1994). *Moving beyond words: Age, rage, sex, power, money, muscles: Breaking boundaries of gender.* New York: Simon & Schuster.

Thorne, B. (1993). *Gender play: Girls and boys in school.* New Brunswick: Rutgers University Press.

Trites, R. S. (2000). *Disturbing the universe: Power and repression in adolescent literature.* Iowa City: University of Iowa Press.

Tyler, S. (1986). Post-modern ethnography: From document of the occult to occult document. In (pp. 122–139).

Usher, P. (2000). Feminist approaches to a situated ethics. In Simmons & Usher (Eds.), *Situated ethics in educational research* (pp. 22–38). New York: Routledge.

Van Bavel, T. (1996). *Augustine* (O. S. A. John e. Rotelle, Trans.). Strasbourg: Editions du Signe.

Weedon, C. (1998). Feminism and the principles of poststructuralism. In J. Storey (Ed.), *Cultural theory and popular culture* (pp. 172–183). Athens: University of Georgia Press.

Weitz, R. (Ed.). (2003). *The politics of women's bodies: Sexuality, appearance, and behavior* (2nd ed.). New York: Oxford University Press.

West, C. , & Fenstermaker, S. (1995). Doing difference. *Gender and Society, 9*(1), 8–37.

West, C. , & Zimmerman, D. H. (1987). Doing gender. *Gender and Society, 1*(2), 125–151.

Willis, P. (1981). *Learning to Labor: How working class kids get working class jobs.* New York: Columbia University Press.

Young, J. P. (2000). Boy talk: Critical literacies and masculinities. *Reading Research Quarterly, 35*(3), 312-337.

Zinn, M. B., & Dill, B. T. (1996). Theorizing difference from multiracial feminism. *Feminist Studies, 22*(2), 321-331.

Zipes, J. (2006). *Why fairy tales stick: The evolution and relevance of a genre.* New York: Routledge.

Index

absolution, 129
affection, 147
agency, 50
alcohol, 146
allegory, 14
anxiety, sexual, 96
athletics
    centrality of, 75
    and fag discourse, 75–80
    and gender, 76–77
    and gender testing, 84
    and girls, 93–94, 95
    hockey, 91–94
    and masculine mystique, 24
    role of, 57
    as social event, 92–93
    team nicknames, 25
    and violence, 77, 78, 79
    wrestling, 78–79
    See also coaches; football
Augustine, 16
Augustinians, 2, 3, 11
Austin, J., 47
autoethnography, critical, 47–50
Avner, 117

Bakhtin, M., 66
Baptism, 102
Ben, 72
Bersani, L., 79
betrayal, 144
Beyond God the Father (Daly), 39
Bible
    allegory in, 14
    and literalism, 108–109
    women in, 109, 110
Biesta, G. J., 17, 34
bitch, use of term, 150
body
    control of, 24
    and gender, 23–26
    in schooling, 32, 33
    and social norms, 23
Bourdieu, P., 18
boys
    differences of with girls, 97–99
    raised as soldiers, 24
    See also masculinity
Britzman, D. P., 31, 48, 50
brotherhood, 99–101, 103, 105–106
bullying, 148–152
Butler, J., 21, 22, 23, 28, 38, 153
Byrne, Mrs., 108

Cameron, D., 28, 71
Campus Ministry, 56, 117
Carnegie Conversation on Catholic Education, 155
carnivalesque, 66, 132
Carroll, James, 41, 157
Catholicism
    mentality of power, 41
    women in, 97, 109, 110 (*See also* Monica of Cascia)
    See also Christianity; religion; schools, Catholic
Chabon, Michael, 6
Channel 1, 57
chapel, 1–3, 77, 80
cheating, 53
Cherryholmes, C. H., 25
Chicago, 8–10
ChiRho, 120
Christianity
    as male space, 131
    women in, 40–41, 110
    See also Catholicism; religion
Christopher, St., 14
Chronos, 120, 130
Chunk, 68, 105, 122, 123, 141

church, Catholic. *See* Catholicism; religion
coaches, 76, 77–79, 87
Colin, 53
community, Christian, 131
confession, 124, 126, 128, 129
Connell, R. W., 5, 23, 25, 26–28, 30, 31, 41, 50, 66, 96
construction, 153
control
    and freedom, 148–149
    of male body, 24
    prayer as, 117
Corbett, K., 25, 85, 142
creeping, 60

Daley, Mrs., 103, 104
Daley, Richard, 10
Daly, M., 39, 97, 109
Dan, 86
De Corpore et Sanguine Domini, 2
Dee, Mr., 92, 95–96
Derrida, J., 49
difference, gendered, 97–99
discourse
    and ethnographic text, 49
    and power, 31, 32
discourse, fag. *See* fag discourse
Donnie, 53, 147, 148
Dunbar, 68, 86, 107, 141, 142

Eagleton, T., 14
education, Catholic. *See* schools, Catholic
Epstein, D., 22
Eucharist, 2
Eve, 109
experience, 49
extracurriculars. *See* athletics; Kairos

Facebook, 60
fag discourse
    absence of during Kairos, 123
    affection in, 147
    and athletics, 75–80
    in cafeteria, 66
    circularity of, 71–72
    condoned by administration, 87
    and frustration, 68
    and girlfriends, 70, 96–97
    and helplessness, 68
    and homophobia, 68
    impermanence of, 82
    and language, 73
    opting out of, 69, 72–73
    in Pascoe's work, 36
    penises, drawing of, 81–87
    permanent status of, 82
    relationships in, 70–71
    and religion, 73–75
    terminology, 80–81
    and tradition, 82
    used to regulate masculinity, 67, 69
    uses of, 67–69
fag/faggot
    specter of, 83–84
    use of term, 67, 80–81, 142 (*See also* fag discourse)
fag identity, 22–23
fag tags, 84
fairy tales, 15
female pollution, 116
feminist inquiry, 45–46
Fendler, L., 28, 29
Ferguson, Ann Arnett, 24, 34, 35
Fiske, J., 33
flash interviews, 58–59, 137, 139, 154–155
football
    centrality of, 54–55, 75
    and fag discourse, 75–80
    pink jerseys, 76
    as social event, 92–93
    See also athletics
Foucault, Michel, 8, 17, 28, 29, 31, 33, 38, 50, 57, 66, 128, 138, 148
fraternities, 153, 154
freedom, 148–149
free will, 26
friendship, male, 100–101
Fromm, ?, 103

Index

frustration, 68
funerals, 101

Garcia, Ms., 103–104
gay, use of term, 67, 142
  See also fag discourse
Gee, James, 33
gender
  assumptions about, 5
  and athletics, 76–77
  and body, 23–26
  as changing, 25–26
  as constructed in interaction, 17
  formulation of in single-sex schools, 154
  and institutions, 27, 30
  performance of, 30
  and regulatory practices, 32
  and schooling, 32–37
  social embodiment of, 23
  See also masculinity
gender construction, 46
gender differentiation, 5, 97–99
gender identity, making of, 35
gender relations, 27–28, 30
gender roles, 27, 39–40
  See also sex differences
gender-role socialization, 22
Gender Trouble (Butler), 22
girlfriends
  and fag discourse, 70, 96–97
  vs. brotherhood, 99–101, 103, 105–106
girls
  at athletic events, 93–94, 95
  differences of with boys, 97–99
  See also girlfriends; relationships; women
Gospels, 109

Hanns, 108, 118
Harris, Ian, 24, 100
helplessness, 68
heterosexual market, 71
heterotopia, 119, 130
Hickey, A., 47
History of Sexuality (Foucault), 33, 38

hockey, 91–94, 95
homecoming, 33–34, 71
homoerotica, 70–71, 86
homophobia
  in all-boys schools, 153–154
  and fag discourse, 68
  in fraternities, 153–154
  rooted in performative masculinity, 21–22
homosexuality
  fag identity, 22–23
  fear of, 21–22 (*See also* homophobia)
  intolerance of, 69
  See also fag discourse
homosociality, 86, 99–101, 103, 105–106
Huey, 66, 67, 99–100, 149
Hughes, John, 8
Hurley, Michael, 8

IALAC (I Am Lovable And Capable), 102
ideals, liberatory, 137
ideology, 29
illness, 78
indoctrination, 7
institutions and gender, 27, 30
interaction, physical, 57
Irish, 8–10
Isocrates, 138

Jack, 122, 123
Jaime, 74
Jake, 144
jerseys, pink, 76
Jerusalem Cross, 125
Jesus, birth narrative, 40, 108, 132
jewelry, 13
Joey, 74
Johnny, 99
Johnson, R., 22
Julie, 82, 87

Kairos
  absence of fag discourse during, 123
  access to, 56

administration's ideal of, 121–122
Burke's, 123–125
as carnivalesque, 132
closing ceremony, 130–131
as confession, 129
as conservative project, 133
counter-site, 130
effectiveness of, 129
expression of love in, 141
fourth day, 131
as heterotopia, 119
hugs during, 128
and link to St. Monica, 126
naked mass, 122–123
origin of term, 120
and parents, 130
purpose of, 126–127
and return to Chronos, 130, 131
secrecy of, 131
sharing during, 128
structure of, 125–126
student leaders of, 127–128
time during, 120
and tradition, 98, 133
value placed on, 121
Keck, 96, 105
Kerygma, 132
Kimani, 54, 69, 79, 80
knowledge
and power, 50
production of, 8
Kobe, 67, 103–104
Krupke, Coach, 77–79, 87

language
and fag discourse, 36, 73
and power, 28–29
Latke, Mr., 106, 108
Lazerson, M., 8
Lefebvre, H., 42
Longhurst, R., 99
Lorder, Audre, 27
Lotti, Monica, 15
See also Monica of Cascia

love, expression of, 141
Luke, 67, 93–94, 107
lunch, 66–67

Mac An Ghaill, M., 22, 24, 34, 35, 96, 98
MacBeth, 108
Mad Max, 93
The Making of Men (Mac An Ghaill), 96
Mancini, Paolo, 16
Mann, Horace, 7
Marist High School, 9, 14
Marks, Mrs., 108
marriage, 34
Mary, 13, 109
masculine mystique, 24
masculinities, multiple, 5, 23, 26, 27, 28
masculinity
  and body, 23–26
  and contempt for women, 103
  hegemonic, 30, 31–32, 66, 96
  and illness, 78
  as performative, 153
  and regulatory practices, 32
  and religion, 38–41
  and weakness, 78
  See also boys; gender
masculinity, black male, 35
masculinity, failed, 76–77
masculinity of moderation, 138
mass, naked, 122–123
Matt, 107
McDonnagh, Tim, 10
Merton, Thomas, 125
Messner, M., 24, 76–77
methodology
  critical autoethnography, 47–50
  feminist inquiry, 45–46
  and partiality, 55
Mick, 86, 107
Miedzian, M., 24, 78
Mika, 82, 87, 110
Mike, 118
ministry, teaching as, 156–157
Monicaman, definition of, 116

Monica of Cascia, 15–17, 109, 117
  See also St. Monica of Cascia High
    School
Mormons, 73
Mount Carmel High School, 6, 14
Murph, 139–142, 147
mythology, 132

NCLB, 156
Nespor, J., 4, 32, 33
New Reformation, 157
Nico, 75, 105, 107, 108, 117
No Child Left Behind, 156
Notre Dame, University of, 155

O'Dea, 141
On Language and Sexual Politics (Cameron),
  28
orientation, new faculty, 81–82

Packer, 85, 104, 144, 146
Pascoe, C. J., 21, 22, 23, 27, 33, 35–36, 37,
  57, 67, 69, 70, 73, 74, 153
passivity, 79, 80, 87
Paterno, Mr., 94
peers, interactions with, 4
penises, drawing of, 81–87
personal as political, 45
phallus
  size of, 85
  symbolism of, 84
phone calls, 145–148
pictures
  Murph's, 139–140
  reasons for drawing, 145
  Scotty's, 149–150
Pinar, W., 5
Plato, 141
poststructuralism, 46, 50
poststructuralism, feminist, 48–49
power
  in cafeteria, 66
  Church's mentality of, 41
  Connell on, 31

  and discourse, 31, 32
  Foucault on, 31
  and knowledge, 50
  and language, 28–29
  moderating, 138
  and resistance, 32
prayer, as classroom management strategy,
  117
Prayer of the Peacemaker, 117

Qualter, 76
Quigley South, 9

Radbertus, 2
Raff, 74, 75, 86, 107, 108, 146, 147, 148, 149
Ratramnus, 2
Ray, 75
relationships
  in fag discourse, 70–71
  lack of discussion of, 69
  oriented around heterosexual norms, 71
  See also girlfriends; girls; women
religion
  and assumptions about becoming a man,
    5
  and assumptions about gender, 5
  and assumptions about sexual possibility,
    5
  as discipline, 117, 119
  and fag discourse, 73–75
  and gender differentiation, 5
  and gender roles, 39–40
  and masculinity, 38–41
  passive resistance to, 117–119
  and sex, 38, 39
  as surveillance, 119
  views of, 59
  See also Catholicism; schools, Catholic
religiosity
  as performative, 153
  of St. Monica students, 74
representation, 50, 153
research
  entextualizing, 57–59

field notes, 55
flash interviews, 58–59, 137, 139, 154–155
and liberatory ideals, 137
methodology, 45–50, 55
notes from students, 140–142
reaction to schedule changes, 143–148
and relationship with students, 139–152
seduction in, 139, 144
students' desire to be included in, 152
title for, 152
writing up, 48
researcher
as bullying victim, 148–152
intentions of, 50
phone calls from students to, 145–148
role of, 47, 138–139
resistance, 30–31, 32, 117–119
retreats. *See* Kairos
Riordan, Cornelius, 36
River High School, 74
See also Pascoe, C. J.
Rob, 118
Robinson, P., 156
Rose, M., 4
Ruhlman, Michael, 36, 37, 104, 105

St. Monica of Cascia High School
athletics at (*See* athletics; football)
demographics of, 10
description of, 9–11
reasons for attending, 73–74
scapulars, 11–14, 125
Scheurich, ?, 50
school
peer interactions in, 4
sex in, 25
schooling
body in, 32
and gender, 32–37
indoctrination in, 7
schools, Catholic
history of, 8–9
indoctrination in, 7
number of students in, 6–7
research on, 7, 155–156
single-sex, 9
as worth saving, 157
See also religion; St. Monica of Cascia High School
schools, single-sex, 36
See also St. Monica of Cascia High School
Scotty, 148–152
Sean, 58–59
seduction, 139, 144, 149
self
mastery of, 149
presentations of, 24
Semenya, Caster, 84–85
sex
discussion of, 72
passive role in, 79, 80, 87
and religion, 38, 39
in schools, 25, 33–34
talking about, 69
sex differences, 26–27
sex role theory, 26
sexual anxiety, 96
sharing, 126, 128
Shulman, Lee, 155
silence, 29
Simon Stock, St., 13
Sisyphus, 31
skin diseases, 78
sleep deprivation, 120
Sleepy, 104
Smithers, A., 156
socialization, gender-role, 22
Socrates, 141
Soja, E. W., 122, 130
soldiers, boys raised as, 24
Spong, John Shelby, 16, 39, 40, 108
sports. *See* athletics
squishes
meaning of term, 105
See also girlfriends; girls; women
structuralism, 46

Superbad, 85
surveillance, 119

tattoos, 74, 125, 133
teachers, female, 103–104, 106, 110–111
teaching, as ministry, 156–157
tests, cheating on, 53
text, ethnographic, 49
theology class, 55
Thorne, Barrie, 34
Tim, 54, 58–59, 76, 77, 78, 86
time. *See* Chronos; Kairos
Token, 105
torture, 120
tradition
    building, 102
    and fag discourse, 82
    and Kairos, 98, 133
    role of, 57
    service to, 101
    and women, 102, 110
transubstantiation, 2, 38
Trites, R. S., 12, 15, 28
Tyler, S., 49, 50

Van Maanen, ?, 48
Vatican council, 157
violence
    and athletics, 77, 78, 79
    male tendency toward, 24–25

Wacquant, L., 18
weakness, 78
Webster, Noah, 7
Weedon, C., 48
West, C., 32
women
    admired by St. Monica students, 110–111
    always-present-absence of, 105
    in Bible, 109, 110
    in Catholic Church, 97, 109, 110
    in Christianity, 40–41, 110
    contempt for, 103
    at funerals, 101
    humanity of, 98
    perceived shortcomings of, 86
    as pollutants, 116
    at St. Monica, 103–104, 106, 110–111
    stereotypes of, 107
    and traditions, 102, 110
    See also girlfriends; girls; relationships
wrestling, 78–79

Xenophon, 141

Zach, 68
Zimmerman, D. H., 32